DATE DUE

MY 1 0 '95			
AP2 5 '95			
OCO 4 '95			
OC2 6 '95			
NO1 4 '95			
FE1 0 '97			
DE 0 8 '98			
MAY 0 2 2002			

DEMCO 38-297

YOUNG PEOPLE
WITH PROBLEMS

YOUNG PEOPLE WITH PROBLEMS
A Guide to Bibliotherapy

JEAN A. PARDECK
AND
JOHN T. PARDECK

Foreword by Jerry G. King

GREENWOOD PRESS
Westport, Connecticut • London, England

Library of Congress Cataloging in Publication Data

Pardeck, Jean A.
  Young people with problems.

  Includes bibliographical references and indexes.
  1. Bibliotherapy. 2. Child psychotherapy.
3. Adolescent psychotherapy. 4. Child psychopathology—
Juvenile literature—Bibliography. 5. Adolescent
psychopathology—Juvenile literature—Bibliography.
I. Pardeck, John T. II. Title.
RJ505.B5P37 1984   616.89'166'088055   83-18601
ISBN 0-313-23836-7 (lib. bdg.)

Library of Congress Catalog Card Number: 83-18601
ISBN: 0-313-23836-7

First published in 1984

Greenwood Press
A division of Congressional Information Service, Inc.
88 Post Road West, Westport, Connecticut 06881

Printed in the United States of America

10 9 8 7 6 5 4 3 2

To Jamie and Jonathan,
our sons

Contents

Foreword ix

Preface xi

Acknowledgments xv

1. Introduction 1
2. Alcohol and Drug Addiction 18
3. Divorce and Separation of Parents 33
4. Emotional and Behavioral Problems 49
5. Moving to a New Home 70
6. Physical Handicaps 78
7. Pregnancy and Abortion 94
8. Serious Illness and Death 106
9. Sexual Awareness 126
10. Sibling Relationships 138
11. Stepparents 153

Author Index 165

Title Index 168

Subject Index 172

Foreword

"Make it relevant"—a misbegotten cliché born of impatience and historical ignorance, or a challenge that is changing therapeutic methods? This book will not resolve that crucial and complex question, but it will help therapists and nontherapists alike find additional resources for dealing creatively with developmental and circumstantial change in children. The authors do this by providing "relevants": points of relevance for today's growing child.

Many books on therapies are written for abstract courses where the major goal is to learn theories and research about the process of behavioral and emotional change. In these areas there is little concern with practical applicability. Other books are written for functional reasons where the primary goal is to learn information that can be used to improve the quality of one's life. This book belongs to the latter group, as its primary objectives are: (1) to identify a number of ideas through literature for dealing with general and specific problems of developing youngsters. The authors use nearly 300 literary works that are pertinent to our changing environment; (2) to describe and illustrate these ideas in language that can be understood without necessarily having prior training in the behavioral sciences; and (3) to identify ways to enhance awareness and insight in applying these ideas to problems facing young people.

As a family counselor, I have found that certain forms of literature are valuable in helping clients seek solutions to interpersonal conflicts as well as emotional stress. Resistance is a major component of any form of psychotherapy. In family therapy, however, dealing with resistance is especially complicated by a variety of subtle *but* dynamic factors. A distinctive feature of this book is the inclusion in each chapter of relevant literature that deals with specific problem areas in the developing child and adolescent. This literature can aid the therapist in breaking down resistance in at least two ways. First, good contemporary writing necessarily confronts enduring human questions and, conversely, good literature frequently has, in addition to its universal values, a particular significance for a particular time.

Relevance is not a special quality in things, in people, or even in the present or future. It is the quality perceived by the mind that enables a person to understand the present and the past as one fabric of experience in which one shares. Jean and John Pardeck's *Young People with Problems: A Guide to Bibliotherapy* is not merely timely, but a significant tool that can be used by therapists and nontherapists in helping our children cope in a changing society.

Jerry G. King, Ph.D.

Preface

PURPOSE

The primary purpose of this book is to provide counselors, psychologists, psychiatrists, social workers, and other helping professionals with readily available information about bibliotherapy, including annotations of recommended books for working with young people with problems. This book is also designed for those not trained in counseling or therapy, such as librarians and teachers, who work with children and adolescents in their daily professional lives. Bibliotherapy in this work is viewed as an approach useful not only for dealing with severe emotional problems and minor adjustment problems, but also as a tool for meeting developmental needs of individuals. By recognizing bibliotherapy as a useful helping tool for treating a variety of problems, its usefulness extends to not only trained counselors and therapists, but also to those not necessarily trained as professional helpers.

For those not having a background in bibliotherapy, an introduction to this emerging field is presented in Chapter 1. A definition of bibliotherapy is presented, the stages of the bibliotherapeutic process are discussed, and a review of the research related to its effectiveness is covered. The value of bibliotherapy and its limitations are presented. The practical application of bibliotherapy, including examples of its use, is also discussed. The practitioner well acquainted with bibliotherapy should also find this chapter to be beneficial.

Ten different issues that have been identified by the authors as major problem areas for young people are covered in this book. They are alcohol and drug abuse, divorce and separation of parents, emotional and behavioral problems, moving, physical handicaps, pregnancy and abortion, serious illness and death, sexual awareness, sibling relationships, and stepparents. Nearly 300 children's books, most of which are fictional, are annotated illustrating all of these problem areas; more than twenty books are presented for each of the problem areas covered.

This book is intended to provide insight into the bibliotherapeutic process for those working with young people. It provides access to a large number of annotated books dealing with major problem areas facing children and adolescents today.

COVERAGE AND SCOPE

The large majority of books annotated in this work were published after 1970, with a few books dated earlier than 1970 included. Many of the books annotated were published in the 1980s. The general criteria established for a book to be annotated were:

(1) the book had to be a children's literary work that related to one or more of the ten major problem areas,

(2) the book had to have either a fictional character or be about a factual character that the reader could identify with, and

(3) the book had to deal realistically with a problem and had to be clearly useful to the implementation of the bibliotherapeutic technique.

Each of the chapters covering a problem area includes a synopsis to help acquaint the reader with a particular problem. These synopses are not meant to be inclusive of all that is known about a particular problem facing young people; rather they are intended to focus on what the authors felt was the most important information available at this point on a problem in brief form. Also included in the synopsis of each problem area are the criteria used to select the books pertaining to that particular problem. These criteria are in addition to the general criteria established above.

ENTRIES

Entries for children's and young peoples' books in this work provide a bibliographic citation, followed by a synopsis of the book and aids to book selection. Each bibliographic citation includes the author, title of book, place of publication, name of publisher, date of publication, and number of pages in the book. For citations of short stories found within a book, the name of the short story and the inclusive pages where it is located within the book are also included. For those book titles that are available in paperback form, the citation includes the name of the paperback publisher and the year of paperback publication. The citation lists the publisher's name for any books that are available in Large Type for use by the visually impaired. Availability of the book for the handicapped in the forms of braille and/or

talking book through the Library of Congress is included in the book citation as well.

The synopsis of each book annotated generally mentions the age and sex
of the book's main character. Other important characters within the book
are presented as they relate to the main character. The problem area or
multiple problems that are a part of the book's theme are stressed within the
synopsis.

The book synopsis is followed by two important elements of book selection, the interest level and the reading level of each book. The interest level,
which is given in terms of age, states the general age range of young people
who would be interested in a particular book. For ease in book selection,
the interest levels fall into the categories of 5-8 years of age, 8-11 years of
age, 11-14 years of age, and 14-18 years of age. An inclusive category of
11-18 years of age is also used as an interest level for suitable books. Age of
the book's main character, complexity of the story plot including relationships between story characters, and explicit sexual content and controversial
language were all considered in determining a book's interest level.

The reading level of each book is stated in terms of grade level (that is, a
book with a reading level of 5.0 could normally be read by an average
reader in fifth grade. This same book could also be read by a below-average
reader in seventh grade, provided the interest level of the book was appropriate). Reading levels for each book were determined through use of a
readability formula. The authors made use of the Harris-Jacobson Readability Formula for books that appeared to be of fourth grade difficulty or
below.[1] This formula is based on difficulty of vocabulary, as measured by
the use of a basic word list, and average sentence length.[2] The Fry Readability Scale was used for books that appeared to be of fifth grade difficulty
or above. This measure of reading level is based on average sentence length
and word difficulty as determined by syllable count.[3]

The authors used several abbreviations for recurring words found within
the annotations. These abbreviations are listed in the table below:

TABLE OF ABBREVIATIONS

IL	Interest level of book
LC	Library of Congress
pap.	paperback book
RL	Reading level of book

ARRANGEMENT

There are eleven chapters in this work, including an introduction to bibliotherapy in Chapter 1, followed by ten chapters covering children's books on a problem area. The annotated entries are arranged within each chapter in alphabetical order by the author's last name. Many of the books listed in a particular chapter that deal with more than one problem area are also cross-referenced in other chapters.

INDEXES

The Author Index is a guide to the individuals who wrote the books annotated in each chapter. The Title Index helps the reader locate a particular work by title. The numbers following the authors and titles in these two indexes refer to the books' main entry numbers within each of the ten chapters.

The Subject Index serves two functions. It helps the user locate materials about a specific subject that may or may not fall within one of the ten problem areas (for example, divorce, a main problem area, is a heading within the Subject Index as are headings such as dieting and depression). It also allows the reader to identify entries about subjects such as counseling which cut across several of the chapters. Like the two other indexes, the Subject Index refers the reader to appropriate entry numbers within each chapter.

NOTES

1. Albert J. Harris and Edward R. Sipay, *How to Increase Reading Ability* 6th ed. (New York: David McKay, 1975), p. 658.

2. Harris and Sipay, p. 461.

3. George R. Klare, "Assessing Readability," *Reading Research Quarterly* (Volume 10, No. 1, 1974-1975): 62-102.

Acknowledgments

The authors would like to thank the staff of the Dean B. Ellis Library, Arkansas State University, for its help in locating children's books for this work. Special thanks go to Margaret Denny for alerting the authors to new selections coming into the library and for help in locating current books dealing with various children's problems. Margarett Daniels, Donna Wells, and Terrie Sypolt of the Inter-Library Loan Department were also helpful in obtaining books from other libraries.

The authors also thank Lois Musick and her junior high school students of the Norborne Elementary School for their suggestions on children's books. Thanks go to Ruth Pardeck and Burl Musick for their encouragement and support.

The authors wish to express appreciation to Dr. Jerry King for writing the Foreword to this work. Special thanks go to Mary Sive of Greenwood Press for her guidance and assistance throughout this project.

Jean A. Pardeck, M.Ed.
John T. Pardeck, Ph.D.

August 1983

ABOUT THE AUTHORS

JEAN A. PARDECK is a Reading Specialist in private practice. She has published in such journals as *Family Therapy, Practice Digest*, and *Group Psychotherapy, Psychodrama, and Sociometry*. Jean received her M.Ed. in Reading from University of Nebraska-Lincoln.

JOHN T. PARDECK is Assistant Professor of Social Work at Arkansas State University and is a Licensed Certified Social Worker. He has published in such journals as *Child Abuse and Neglect, International Journal of Social Psychiatry*, and *Social Work*. John received his Ph.D. in Social Work from Saint Louis University.

1.
Introduction

Written words have influenced the decisions, attitudes, and behaviors of mankind since the beginning of recorded history. Even before the invention of books as we presently know them, teachers used reading materials to help individuals solve their personal adjustment problems. In fact, if we look to early American schoolbooks, such as the *McGuffey Readers* and *The New England Primer*, an important purpose of these books was to develop character and positive values in students, with the goal that reading these books would impact personal adjustment.

Modern educators, as well as a variety of helping professionals, including psychologists, psychiatrists, and social workers, have begun to realize that books not only impact the personal adjustment of people, but also can be a useful tool in treating behavioral and emotional problems. The process of using books in this fashion has come to be known as bibliotherapy.

Using bibliotherapy as an approach to treatment literally means to treat through books. Even though several definitions have emerged in the literature for bibliotherapy, all of them encompass this literal definition in some form. For example, Russell and Shrodes define bibliotherapy as a process of dynamic interaction between the personality of the reader and literature.[1] When this interaction between the reader and literature is carried out under the guidance of a skilled helper, therapeutic change can occur.

Others have defined bibliotherapy as a process that can be used at a variety of intervention levels, including therapy with the emotionally ill, as well as at a level where everyday problems of people can be dealt with. Lindeman and Kling have made such a distinction with their definition of bibliotherapy. They distinguish three types of bibliotherapy: (1) that for the mentally ill, (2) that for dealing with minor adjustment problems, and (3) that of using it as a tool for developmental needs of children.[2] By recognizing bibliotherapy at these three levels with varying goals for its use at each level, it becomes obvious that bibliotherapy can be implemented by psychologists, psychiatrists, and social workers, as well as teachers and librarians.

Process of Bibliotherapy

Bibliotherapy is far more than matching a book with a reader, even though this matching takes skill and insight by the helping person. When used as a form of therapy, the reader must be able to identify with the character in the book who is experiencing a problem similar to the reader's. Similarities between the reader and this character must be evident to the reader. The reader must also interpret the motives of the character and must assess the relationships between the story characters. At this point of the process, the reader makes inferences regarding the meaning of the story and is guided by the helper in applying this meaning to the problem confronting the reader. This *identification and projection* stage occurs before the other stages of bibliotherapy can proceed.

When the reader has identified with the character of the story and projection has occurred, *abreaction and catharsis* is the next stage of the bibliotherapeutic process. In order for catharsis to occur, the reader must experience an emotional release that may be expressed verbally or nonverbally. It is imperative that a therapist guide and support the client during the cathartic experience. The involvement of the therapist is the critical element that distinguishes bibliotherapy from the normal reading process. The therapist must monitor such things as the client's reaction to the literature, the degree of similarity between the client's own emotional experience and the problem being considered, and the emotional experiences of the client through the identification with the story character.

Insight and integration is the final step of the treatment process. The client gains insight while being guided to recognize the self and significant others in the characters in the book. This guidance is aimed at helping the client develop new insight into a problem and being able to come up with possible solutions for it.

The above steps closely correspond to the phases of Freudian psychotherapy, one of the bases from which bibliotherapy draws its theoretical roots. A pioneer in bibliotherapy, Shrodes, describes the process in Freudian psychotherapy terms as follows:

> Identification is generally defined as an adaptive mechanism which the human being utilizes, largely unconsciously, to augment his self-regard. It takes the form of a real or imagined affiliation of oneself with another person, a group of persons, or with some institution, or even with a symbol. There is usually involved admiration for the object of one's identification, a tendency to imitate, and a sense of loyalty and belongingness.
>   Projection has two common usages in the literature. It consists of the attribution to others of one's own motives or emotions in order to ascribe blame to another instead of to oneself. The term is also used to describe one's perception, apperception, and cognition of the world and people. Catharsis is used synonymously with abreaction to denote the uncensored and spontaneous release of feelings: in the Aristotelian sense it means the purging of emotions. Insight is commonly used in psychotherapy to indicate emotional awareness of one's motivations, experiences, and subsequent abreaction.[3]

Bibliotherapy also draws on theoretical constructs developed in learning theory. As learning theorists assume, the human species learns by imitation; if we apply this principle to bibliotherapy, the client, by being presented fictional characters in books, is offered models of positive, adaptive behavior to identify with. This approach can be especially useful for children lacking positive role models in their social environment.[4]

Finally, it must be kept in mind, going back to the Lindeman and Kling definition, that bibliotherapy can be used at several different levels when working with people. The above three stages describing the total bibliotherapeutic process would probably all be used by the advanced therapist. If a teacher or librarian uses bibliotherapy as a helping modality, it is important that this kind of helper not go through all three stages of the process. Those not trained in advanced treatment techniques may want to use bibliotherapy as an approach for assisting people with minor adjustment problems or for helping a child with a developmental need. By using bibliotherapy at this level, the helper would probably go through the *identification and projection* stage of the bibliotherapeutic process and not proceed to the advanced stages of *abreaction and catharsis* and *insight and integration*. Even at this lower stage, much can be accomplished in helping a person deal with a problem.

Values of Bibliotherapy

Counselors and therapists who work with clients experiencing problems see such values in bibliotherapy as: helping the client to gain greater insight into problems, providing the client with techniques for relaxation and diversion, creating a medium through which the client can discuss problems, helping the client to focus attention outside of the self, and creating a helping environment in which the client can objectively discuss a situation occurring in a story which is similar to the client's own situation.

Even though helping professionals have found bibliotherapy to be useful, critics of this emerging technique have criticized it on the grounds that it is not an exact science. Much of this criticism is unwarranted because virtually all of the helping therapies are far from exact; bibliotherapy is no exception. However, bibliotherapy may be more complex than other current therapies in that one not only must be skillful in selecting literature that parallels the problem faced by a person, but also must be able to use this literature as a therapeutic medium. Because of the need for this combination of skills, some have argued that bibliotherapy is not a useful technique for teachers, librarians, and others not necessarily trained in therapy.

However, as mentioned previously, bibliotherapy can be useful for those not trained to do therapy if they do not attempt to move the person seeking help into the advanced stages of the bibliotherapeutic process involving *abreaction/catharsis* and *insight/integration*. The beginning stage of the bibliotherapeutic process, *identification/projection*, can be implemented by those working with various individuals who lack advanced therapeutic training. In a certain sense non-therapists such as librarians and educators who know and use books in their professional work are already using bibliotherapy in an elementary form even though they may not be aware of the bibliotherapeutic approach. Since we know that reading affects one's own feelings, attitudes, and self-development, the teacher or librarian who recommends books to readers is involved in the process of helping people. By becoming familiar with bibliotherapy, the non-therapist can be even more effective in working with people.[5]

Bibliotherapy can be valuable for individuals needing help with interpersonal relationships. For those having problems with family and peer relationships, bibliotherapy can help in developing a tolerance and understanding of others, in creating a readiness to accept differences in others, and in formulating a more objective approach to human problems.[6] After reading about other family units, individuals with problems related to family life can recognize that they are not alone in their problems and that their problems do have solutions.[7] The many ways in which family members react to each other, ranging from conflict to cooperation, can be better understood. Likewise, those individuals having problems with peers can gain insight into the complexities of peer relationships through reading about other peer situations. The powerfulness of peer pressure and the wholesome as well as the disturbing influence of peers on an individual can be recognized.[8]

Bibliotherapy has much value in helping those faced with a physical handicap as well. By reading about one's handicap in literature and seeing how the character in the story copes with the same problem, great insight can be gained. The handicapped person can learn to accept and live with a handicap by reading about how a character in literature has met a similar challenge. The physically handicapped person may learn that many others have faced the same problem, had similar feelings of inadequacy and failure, and yet have found a way to some degree to succeed and develop self-realization about the problem. Handicapped individuals may even see improvement with their handicap as they read about the problem.[9]

Finally bibliotherapy can be viewed as a preventative tool. It may help to prevent such problems as neurotic tendencies and other psychological disorders through the vicarious participation of the reader in a story character's problems. An example of this would be the potentially rebellious adolescent who gains insight through literature about this kind of problem and finds ways of preventing the problem's further development through literature. Young people having typical concerns about their sexual or psychological development may benefit through reading about the way in which characters in literature have dealt with similar concerns. Such insight might well prevent emotional or psychological problems for these children. Indeed literature may be the only way that some individuals can see that many of their problems are "normal;" literature can thus help them in preventing the development of more serious emotional or psychological disorders.

Effectiveness of Bibliotherapy

Much research has been conducted on the effectiveness of bibliotherapy. The findings of this research report that bibliotherapy appears to work for certain kinds of problems and not for others. Like most other current therapies developed in the behavioral and social sciences, much more research needs to be conducted on testing the effectiveness of bibliotherapy. Presently, the research on bibliotherapy falls roughly into the following categories: academic achievement, assertiveness, attitude change, behavioral change, marital relations, reducing fear, self-concept and self-development, and therapeutic usefulness.

Academic achievement. Most of the findings on bibliotherapy suggest
that it may not increase academic achievement; however, a few studies
do show bibliotherapy to have a positive effect on this factor. Whipple
found that the use of bibliotherapy as a therapeutic adjunct raised academic achievement in the biological sciences of students in a state reformatory.[10] King found that underachieving boys who received bibliotherapy in addition to regular language arts classes showed significant gains
over other underachieving boys who attended only language arts classes.[11]
A study by Lundstein found that bibliotherapy helped increase communication skills of elementary school students.[12]

Five studies found that bibliotherapy did not affect academic achievement. Bigge and Sandefur found that bibliotherapy did not impact the
academic achievement of a study group of high-school students.[13] Study-
ing a group of fifth and sixth grade students, Dixon concluded that bibliotherapy in conjunction with a remedial reading instruction program did
not increase reading skills.[14] Livengood reports that a bibliotherapy
program failed to increase the reading skills of a group of sixth grade
students.[15] A study by Ponder discovered that bibliotherapy did not
affect reading achievement in a group of poverty level students.[16] Research reported by Schultheis found that fifth and sixth grade classes
that received bibliotherapy and guidance did not gain in reading achievement over students not receiving the same treatment.[17]

Assertiveness. Allen and Nesbitt found that bibliotherapy can increase
assertive behaviors.[18] McGovern found that bibliotherapy increased assertiveness levels in subjects subsequent to assertiveness training over
those who did not experience bibliotherapy.[19] Even though the research
is limited in this area, the findings suggest that bibliotherapy may impact
assertiveness levels.

Attitude change. Bibliotherapy has been found useful for bringing about
attitude change. Studies by Jackson, Litchner and Johnson, and Standley and Standley have found that bibliotherapy programs positively
changed attitudes of majority group members toward blacks.[20] Smith
found that students could report ways that bibliotherapy changed their
attitudes.[21] Tatara found that bibliotherapy could be successful in mod-
ifying students' attitudes toward scientists.[22] One final study by Wilson
on the positive effects of bibliotherapy reports that it was found useful
for changing severe attitudinal problems.[23]

Behavioral change. The findings suggest that bibliotherapy can change
the behavior of individuals. Several major research studies have been
done on changing behavior through bibliotherapy. One study found that
reading short stories by sixth graders increased the expression of aggressive behaviors but did not decrease selfish behaviors.[24] A study by
Shirley found that students were able to report ways in which articles,
books, etc. changed their behaviors.[25] McClasky reported that bibliotherapy positively modified behaviors in emotionally disturbed patients.[26]

Marital relations. Most research has found that bibliotherapy does not
apparently improve marital relationships. Carr evaluated the effectiveness of bibliotherapy with other methods in teaching problem solving behaviors for dealing with marital conflict. Carr found bibliotherapy to be

one method that was not useful for learning problem solving behaviors
in dealing with marital conflict[27]   Barton found bibliotherapy not to be
useful as a technique for learning marital problem solving skills as well.[28]
A study by Baum reported that a self-help bibliotherapy group for marital enrichment did not differ significantly from those groups using a more
typical and structured format.[29]   Consequently, at this time, there is
little evidence reported in the literature suggesting that bibliotherapy is
useful for improving marital relations.

Reducing fear.   Little support is reported in the research implying that
bibliotherapy reduces certain fears in people.   Webster found that bibliotherapy reduced fears in first grade children;[30] however, Dixon and
Link did not find bibliotherapy effective in reducing fear and anxiety in
the subjects they studied.[31]

Self-concept and self-development.   The research is mixed on the impact
of bibliotherapy on self-concept and self-development.   Studies by Kanaan, King, and Penna reported that bibliotherapy had a positive impact
on the self-concepts of children.[32]   However, studies by Caffee, Dixon,
Roach, and Shearon did not show bibliotherapy to enhance the self-concepts of the students studied in their research.[33]

Studies have reported that bibliotherapy can positively impact self-
development however.   Appleberry found bibliotherapy useful for improving the mental health of a non-clinical population of third grade children.[34]
Amato found that bibliotherapy helped college students to improve problem solving, develop insight, resolve stress, as well as several other
positive characteristics.[35]   Mattera found that reading books helped children in their problem solving.[36]   Finally, a study by Herminghaus reported that bibliotherapy helped to produce desirable personal behaviors
among a group of children studied.[37]   A limited number of studies have
found bibliotherapy not very useful for self-development.   Bigge and
Sandefur reported that the personalities of a non-clinical population of
high-school students were not impacted by bibliotherapy.[38]   A study of
sixth graders by Stephens concluded that bibliotherapy did not increase
self-reliance in these students.[39]

Therapeutic usefulness.   Most research on bibliotherapy reports that it
can be a valuable therapeutic technique for helping people.   As a therapeutic tool, Whipple found that bibliotherapy helped as a medium in improving the mental health of inmates.[40]   A study by Muehleisen found
that bibliotherapy reduced psychiatric symptoms and improved ego
strengths in patients.[41]   Saper found that bibliotherapy in combination
with group therapy created greater involvement, problem solving behaviors, and insight in subjects than group therapy alone.[42]   In summary,
the research suggests that bibliotherapy can be a valuable component to
the therapeutic process.

Bibliotherapy has been found to be relatively effective in the following areas: assertiveness, attitude change, behavioral change, self-development, and as a therapeutic method.   The usefulness of this approach
for academic achievement, marital relations, reducing fear, and changing
self-concept is not strongly supported in the research.   Many of the
studies that have found bibliotherapy to be useful involved children and
adolescents.   These findings should give added confidence to the helping
person wishing to use bibliotherapy with young people.

Application of Bibliotherapy with Young People

Concerned adults who wish to use bibliotherapy to help children with their problems must have an interest in and a concern for children as well as a willingness to become familiar with children's books.[43] The use of books can be simple or complex, depending on the child's needs and on the background of the helping person. Classroom teachers and librarians can search for books that mirror a developmental need or adjustment problem they wish to help a child with.[44] If a child's problem is more severe, a trained therapist can make use of books to guide and support a child in reading about problems which are similar to the child's own.

Helping individuals need to consider the important factor of readiness on the part of the young person they wish to utilize bibliotherapy with. Inappropriate timing may impede the bibliotherapeutic process and even provoke annoyance on the part of the young person. A teacher, librarian, or trained therapist should not suggest that a child read certain books too early in the relationship between them. An adequate working relationship based on rapport, trust, confidence, and mutual understanding must first be established. Otherwise the child may feel that the suggestion to read certain books about a problem the child is experiencing is a way of avoiding the problem on the part of the helping individual.[45]

Another poor time for utilizing bibliotherapeutic techniques is when the individual is deeply involved in wrestling with a problem or when the person is speedily moving toward the resolution of the problem. Typically, the individual is most ready for the initiation of bibliotherapy when the following conditions have been met: (a) a working relationship involving mutual trust has been developed, (b) the presenting problem has been agreed upon by the young person and the helping individual, (c) some preliminary exploration of the problem has occurred, and (d) the young person is exhibiting low resistance to the helping process.[46]

Selection of books. Although bibliotherapy, to be most effective, demands more than just matching books to a particular child, that is certainly the first step. The most important factor in selecting a book, of course, is knowledge of the problem a young person is facing. However, the young person's age and reading level, as well as the book's form of publication, must also be taken into consideration by the helping individual.

The problem a young person is facing is the starting point in selecting appropriate materials for bibliotherapy. This problem may be a developmental need, a minor adjustment problem, or a problem of more intensity. Later chapters of this book include ten problem areas common to many young people. The helping individual is usually aware of a young person's problem through previous association with the child. The problem can also be discovered or be more fully understood through the consulting of school records[47] or by talking with significant individuals close to the young person.

Once the problem has been identified, appropriate books must be located which focus on the particular need or center on the problem facing the child. Presently there is almost no topic that is unmentionable in children's books.[48] Controversial topics such as sexual awareness, terminal illnesses and dying, and mental illness are all found in certain children's books. It is important that the book chosen on a particular problem also make use of realistic approaches and plausible solutions and that the characters within the book are lifelike.[49]

Another important consideration in choosing books is the young person's age. Children five years of age and under are already faced with problems such as moving, sibling relationships, etc. and books are readily available on these topics for young children. However, these same topics are the focus of many adolescent books as well. Therefore, in selecting books for a young person, the helper must be aware of the interest level of the book, usually expressed in terms of age.

Chronological age by itself cannot determine book selection. Maturity of the reader, as far as the ability to identify with book characters, is also important. An appropriate interest level for a thirteen-year old, for example, may be in the 11-14 year old range or the 11-18 year old range, depending on the thirteen-year old's level of maturity.

The reading ability of the young person must also be considered. A child's reading level may be ascertained through standardized tests and grades, both available from school records.[50] A classroom teacher is also aware of a student's reading capabilities and other helping individuals who wish to use bibliotherapy may be advised to consult with a child's teacher.

Although a child is often capable of reading slightly beyond capacity [51] when the subject matter of a book is particularly interesting to the child, a too difficult book can greatly hamper the bibliotherapeutic process. Likewise, a book with a reading level which is much too low may prove insulting to a child. This is not to say that a young person with a reading level of 9.0 (approximately 9th grade level) will not enjoy a book with a 7.5 reading level; however, dropping down to a book with a 5.0 reading level which has a more simplified vocabulary may not be appropriate for this individual. When in doubt about a young person's reading level, it is generally best for the helping individual to initially use a book which is at least two years below the child's present grade placement;[52] succeeding books during the course of bibliotherapy can either remain at that level if it seems appropriate or can be of a higher or lower reading level, depending on the assessment of the bibliotherapist.

Bibliotherapeutic techniques have been found to be most effective with children whose reading abilities are average or above-average.[53] These young people are generally more comfortable with reading and have experienced more success with it. This does not mean, however, that bibliotherapy is not possible with the below-average reader. If the helping individual ascertains that a below-average reader can benefit from and will be amenable to bibliotherapy, books are available for these young people. It is possible, for example, to find books appealing to high-schoolers, dealing with problems such as pregnancy and abortion and alcohol/drug abuse, with reading levels of sixth grade and lower.

One final element of book selection is the book's form of publication. Many books have been developed in the forms of braille and talking books by the Library of Congress and are available to the handicapped through regional libraries. Certain publishing companies develop books in Large Type form for use with those who are visually impaired. Many books are also available in paperback form, which may be more appealing to certain young people.[54]

Once the problem facing the young person, as well as the child's reading level and interest level, have all been considered, the helping individual can turn to several sources in selecting appropriate book titles. The location of books on a particular problem can be accomplished through a search of subject headings in a card catalog, but it is more easily done by checking annotations of children's books. Sources are available on children's books which provide annotations including interest levels for various books. Certain sources also provide annotations with both interest levels and reading levels for each book, such as those annotations found in later chapters of this book.

Selection of books for group bibliotherapy. In using bibliotherapy with small groups of children, the same principles of book selection should be followed. However, there must be consideration of the individual needs and characteristics of group members. Each member of the group must be faced with the same general problem, such as a group of children with divorced parents or several adolescents who are all experiencing problems with siblings. The helping individual must also assess the readiness of each group member for bibliotherapy, in terms of having a good working relationship with the helper and in agreeing that a problem exists.

Group members need to be fairly close in age chronologically or at approximately the same developmental level so that any books selected will be suitable for all group members. The reading level of each individual must be known, with any book selected not too difficult for the lowest reader in the group. Multiple copies of the book selected must be available, of course, and alternate forms of publication, such as Large Type or braille, must be obtained for any individuals in the group who need them.

Introducing the book(s). Once the child appears to show readiness for the bibliotherapeutic process and the book selection has been completed, the problem arises of how the helping individual should introduce the book to the child. Most practitioners feel that it is best to suggest books rather than to prescribe them to the individual faced with the problem.[55] This makes the reading of the book seem less like a school assignment.[56] The ideal situation would be for the helping individual to have on hand several appropriate books dealing with a certain problem that the reader could choose from.

It is quite important that the helping individual possess at least a general familiarity with the book(s) being suggested.[57] If a detailed annotation of the book has not been previously read, the helping individual needs to read the book jacket and/or skim the contents of the book. Then an aspect of the plot which is particularly interesting or the mention of a character similar to the young person can perhaps help the child in choosing a book. Getting another young person who has read one of the books to recommend it may also be helpful.[58]

Use of follow-up strategies. There is agreement among virtually all studies on bibliotherapy that the reading of a book must be accompanied and/or followed up by discussion and/or counseling.[59] Although it is sometimes possible for the reader to experience *identification/projection* through merely reading a book, normally the three stages of the bibliotherapeutic process, especially the advanced stages of *abreaction/catharsis* and *insight/integration*, occur only as the result of interaction between the reader and a helping person.[60] Guidance by the helping person is essential, not only in the selection of appropriate books, but also in e- voking active reactions, in discussion of the reader's insights, and even in the role-playing and dramatization of critical incidents of the story.[61]

Classroom teachers and librarians may select appropriate books for a certain child who is experiencing a problem or they may draw together a group of young people known to have a common concern. A trained ther- apist may use bibliotherapy as a part of individual counseling or as a way to supplement or enrich a small group experience.[62] There are many thought-provoking activities that can follow the reading of a book.[63] Some of these follow-up strategies are best suited for individuals; others require a small group approach. The helping individual could make use of only one follow-up strategy after the reading of a book or several could be used.

Certain problems illustrated in books are more congenial to follow-up than other problems. For example, many of the follow-up strategies listed below could be used with books on divorce or sibling relationships; more caution must be used in selecting follow-up activities for books dealing with death or mental illness because of the seriousness of these problems. To aid in explanation of these strategies, the ten different problem areas covered in this book are mentioned as examples of possible use with each strategy. This is not to preclude use of these strategies with any other problem the helping individual deems suitable.

1. Develop a synopsis of the story, either written or tape recorded, using the point of view of a character other than the one who told the story. A new baby could relate how it feels to suddenly have an older sibling rather than vice versa or an alcoholic parent could describe their family life rather than having their child's view of it.

2. Make a daily schedule for the main character of the book and for yourself. Compare the two. The character with diabetes would have a schedule complete with injections, urine testing, etc. A character with behavioral problems might have a visit to a probation officer included in the schedule.

3. Compose a diary for a book character. The pregnant teenage character or her boyfriend would both have insightful diary entries, as would a character faced with a terminal illness.

4. Write a letter from one of the book characters to another charac- ter. A child character angry at a new stepparent, for example, or a young person wishing that a mother would more fully explain a father's serious illness.

5. Make a map illustrating story events, using your imagination to come up with details not given in the book. This could be useful for a story about a child who moves with new streets, buildings, etc. included or for a story about a handicapped child who needs to be able to nego- tiate a public school building.

6. Make a time line of story events and compare it to your own time line; i.e., the sequence of events leading to the separation of a charac- ter's parents or the physical changes leading to puberty in a character.

7. Think up a different ending for a story or stop reading before the last chapters of a book and come up with your own ending. This can be either written or tape recorded. A different ending could be done for a story about a teenage alcoholic, for example, or for a story about a child who has a retarded sibling.

8. Send a telegram to one of the story characters, either from another character or from yourself. This can be quite serious, such as condolences sent to a character whose parent has died, or in fun, such as congratulations sent to a character for surviving a move to a new neighborhood.

9. Compose a "Dear Abby" letter that a character in the story could have written about a problem situation. A character who has discovered that a sibling is a shoplifter, for example, or a girl concerned about her menstruation beginning.

10. Hold a round-table discussion or panel concerning a decision one of the book characters is faced with. A teenage girl's decision about what to do when she discovers she's pregnant or an adolescent's decision about whether to use a drug could both be discussion topics for a group.

11. For younger readers, construct puppets or make soap or clay models of story characters to re-enact a scene with. This could be used to re-enact sibling squabbles in one of the books or to re-enact the reaction of classmates to a handicapped child being mainstreamed into their school.

12. Draw pictures in sequence or make a TV scroll of important incidents of the story; i.e., the arrival of a new baby in a family or the first meeting of a child with its new stepparent.

13. Role-play an interesting part of the book. Take the part of an adult rather than a character who is a young person. For example, take the part of a recently divorced mother telling her child she is going out on a date or the part of a father who has discovered that his child is using marijuana.

14. Make two columns and list the strong points, as well as areas that need improvement, for a character. Then make the same two lists about yourself. The character who is handicapped would have obvious areas that need improvement as well as strong points, as would the character suffering from a low self-concept.

15. Hold a mock trial concerning an incident in a book with one person in the group playing the part of a defendant on the stand and others playing the parts of lawyer, judge, jury, witnesses, etc. The defendant could be a character who has participated in vandalism or one who has been truant from school.

16. Using a box with a slit cut in it, write either suggestions or questions you have directed toward one of the book characters. A different reader of the same book can respond to any questions. Suggestions could be directed toward a character having a drug abuse problem or questions could be directed toward a child character whose parent has received treatment for mental illness, for example.

17. Glue pictures and/or words cut from a magazine on a piece of cardboard to make a collage illustrating different parts of the story. The collage could illustrate a story about young siblings learning to share or a story about a child who is moving to a new home.

18. Rewrite the first or last chapter of a book. New characters, new problems, different incidents, and new solutions can be used. This could be used to give a new twist to a story about gang involvement or a story dealing with physical abuse of a young person.

19. Make a mobile that represents key events in a story using your own drawings or pictures cut from magazines. A mobile could represent a day spent with a non-custody divorced parent, for example, or could represent the accomplishments of a handicapped child.

20. Write a news report concerning an incident in a book; i.e., a character's first visit to a social worker or psychologist or a truce called between two rival siblings.

In using any of the previous follow-up strategies, the helping individual must keep several things in mind. The maturity of the young person must be considered. Certain activities are more suitable for younger children, while others require the advanced thinking and writing skills of an older child. Many of the activities involve writing; if a young person dislikes writing, the same activity can generally be accomplished with a tape recorder. Other strategies are best suited to a child who enjoys artistic activities. The same principle can be used here as in introducing a book; several follow-up strategies can be suggested with the child selecting one or more that the child is interested in.

Examples of utilizing bibliotherapy with young people. In order to illustrate the three stages of the bibliotherapeutic process and the use of some of the follow-up strategies, books about a problem situation facing many young people today, the separation and divorce of their parents, will be used. Although certain books dealing with divorce will be used to illustrate the three stages of the bibliotherapeutic process, it should be kept in mind that these books are not limited to any one stage of the bibliotherapeutic process. In other words, a book used to illustrate the lower stage of the process could also be used in the advanced stages with the guidance of a therapist. Likewise, the use of any follow-up strategies for a particular book does not mean that other follow-up strategies could not be used with this book as well.

Teachers and librarians are in an excellent position to provide children whose parents are going through separation and divorce with books on this problem. For young children not yet able to read books on their own, a classroom teacher could draw together several students facing this problem to read aloud a book such as *Mommy and Daddy are Divorced*.[64] Children in a small group like this could quite easily experience *identification and projection* as they hear about the two main characters of this book, Ned and his little brother. Children whose parents have divorced, like Ned and his brother, may also have eagerly anticipated spending the day with their father and later become upset when their father brings them back home. A teacher or librarian could have children make a TV scroll or draw pictures from this story in sequence as a follow-up strategy with this book. The children should, of course, be encouraged to make variations in the pictures if they wish so that the pictures represent the child's own situation.

A therapist may wish to be more specific in selecting books for young people on the topic of divorce if the therapist wants the client to move into the higher stages of bibliotherapy. A therapist could select a book such as *Something to Count On*[65] for a young person who has developed behavioral problems after the child's parents divorce. A pre-adolescent child with behavioral problems following a divorce could easily *identify* and experience *projection* with ten-year old Lorraine, the main character in this book. Lorraine finds her mother aloof after her parents divorce and her father keeps canceling weekend visits with Lorraine, leading Lorraine to misbehave at school. A young person with a similar parental situation after a divorce may react quite strongly to Lorraine's turmoil at this time. The reader of this book could perhaps experience *abreaction and catharsis* if the therapist uses a follow-up strategy such as having the child write a letter to Lorraine's mother or father expressing anger at their ignoring Lorraine's needs.

After reading this book, a young person with a parental situation like Lorraine's might also be able to move to the final stage of bibliotherapy, *insight and integration*, with the help of a therapist. Ignored by her parents, Lorraine turned to an understanding teacher to help her with her problems. Similarly, young people whose parents are not helping them adjust to divorce could be guided by a therapist into coming up with some solutions on their own. This might be an instance when the reader could write or tape record a different ending for this book which would show a different solution to Lorraine's problem.

An adolescent whose parents share joint custody after a divorce may *identify* and experience *projection* with fourteen-year old Phoebe who is in the same situation in *The Divorce Express*.[66] Phoebe shuttles back and forth between her mother's city apartment and her father's home in the country. A young person reading this book may wish to draw a map illustrating Phoebe's weekly journey from the home of one parent to the other.

A young person whose divorced parents are dating may also share the hostility and confusion felt by Phoebe when each of her parents begins dating other people. The reader of this book could perhaps be guided to move into *abreaction and catharsis* through the use of a follow-up strategy such as role-playing a scene from the book where Phoebe and her mother are waiting for her mother's date to arrive. Changes could be inserted in the book's conversation to reflect the youngster's own situation with a parent dating.

When her mother makes the decision to remarry, Phoebe confides in a friend whose parents are also divorced. This friend offers much-needed support to Phoebe at this time of change in her life. A reader of this book could possibly be helped by a therapist in experiencing *insight and integration* if the young person wrote suggestions to Phoebe about other ways to resolve her problems. These suggestions might reflect ways of coping that the young person could use as well in the aftermath of a parental divorce.

These are but a few of the children's books available on the area of separation and divorce of parents; some are quite general while other books point out specific factors related to this problem facing many young people. As illustrated above, a classroom teacher or librarian can expose a young person or a small group of children to suitable books on a certain problem through which the child(ren) can experience *identification and projection*. For the higher stages of the bibliotherapeutic process, *abreaction and catharsis* and *insight and integration*, it is highly advisable for a therapist to be involved in the process of treatment.

Limitations of Bibliotherapy

As with most treatment techniques, there are limitations and precautions when using bibliotherapy. Bibliotherapy should not be used as a single approach to treatment, as it appears to be most effective when used in conjunction with other therapeutic approaches.

The helping person should realize that fears and anxieties may be aggravated by reading about mental health problems. This possibility must be closely monitored by the helping person.

Bibliotherapy appears to be most effective when used with children or adults who are in the habit of reading. It is important that the helping person know the client well enough to judge the client's reading ability and interest level. If the helping person does not match the client with the correct reading material, frustration is likely to occur.

Another limitation is that the client may intellectualize about problems when reading about them. In other words, the client fails to *identify* with a character in the story, resulting in a form of *projection* that only serves to relieve the client of any responsibility for resolution of problems.[67] The possibility of this occurring with younger children is not as great because of their limited cognitive development, but it becomes an important potential phenomenon with older children and adults.

The possibility of the relationship with the helping person as the cause of the resolution of a problem must also be taken into consideration.[68] As has been found for many therapeutic modalities, this can be best monitored by careful assessment of the impact of the therapeutic relationship versus the impact of bibliotherapy on the client's problem.

NOTES

1.   David H. Russell and Caroline Shrodes, "Contributions of Research in Bibliotherapy to the Language-Arts Program," *School Review* (Volume 58, 1950): 411-420.

2.   Barbara Lindeman and Martin Kling, "Bibliotherapy: Definitions, Uses, and Studies," *Journal of School Psychology* (Volume 2, 1969): 36-41.

3.   Caroline Shrodes, *Bibliotherapy: A Theoretical and Clinical-Experimental Study* (Doctoral Dissertation: University of California, 1949).

4.   Frank Fischer, "Influence of Reading and Discussion on Attitudes of Fifth Graders Towards American Indians," *Journal of Educational Research* (Volume 62, 1968): 25-32.

5.   Paul A. Witty, "Meeting Developmental Needs Through Reading," *Education* (Volume 84, 1964): 451-458.

6. George D. Spache, *Good Reading for Poor Readers* 9th revised ed. (Champaign, Illinois: Garrard Publishing, 1974), p. 23.

7. Marsha Kabakow Rudman, *Children's Literature: An Issues Approach* (Lexington, Massachusetts: D.C. Heath and Company, 1976), p. 6.

8. Eileen Tway (ed.), *Reading Ladders for Human Relations* 6th ed. (Washington, D.C.: American Council on Education, 1981), p. 148

9. Edith S. Clarke, *Stories About Retarded Readers for Use in the Junior High School* (Doctoral Dissertation: Columbia University, 1967).

10. C. Whipple, *The Effect of Short-Term Classroom Bibliotherapy on the Personality and Academic Achievement of Reformatory Inmate Students* (Doctoral Dissertation: University of Oklahoma, 1978).

11. N. King, *The Effects of Group Bibliocounseling on Selected Fourth-Grade Students Who Are Underachieving in Reading* (Doctoral Dissertation: University of the Pacific, 1972).

12. S.W. Lundstein, "A Thinking Improvement Program Through Literature," *Elementary English* (Volume 49, 1972): 505-512.

13. J. Bigge and J.T. Sandefur, *An Exploratory Study of the Effects of Bibliotherapy on the Behavioral Pattern of Adolescents* (Emporia, Kansas: Kansas State Teacher's College, 1966).

14. J. Dixon, *The Effects of Four Methods of Group Reading Therapy on the Level of Reading, Manifest Anxiety, Self-Concept, and Personal-Social Adjustment Among Fifth and Sixth-Grade Children in a Central City School Setting* (Doctoral Dissertation: State University of New York-Buffalo, 1974).

15. D.K. Livengood, *The Effect of Bibliotherapy Upon Peer Relations and Democratic Practices in a Sixth Grade Classroom* (Doctoral Dissertation: University of Florida, 1961).

16. V. Ponder, *An Investigation of the Effects of Bibliotherapy and Teachers' Self-Others Acceptance on Pupils' Self-Acceptance and Reading Achievement Scores* (Doctoral Dissertation: University of Southern Mississippi, 1968).

17. M. Schultheis, *A Study of the Effects of Selected Readings Upon Children's Academic Performances and Social Adjustment* (Doctoral Dissertation: Ball State University, 1969).

18. R.D. Allen, *An Analysis of the Impact of Two Forms of Short Term Assertive Training on Aggressive Behavior* (Doctoral Dissertation: Southern Illinois University, 1978); E.B. Nesbitt, *Comparison of Two Measures of Assertiveness and the Modification on Non-Assertive Behaviors* (Doctoral Dissertation: University of Tennessee, 1977).

19. C. McGovern, *The Relative Efficacy of Bibliotherapy and Assertion Training on the Assertiveness Levels of a General Population and a Library Personnel Population* (Doctoral Dissertation: Northwestern University, 1976).

20. E.P. Jackson, "Effects of Reading Upon Attitudes Toward the Negro Race," *Library Quarterly* (Volume 14, 1944): 47-54; J.H. Litcher and D.W. Johnson, "Changes in Attitudes Toward Negroes of White Elementary School Students After Use of Multiethnic Readers," *Journal of Educational Psychology* (Volume 60, 1969): 148-152; F. Standley and N. Standley, "An Experimental Use of Black Literature at a Predominantly White University," *Research in Teaching English* (Volume 4, 1970): 139-148.

21. N.B. Smith, "Some Effects of Reading on Children," *Elementary English* (Volume 25, 1948): 271-278.

22. W. Tatara, "Effects of Novels on Ideas About Scientists," *Journal of Educational Research* (Volume 58, 1964): 3-9.

23. J. Wilson, "The Treatment of Attitudinal Pathosis by Bibliotherapy, A Case Study," *Journal of Clinical Psychology* (Volume 7, 1951): 345-351.

24. I. Lewis, *Some Effects of the Reading and Discussion of Stories on Certain Values of Sixth-Grade Pupils* (Doctoral Dissertation: University of California-Berkeley, 1967).

25. F. Shirley, *The Influence of Reading on the Concepts, Attitudes, and Behavior of Tenth-, Eleventh-, and Twelfth-Grade Students* (Doctoral Dissertation: University of Arizona, 1966).

26. H. McClasky, *Bibliotherapy with Emotionally Disturbed Patients: An Experimental Study* (Doctoral Dissertation: University of Washington, 1970).

27. R. Carr, *The Effects of Bibliotherapy and Modeling, Videotaped Feedback on Problem-Solving Behaviors in Marital Conflict* (Doctoral Dissertation: East Texas State University, 1975).

28. G. Barton, *Treating Marital Conflict: The Effects of Bibliotherapy Versus Videotaped Feedback and Bibliotherapy on Problem-Solving Behaviors in Marital Conflict* (Doctoral Dissertation: Brigham Young University, 1977).

29. M. Baum, *The Short-Term, Long-Term, and Differential Effects of Group Versus Bibliotherapy Relationship Enhancement Programs for Couples* (Doctoral Dissertation: University of Texas, 1977).

30. J. Webster, "Using Books to Reduce the Fears of First-Grade Children," *Reading Teacher* (Volume 14, 1961): 159-162.

31. Dixon; M. Link, *The Effect of Bibliotherapy in Reducing the Fears of Kindergarten Children* (Doctoral Dissertation: Ball State University, 1977).

32. J. Kanaan, *The Application of Adjuvant Bibliotherapeutic Techniques in Resolving Peer Acceptance Problems* (Doctoral Dissertation: University of Pittsburg, 1975); King; R. Penna, *The Relative Effectiveness of the Classroom Discussion Approach and the Tutorial Approach to Literature for the Development of Adolescent Ego-Identity* (Doctoral Dissertation: Fordham University, 1975).

33. C.L. Caffee, *Bibliotherapy: Its Effect on Self-Concept and Self-Actualization* (Doctoral Dissertation: East Texas State University, 1975); Dixon; L.E. Roach, *The Effects of Realistic Fiction Literature Upon the Self-Concept of Elementary School Students Exposed to a Bibliotherapeutic Situation* (Doctoral Dissertation: University of Akron, 1975); E. Shearon, *The Effects of Psychodrama Treatment on Professed and Inferred Self-Concepts of Selected Fourth Grades in One Elementary School* (Doctoral Dissertation: University of Florida, 1975).

34. M. Appleberry, *A Study of the Effect of Bibliotherapy on Third-Grade Children Using a Master List of Titles from Children's Literature* (Doctoral Dissertation: University of Houston, 1969).

35. A. Amato, *Some Effects of Bibliotherapy on Young Adults* (Doctoral Dissertation: Pennsylvania State University, 1957).

36. G. Mattera, *Bibliotherapy in a Sixth Grade* (Doctoral Dissertation: Pennsylvania State University, 1961).

37. E. Herminghaus, *The Effect of Bibliotherapy on Attitudes and Personal and Social Adjustment of a Group of Elementary School Children* (Doctoral Dissertation: Washington University, 1954).

38. Bigge and Sandefur.

39. J. Stephens, *An Investigation into the Effectiveness of Bibliotherapy on the Reader's Self-Reliance* (Doctoral Dissertation: University of Oklahoma, 1974).

40. Whipple.

41. R. Muehleisen, *Reducing the Risks of Health Change Associated with Critical Life Stress* (Doctoral Dissertation: Ohio University, 1976).

42. M. Saper, *Bibliotherapy as an Adjunct to Group Psychotherapy* (Doctoral Dissertation: University of Missouri, 1967).

43. Sharon Dreyer, *The Bookfinder: Volume 2* (Circle Pines, Minnesota: American Guidance Service, 1981), p. xii.

44. Rudman, p. 4.

45. Joseph S. Zaccaria and Harold A. Moses, *Facilitating Human Development Through Reading: The Use of Bibliotherapy in Teaching and Counseling* (Champaign, Illinois: Stipes Publishing, 1968), pp. 77-78.

46. Zaccaria and Moses, p. 78.

47. Eleanor Brown, *Bibliotherapy and Its Widening Applications* (Metuchen, New Jersey: The Scarecrow Press, 1975), p. 183.

48. Rudman, p. 4.

49. Patricia Cianciolo, "Children's Literature Can Affect Coping Behavior," *Personnel and Guidance Journal* (Volume 43, 1965): 898.

50. Zaccaria and Moses, p. 81.

51. Albert J. Harris and Edward R. Sipay, *How to Increase Reading Ability* 6th ed. (New York: David McKay, 1975), p. 522.

52. Harris and Sipay, p. 644.

53. Zaccaria and Moses, p. 80.

54. Daniel N. Fader and Elton B. McNeil, *Hooked on Books* (New York: Berkley, 1968).

55. Zaccaria and Moses, p. 78.

56. Brown, p. 189.

57. Zaccaria and Moses, p. 76.

58. Brown, p. 188.

59. Zaccaria and Moses, p. 82.

60. Spache, p. 24.

61. Ibid.

62. Fredrick A. Schrank, "Bibliotherapy as an Elementary School Counseling Tool," *Elementary School Guidance and Counseling* (February 1982): 223.

63. Brown; *Fifty Creative Ways to Use Paperbacks in the Middle Grades* (New York: Scholastic Book Services, 1980); Bruce Raskin (ed.), *The Reading Idea Book* (Palo Alto, California: Education Today Company, 1978); Rudman; Alma E. Russell and William A. Russell, "Using Bibliotherapy with Emotionally Disturbed Children," *Exceptional Children* (Summer 1979).

64. Patricia Perry and Marietta Lynch, *Mommy and Daddy are Divorced* (New York: The Dial Press, 1978).

65. Emily Moore, *Something to Count On* (New York: E.P. Dutton, 1980).

66. Paula Danziger, *The Divorce Express* (New York: Delacorte Press, 1982).

67. Zaccaria and Moses.

68. Brown.

2.
Alcohol and Drug Addiction

Alcohol, like many other drugs, is widely abused. Alcohol is the most commonly used and abused drug in the United States; about 50 percent of the population consumes alcohol from time to time.[1] Other drugs besides alcohol are being used by larger numbers of the general population as well. Such drugs as stimulants, amphetamines, depressants, hallucinogens, etc. are being abused by both young people and adults. The reaction by much of society to the abuse of these kinds of drugs has been harsh, thus making treatment very difficult for professional helpers.

Among those who do abuse drugs, a dominant personality type has not emerged that would assist practitioners in their treatment efforts. However, limited evidence does suggest that the passive-aggressive personality type is more predominant among alcoholics and the anti-social personality type seems to be characteristic of certain drug addicts.[2]

Alcoholism

Alcoholism is a major health problem and is a chief cause of traffic accidents, liver disease, and a variety of other social problems.[3] It is often viewed as a disease where the person drinks too much resulting in personal and family problems. Alcoholism is a progressive disease that, without sobriety, may end in institutionalization, mental and/or physical deterioration, and possibly death.

It is estimated that there are 10 million alcoholics in America; each one affects at least four other key individuals, including the spouse, other family members, or the employer.[4] Alcoholics often lose control of their lives and only gain control again by ending their abuse of alcohol.

Alcoholism has a powerful effect on the family. The impact of the alcoholism on the family is usually gradual and the response of family members is influenced heavily by their respective personality structures and family roles. The effects of alcoholism on the family have been mainly viewed from the way in which the husband-father alcoholic disrupts family life.[5]

Children, more so than other family members, are affected by the alcoholic. The child with an alcoholic father or mother must live with conflict and parental roles that are distorted. The alcoholic parent shows little adequate adult behavior.[6] Children of alcoholic families also feel the stigma attached to their families by much of society.

The abuse of alcohol is also common among children as well. Many children learn to drink by observing their parents or other adults. Drinking among adolescents is widespread and appears to be reinforced by pressures to conform to the adolescent group. Studies suggest in fact that it is unusual for the adolescent not to drink.[7] The use of alcohol among young people can lead to alcoholism as well as to other problems related to abuse, such as traffic accidents.

Most adolescent drinking reflects the practices and sanctions of family, friends, and other various reference groups. For some young people, however, drinking alcohol involves breaking with family or religious convictions. The act of drinking, the effects of drinking, and the behavior of drinking companions may create feelings of personal conflict or guilt. The reaction to these feelings may actually be relieved temporarily by drinking. Thus a cycle of conflict and confusion is produced that is relieved temporarily when the young person drinks.

Other problems for young people who drink revolve around their lack of experience in coping with the effects of alcohol. Since intoxication often takes place in public, the young person is likely to be involved in some difficulty which is highly visible. Thus the problems related to drinking are intensified because of where the child is likely to drink, in public, and the strong probability that the child will be involved in a drinking related problem.

Drug Addiction

Drugs are substances that affect the mind and/or body, resulting in behavioral or physical change. The development of drug addiction varies depending on such factors as environmental circumstances, feelings of inadequacy, insecurity, and isolation. Drugs can lead to compulsive abuse and dependence, both physical and psychological.

Physical dependence results when certain drugs are taken on a regular basis over a period of time in which the body begins to need the drug to carry out normal functioning.[8] Psychological dependence is a state in which a person feels a need for a drug. This may occur with or without physical dependence. The seriousness of dependence varies with the type of drug, the length of time the drug is taken, and the personality make-up of the user.[9]

One of the most used drugs among young people is marijuana. Marijuana produces a feeling of well-being, relaxation, sociability, and talkativeness for the user. Like alcohol, there is much pressure among the peers of young people to use marijuana.

PCP or "angel dust" is one of the most dangerous drugs used by some young people. This drug creates a feeling of weightlessness and of being out of touch with one's immediate environment. It will intensify overt or latent psychotic tendencies - flashbacks are also common in the user of this drug.

Speed, another drug currently being abused by many youth, can create paranoid reactions and violent behavior, as well as unpredictable mood changes. The problems related to speed are intensified in that it is a legitimate drug that often finds its way to the streets through illicit means.

Another abused drug among youth is heroin. This drug creates a high that gives the person a false sense of well-being. Addiction to this drug is often related to criminal acts that are done to support one's habit. Addicts often neglect themselves and are normally susceptible to infection and malnutrition. Heroin tolerance develops rapidly and increasing doses are needed to produce the desired effect.

All of the above drugs, as well as other drugs not mentioned, continue to be a major social problem in society. As the pressures of modern day living increase and the lives of young people and adults become more complex, the use of drugs will continue to be a problem. There is little to suggest that this trend will reverse in the near future.

Criteria for Book Selection

In this chapter, books were selected illustrating young people with alcohol or drug abuse problems. Books were also included that deal with the problems young people face if they have an alcoholic parent. The books annotated treat the problems of alcohol and drug abuse realistically, emphasizing the pressures that lead to abuse and the impact on other lives because of it.

Although the books selected for this chapter concerning parental alcoholism did not dwell on the parents' reasons for drinking, certain factors such as parental unemployment, loneliness, and other everyday pressures were at least mentioned in most of the books. The effects of parental alcoholism on children and other family members are illustrated in these books. Children who are characters in these books are often neglected and left to fend for themselves. They are usually friendless due to the shame and embarrassment these children feel concerning their alcoholic parent. A few books show children who are abused, either physically or sexually, as a result of their parents' alcoholism.

Books selected for this chapter where a young person is an alcoholic similarly illustrate how the young person's drinking affects parents and siblings. Certain books point to pressures at school related to sports or academic achievement as leading to a young person's alcoholism. Other alcoholic youth who were characters in some of the books suffered from a lack of social confidence and insecurity. The most helpful books on adolescent alcoholism stressed the tremendous peer pressure for young people to drink.

Peer pressure is also emphasized as a motivation for use of other drugs such as marijuana, speed, heroin, and angel dust in many of the books selected for this chapter. The possible parental and school conflicts that can result from drug abuse are pointed out. A few young people who are drug abusers in these books become involved with drug pushing. Most of the books showing a young person involved with drug abuse also mentioned a confrontation with the law without being preachy.

For bibliotherapy purposes, most of the books on alcoholism and drug abuse selected for this chapter have characters that young people with these problems can readily identify with. The books also generally hint at a possible solution to these problems. Certain books referred to a parent's alcoholism as a "disease" which is most helpful for children to understand. Solutions such as AA (Alcoholics Anonymous) or other rehabilitation programs were explored in many of the books. Books giving the impression that there is an easy solution to alcoholism or drug abuse were avoided. As a way of dealing with an alcoholic parent, some children merely avoided that parent and tried to rely on siblings or looked beyond the home for solace.

NOTES

1. Armand L. Mauss, *Social Problems as Social Movements* (New York: J.B. Lippincott Company, 1975), p. 285.

2. American Psychiatric Association, *Diagnostic and Statistical Manual of Mental Disorders* 2d ed. (Washington, D.C.: The Association, 1968), p. 43.

3. Ogden Tanner, *Stress* (New York: Time/Life, 1976), p. 142.

4. Charles Zastrow, *Introduction to Social Welfare Institutions* (Homewood, Illinois: The Dorsey Press, 1982), p. 395.

5. Robert R. Bell, *Social Deviance* (Homewood, Illinois: The Dorsey Press, 1976), p. 162.

6. Joan K. Jackson, "Alcoholism and the Family," in *Marriage and the Family* (Itasca, Illinois: F.E. Peacock, 1969), p. 277.

7. Bell, p. 164.

8. Zastrow, p. 399.

9. Ibid.

BOOKS

2.1   Anonymous. *Go Ask Alice*. Englewood Cliffs, NJ: Prentice-Hall,
       1971. 189 pp. Avon, 1971 pap. LC, braille and talking book.

       Alice, who is fifteen years old, is excited about her parents' move
       to a new city; however, she has problems making friends at her
       new school. Alice decides to return to her home town for the sum-
       mer and stay with her grandparents. There some of her old
       friends introduce Alice to various kinds of drugs and she also be-
       comes very promiscuous. Confused about whether she wants to
       continue using drugs, Alice goes back to her parents' home. Once
       school starts, Alice gets involved in the drug scene at her new
       school and begins pushing drugs to elementary school students.
       Alice begins running away periodically and living on the streets,
       taking all kinds of drugs and continuing to act out sexually. When
       she hits bottom, Alice returns home where her parents try to help
       her and have her go for counseling. The drug counseling helps
       Alice but her old drug crowd keeps trying to lure her back into
       the drug scene. Alice eventually dies from a drug overdose, with
       no one knowing whether it was suicide or a deliberate overdose
       forced on Alice by her drug using friends.

       IL: Ages 11-18   RL: 8.0

2.2   Barness, Richard. *Listen to Me!* Minneapolis: Lerner Publications
       Company, 1976. 95 pp.

       Neglected by her widowed mother, thirteen-year old Sally begins
       using speed at parties so that she can forget her poverty and
       make friends. Sally and her best friend Cindy start shoplifting
       to obtain money for speed and eventually burglarize houses. By
       the age of sixteen, Sally has quit school and has been taken to a
       juvenile detention center many times. After Sally is charged with
       possession of drugs and her sentence is suspended, she tries
       working a full-time job. But soon Sally and Cindy are pushing
       drugs to support their habit. When the two girls are picked up
       by a narcotics agent, they spend six months in a workhouse and
       are put on parole for a year during which time they stay clean.
       However, Sally and Cindy go back to using speed and heroin,
       rolling drunks outside bars for money and driving a car for Bobby,
       a friend who holds up drug stores. When Cindy dies of an over-
       dose at a party, Sally decides to move back home with her mother.
       During Sally's last drive to a pharmacy for Bobby, he is shot and
       killed. At twenty, Sally faces a prison sentence with possible pa-
       role in three years.

       IL: Ages 11-18   RL: 5.0

2.3   Berry, James. *Heroin Was My Best Friend*. New York: Crowell-
       Collier, 1971. 128 pp. Macmillan, 1974 pap.

       A drug rehabilitation center and its workings are described. Seven
       young ex-addicts are interviewed; they relate the different reasons
       why they started taking heroin and what life was like once they

(Berry, James)

became addicted to it. Family relationships, peer groups, and police involvement are all mentioned. A mother of two addicts is also
interviewed.

IL: Ages 11-18   RL: 7.0

2.4   Blue, Rose. *Nikki 108*. New York: Franklin Watts, 1972. 49 pp.

With her family deserted by her father and her mother feeling
hopeless and depressed in their ghetto neighborhood, eleven-year
old Nikki has only her eighteen-year old brother Don to turn to
for advice and support. Therefore, Nikki becomes upset when Don
begins experimenting with drugs and eventually becomes a heroin
addict. When Nikki finds Don dead of an overdose, she is overwhelmed with grief but Nikki's mother seems to have expected it.
After seeking out some of Don's friends, most of whom live in poverty and despair, Nikki decides to make something of her life and
turns to an encouraging and helpful teacher at school.

IL: Ages 11-14   RL: 3.5

2.5   Butterworth, William E. *Under the Influence*. New York: Four
       Winds Press, 1979. 247 pp.

Allan and Keith, high school seniors, become friends when they
both transfer to a different school. Allan is surprised at the way
Keith drinks beer so frequently, any time of the day, and at how
Keith seems offended if Allan doesn't join him in drinking. When
Keith disrupts two parties he attends and is involved in an automobile accident, Allan is aware that Keith had been drinking excessively on each occasion. There is a court case involving
Keith's accident which causes him much anxiety and he gets drunk
once again. After viewing together a series of driver-ed films on
drunken driving, Keith promises Allan he will go on the wagon but
during a tense moment, he starts drinking again. Keith and his
girlfriend are involved in an automobile accident which kills her
and unable to deal with what has happened, Keith goes into a private mental hospital.

IL: Ages 14-18   RL: 7.0

2.6   Childress, Alice. *A Hero Ain't Nothin' but a Sandwich*. New York:
       Coward, McCann, and Geoghegan, 1973. 126 pp. Avon, 1977 pap.
       LC, talking book.

Benjie, a thirteen-year old black heroin addict, lives with his
mother, grandmother, and "stepfather." Two teachers at his
school turn him in for drug use and Benjie must go to a drug
rehab center. Once he is out, Benjie goes back to heroin again,
always denying that he is "hooked." When Benjie steals his stepfather's clothes to buy heroin, his stepfather moves out of the
house and refuses to have anything to do with Benjie. However,
Benjie's stepfather eventually saves Benjie's life and finds out how
desperately Benjie needs a father figure. Benjie, apparently

(Childress, Alice)

wanting to go straight, goes back to the rehab center, this time accompanied by his stepfather.

IL: Ages 11-18   RL: 7.0

2.7   Dixon, Paige. *Walk My Way*. New York: Atheneum, 1980.   139 pp.

Fourteen-year old Kitty is unhappy living with her widowed father who drinks heavily.   When one of her father's friends attacks Kitty, she knocks him down during the struggle and Kitty flees, fearing she has killed him.   Kitty decides to run away to live with Aunt Lee, an old friend of her mother's.   Along the way she befriends a dog and comes in contact with many helpful people, including an old man who is dying and his grandson.   When Kitty finally arrives at Aunt Lee's, she is welcomed and Kitty calls her father to tell him she will not live with him anymore.

IL: Ages 11-14   RL: 7.0

2.8   Donovan. *I'll Get There. It Better Be Worth the Trip*. see Ch. 8.

2.9   Fox. *Blowfish Live in the Sea*. see Ch. 10.

2.10 Greene, Shep. *The Boy Who Drank Too Much*. New York: The Viking Press, 1979.   149 pp.

Fifteen-year old Buff, who is an outsider at school, plays on the hockey team only to please his father.   Buff's father, who was once a great hockey player, was unable to continue playing after Buff's mother died in an automobile accident.   When Buff gets injured during a game and decides to quit hockey, his drunken father beats him up.   Buff makes a few friends and begins going to parties but he drinks anything he can get his hands on.   He begins to have problems at school and finds he must drink before and during his hockey games to steady his nerves.   After being beaten by his father one night, Buff runs away and is found by his friends in a drunken stupor.   Ready to flee again, Buff is persuaded by his friends to stay with a kindly older woman and start going to a rehab program for alcoholism.

IL: Ages 11-18   RL: 6.0

2.11 Hamilton, Dorothy. *Straight Mark*. Scottsdale, PA: Herald Press, 1976.   126 pp.   Herald Press, 1976 pap.

Eighth-grader Mark is shocked when he discovers that a high-school star basketball player is selling drugs.   When a policeman appears in the hallways of their school, Mark and his friends are even more disturbed.   Following the arrests of three students charged with selling drugs, Mark joins a student group concerned with the drug problem at their school.   One girl whose older sister had been involved with drugs works as a decoy for the police.   A friend of Mark's tells how he once used marijuana when he was angry with his father.   Teachers and concerned parents join the

(Hamilton, Dorothy)

students in trying to fight the drug problem at Mark's school.

IL: Ages 11-14   RL: 6.0

2.12   Hanlon.   *It's Too Late for Sorry*.   see Ch. 4.

2.13   Hinton, Susan E.   *That Was Then, This Is Now*.   New York: The Viking Press, 1971.   159 pp.   Dell, 1972 pap.   LC, talking book.

Sixteen-year old Mark, whose parents are dead, lives with his best
friend Bryon and Bryon's mom in the inner city.   Bryon's mother
is ill and the two boys spend their time hustling pool halls, street
fighting, and hot wiring cars.   They also get drunk fairly often
but stay away from drugs.   When Bryon starts dating Cathy, he
begins reconsidering some of his delinquent activities.   A friend's
death during an alley fight also upsets Bryon and he and Mark
begin to grow apart.   When Cathy's younger brother runs away,
she and Bryon search for him and find him hallucinating on a bad
LSD trip.   Upset over Cathy's brother who is hospitalized, Bryon
is further shocked when he discovers that his friend Mark has
drugs in his possession and has become a pusher.   After much
painful deliberation, Bryon turns Mark into the police and Mark is
sent to prison for five years.

IL: Ages 11-18   RL: 6.0

2.14   Holland, Isabelle.   *Heads You Win, Tails I Lose*.   Philadelphia: J.B.
Lippincott Company, 1973.   159 pp.   Dell, 1977 pap.   LC, braille.

Fifteen-year old Melissa, who is overweight, is upset over her parents' constant battles.   However, Melissa is thrilled when she gets
a part in the school play.   Her drama coach encourages Melissa to
start on a safe diet.   When her father moves out of the house and
her mother begins drinking heavily, Melissa becomes very resentful.   She steals diet pills and sleeping pills from her mother and
begins taking both.   Caught up in a cycle of continually taking
pills, Melissa experiences a "bad trip" witnessed by her boyfriend.
At her boyfriend's encouragement, Melissa tells her mother about
the pills and promises to stop taking them.   She visits a doctor
for help with her weight and the doctor suggests that Melissa
tell her father about her mother's continued drinking.   Melissa's
father promises to go back home temporarily to help Melissa's mother deal with her problems.

IL: Ages 11-18   RL: 7.0

2.15   Holland, Isabelle.   *Now Is Not Too Late*.   New York: Lothrop, Lee,
and Shepard Books, 1980.   159 pp.

Cathy, who is eleven years old, spends the summer with her grandmother while her father and stepmother take their own vacation.
Cathy believes her mother to be dead and she can not understand
why members of her family are reluctant to talk about her mother.
When Cathy begins posing for a woman who is an artist, she finds

(Holland, Isabelle)

herself disobeying her grandmother in order to spend more time
with this woman. Cathy begins having nightmares at this time a-
bout a horrible looking lady chasing her. Only when Cathy and
her friends spy on an AA meeting and hear the woman artist speak
about being an alcoholic, does Cathy realize that this woman is
really her mother. Cathy is hurt by the realization that her father
lied to her about her mother's death and she begins to remember
the cruelty and verbal abuse she suffered from her mother as a
young child. Cathy's grandmother helps her to piece together the
story of her early childhood and to try to establish a renewed relationship with her mother.

IL: Ages 11-14   RL: 7.0

2.16 Hunt. *The Lottery Rose: A Novel.* see Ch. 4.

2.17 Kenny, Kevin and Helen Krull. *Sometimes My Mom Drinks Too Much.*
      Milwaukee: Raintree Publishers, 1980. 31 pp.

A young girl, Maureen, relates how she feels about her alcoholic
mother. Sometimes Maureen is afraid of her mother or embarrassed
by the things her mother does after she's been drinking. Maureen
also feels that her mother doesn't like her and that maybe she is
the reason her mother drinks. However, Maureen's father convinces her otherwise. Maureen spends a lot of time with friends and
gets much support from her teacher. When Maureen's mother is
hospitalized for her alcoholism, Maureen and her father plan how
they can help Maureen's mother with her problem once she returns
home.

IL: Ages 8-11   RL: 3.0

2.18 Kerr. *Dinky Hocker Shoots Smack.* see Ch. 4.

2.19 Kingman, Lee. *The Peter Pan Bag.* Boston: Houghton Mifflin Com-
      pany, 1970. 219 pp. Dell, 1971 pap. LC, talking book.

When seventeen-year old Wendy asks her parents to let her stay
with a friend so she can "find herself," they refuse and she runs
away. Wendy's friend has gone away for the summer so Wendy decides to stay with her friend's older brother, Peter. Peter and
Wendy stay with several of his friends, one of whom is a Vietnam
veteran who takes drugs. Wendy initially likes this group of people and begins to experiment with pot and other drugs. However,
she is not sure whether this life-style suits her; some of her new
acquaintances seem dirty and irresponsible and she hates their
pan-handling for money to live off of. When one of Wendy's
friends is arrested, he can not handle it emotionally and has to be
committed to a mental hospital. Another friend dies in an accidental drowning which may have really been suicide. Wendy is very
disturbed by these events and decides to return home for a while.

IL: Ages 14-18   RL: 6.0

2.20 Luger. *The Elephant Tree*. see Ch. 4.

2.21 Mathis. *Listen for the Fig Tree*. see Ch. 6.

2.22 Mazer, Harry. *The War on Villa Street*. New York: Delacorte Press, 1978. 182 pp. Dell, 1979 pap. LC, talking book.

Willis, an eighth grader, has always been an outsider. His family has moved frequently and Willis has always been teased by his classmates about his abusive, alcoholic father. Willis's only outlet is running just for the fun of it. After beating Willis practically unconscious one night, Willis's father is horrified at the bruises Willis has the next day and vows to remain sober. The next few weeks things seem to be looking up; however, a gang Willis has refused to join beats him up. Trying not to let the gang bother him, Willis decides to enter a running event. The appearance of Willis's drunken father causes Willis to lose the running event. At home afterwards, Willis's father begins to beat him and Willis strikes back. Willis runs away from home but returns the next day, determined to be known for what he can accomplish rather than for his father's behavior.

IL: Ages 11-14   RL: 5.0

2.23 Mazer, Norma Fox. "Chocolate Pudding" in *Dear Bill, Remember Me*. New York: Delacorte Press, 1976. 195 pp. Dell, 1978 pap. LC, talking book.

Sixteen-year old Chrissy lives in a dilapidated trailer with her widowed father and uncle, who are both alcoholics. She has no friends at her high school and is often left alone for several days at a time when her father and uncle go on a binge. Although Chrissy misses their company, she does not look forward to the two men coming back sick and crying with dirty clothes for her to wash. Chrissy is encouraged when she develops a friendship with a boy from her high school.

IL: Ages 11-18.   RL: 7.5

2.24 Mohr, Nicholasa. *In Nueva York*. New York: The Dial Press, 1977. 192 pp.

Rudi's diner is the hub of a poor ethnic neighborhood on New York's Lower East Side. Stories are told of many different people in the neighborhood with the diner serving as the place where their lives intersect. Alcohol and drug abuse are problems for several of the people. The difficulties of a homosexual couple are presented. Rudi's diner is robbed by teenagers; one of them is killed. This book is very frank in its use of street language.

IL: Ages 14-18   RL: 7.0

2.25 Myers, Walter Dean. *It Ain't All for Nothin'*. New York: The Viking Press, 1978. 217 pp. Avon, 1979 pap.

(Myers, Walter Dean)

Twelve-year old Tippy, whose mother died when he was born, has
always lived with his grandmother. When his grandmother becomes
ill and enters a nursing home, Tippy goes to live with his father,
Lonnie, in his squalid apartment. Lonnie and his friends steal for
a living in order to buy liquor and drugs and soon Tippy is forced
to take part in a robbery. Feeling guilty about the robbery,
Tippy begins to drink as well, one day to the point of blacking
out. However, Tippy meets the Sylvesters, a kindly couple who
tell Tippy he can come to them if he's ever in trouble. Eventually
Lonnie and his friends involve Tippy in an armed robbery, during
which one of the men is hurt. Afraid that his father's friend will
die, Tippy goes to the police and is put in a detention center.
Although his father is sent to prison, Tippy is cleared of all charges and goes to live with the Sylvesters. He unrealistically dreams
of having a good father-son relationship with Lonnie some day.

IL: Ages 11-14   RL: 6.0

2.26 Neville, Emily Cheney. *Garden of Broken Glass*. New York: Delacorte Press, 1975. 215 pp.

Thirteen-year old Brian wanders the streets of his poverty-stricken
neighborhood in St. Louis to escape his home life. Brian's divorced mother is an alcoholic, who neglects her children's needs,
and Brian's older sister and younger brother seem to quarrel with
him all the time. Three neighborhood teenagers, who are black,
try to befriend Brian, who is withdrawn and lonely. Brian also
begins to care for a stray dog and develops feelings of affection
for it. When Brian's mother collapses in a drunken stupor and has
to be hospitalized, Brian and his siblings are drawn together in
their concern over what will happen to them. His mother returns
home on medication to keep her from drinking, but she goes on a
binge one day and strikes Brian. Brian runs away from home,
turning to the stray dog and his neighborhood friends for comfort.
When Brian returns home to find his mother drinking steadily once
again, he and his siblings realize that they must rely on each other
to try to keep their family together.

IL: Ages 11-14   RL: 4.5

2.27 Norris, Gunilla Brodde. *Take My Waking Slow*. New York: Atheneum, 1970. 99 pp. LC, talking book.

Thirteen-year old Richie, who has moved many times in the past,
doesn't believe that things will be any better when his parents
move into a public housing project. Richie's father, who is dis-
abled and an alcoholic, promises to stop drinking and go to work
this time. But life falls into the same pattern as before - Richie's
father quits his job and starts drinking again and his mother works
so hard that she becomes ill. Richie begins fighting with other
children and is caught shoplifting at a deli. Richie's father beats
him occasionally and one day Richie strikes back, hitting his father
until he becomes unconscious. Richie runs away, afraid he has
killed his father, but returns soon afterward to find his father

(Norris, Gunilla Brodde)

still alive. With his father seemingly unable to change his ways
and his mother growing more ill, Richie decides that he is on his
own to make a better life for himself.

IL: Ages 11-14   RL: 4.0

2.28 O'Dell, Scott. *Kathleen, Please Come Home*. Boston: Houghton Mifflin, 1978. 196 pp. Dell, 1980 pap. LC, braille and talking book.

Fifteen-year old Kathy becomes friends with Sybil, a new girl at
school who is into heavy drug use. Soon afterwards Kathy meets
a young Mexican alien named Ramon whom she helps to obtain a
job. Ramon persuades Kathy to stay away from drugs. Soon the
two fall in love and Kathy tells her mother that Ramon wants to
marry her. Kathy's mother has Ramon picked up by the immigra-
tion authorities and he is killed during a border ambush. A grief-
stricken Kathy runs away to Tijuana with Sybil, hiding out when
her mother tries to find her. Using drugs including heroin herself now, Kathy tries to stop her drug usage when she discovers
she is pregnant with Ramon's child. When Sybil and Kathy return
to the States with a load of heroin, they are involved in a car accident. Sybil dies and Kathy is not seriously injured, but she
loses her baby. Kathy is sent to a detoxification center to live for
awhile. When she finally decides to return home, she finds her
mother gone in search of Kathy.

IL: Ages 11-18   RL: 4.5

2.29 O'Hanlon, Jacklyn. *Fair Game*. New York: The Dial Press, 1977.
94 pp. Dell, 1978 pap.

With her own father in a sanitarium, fourteen-year old Denise dislikes her new stepfather who drinks heavily. When Denises's stepfather spies on her while she is showering and subsequently begs
her not to tell anyone, Denise is in a state of turmoil. She suffers
from nausea whenever she thinks about her stepfather and Denise's
grades begin to fall at school. Denise's mother and younger sister
are seemingly oblivious to the stepfather's frequent drunkenness
and they can not understand the change in Denise. Once she gets
her mother to recognize her stepfather's alcoholism, Denise is able
to concentrate on her schoolwork. Denise discovers, however, that
her stepfather has made sexual advances toward one of her friends
and he later approaches Denise's eleven-year old sister. Denise's
mother forces her husband to leave and feels guilty over what has
happened to her daughters. However, Denise tries to pick up her
life and reestablish the close relationship she has always had with
her mother and sister.

IL: Ages 11-18   RL: 6.5

2.30 Orr. *Gunner's Run*. see Ch. 4.

2.31 Petersen. *Would You Settle for Improbable?* see Ch. 4.

2.32   Platt. *Headman*. see Ch. 4.

2.33   Reynolds, Pamela. *Will the Real Monday Please Stand Up*. New
        York: Lothrop, Lee, and Shepard Company, 1975. 184 pp. Arch-
        way, 1976 pap.

        Fourteen-year old Monday is indirectly responsible for her older
        brother's arrest for possession of marijuana. Concerned about
        their social status, Monday's wealthy parents are horrified and
        angry at Monday, rather than her brother Johnny. Sensing Mon-
        day's feelings of guilt and regret, a family court investigator has
        Monday use a tape recorder to tell about her troubling relationships
        with her parents and her brother. In the past, Monday's parents
        have given their children many material advantages, including pri-
        vate schools and camp. However, they are rarely at home and
        Monday craves attention and a feeling of togetherness. His par-
        ents' favorite child, Johnny has always been cruel to Monday and
        has made her feel inferior. Monday considers running away from
        her family, but decides to attempt to work out some of her diffi-
        culties with the family court investigator's help.

        IL: Ages 11-18   RL: 7.5

2.34   Samuels, Gertrude. *Run, Shelley, Run!* New York: Thomas Y.
        Crowell, 1974. 174 pp. New American Library, 1975 pap. LC,
        talking book.

        Shelley, who is sixteen, has been running away from situations
        since the age of ten. Placed in foster care at ten due to her moth-
        er's alcoholism, Shelley runs back home to her neglectful mother.
        At twelve she is caught at a pot party and sent to a juvenile cen-
        ter where Shelley runs away from the brutality and homosexuality
        of the other girls. Put in foster care again when she is apprehen-
        ded, Shelley runs back to her still alcoholic mother but finds that
        her mother has remarried. For two years, Shelley lives in fear of
        being sexually abused by her stepfather; finally she leaves this
        situation but is eventually put in a state center for girls. Shelley
        and a friend flee the state center and obtain jobs, but Shelley's
        stepfather turns them in. Sent to a maximum security institution
        this time, Shelley is horrified to learn her friend committed suicide
        to avoid returning to detention. Finally an understanding judge
        places Shelley in the home of a neighbor woman she has always
        loved. Shelley decides to try to forget about her mother and build
        her own life.

        IL: Ages 11-18   RL: 7.5

2.35   Scoppettone, Sandra. *The Late Great Me*. New York: G.P. Put-
        nam's Sons, 1976. 256 pp. Bantam, 1977 pap.

        Seventeen-year old Geri, who is shy and wishes to be popular like
        her mother was, is delighted when Dave becomes her boyfriend.
        Dave introduces Geri to drinking and suddenly Geri finds that she
        has much social confidence at parties and is gaining many friends.
        However, soon Geri feels that she must drink to get through the
        school day and she begins to experience blackouts and terrible

(Scoppettone, Sandra)

hangovers. Geri's father and her mother, who is depressed and withdrawn, ignore the changes in Geri; only Geri's older brother confronts her about her drinking. One of Geri's teachers, who is a nondrinking alcoholic, suggests to Geri that she may be an alcoholic as well and the teacher offers her help. Geri tries to limit her drinking, but when her mother is institutionalized for mental illness, Geri begins to drink heavily with Dave and her friends once more. Two things finally convince Geri to seek her teacher's help - Dave's alcoholic mother dies because of her drinking and Geri suffers a blackout and is beaten up by a strange man in a hotel room. Geri begins attending Alcoholics Anonymous and her father and brother go to Alanon. Geri visits her mother at the hospital and they agree to try to understand each other's illnesses.

IL: Ages 11-18   RL: 5.5

2.36   Seabrooke, Brenda. *HOME is Where They Take You In*. New York: William Morrow and Company, 1980. 190 pp.

Fearful of and disgusted with her alcoholic mother and her mother's shiftless boyfriend, Benicia spends much time hiding in the woods near her home. She befriends James, a sixth grader like herself, who lives in poverty and is constantly taunted by his classmates much as Benicia is. When Benicia meets a friendly young neighboring couple, she pours out the story of her family situation and the couple help her to realize that her mother's alcoholism is a disease. After a violent argument with Benicia, her mother and her mother's boyfriend rob a store and flee, leaving Benicia behind. Benicia is forced to hide out, afraid of the police. She finally turns to the neighbor couple who decide to try to get custody of Benicia.

IL: Ages 8-11   RL: 7.0

2.37   Smith. *Tough Chauncey*. see Ch. 4.

2.38   Strasser, Todd. *Angel Dust Blues*. New York: Coward, McCann, and Geoghegan, 1979. 203 pp. Dell, 1981 pap.

Seventeen-year old Alex gets involved with drugs during his senior year, partly to get back at his affluent and never-at-home parents. He becomes friends with Michael, a tough kid who carries a gun, and the two start to deal together in marijuana and eventually angel dust. Alex's grades fall and he drops out of sports. He neglects to apply to any colleges much to his parent's concern. Michael suddenly disappears and Alex learns that his friend is at a drug abuse clinic. Alex gets arrested for drug dealing and accuses Michael, who has since been discharged from the clinic, of making a deal with the police. Michael almost dies from an overdose of drugs. Alex, whose charges are reduced, feels lucky and decides to try to attend college.

IL: Ages 14-18   RL: 8.0

2.39   Trivers, James. *I Can Stop Any Time I Want.* Englewood Cliffs,
       NJ: Prentice-Hall, 1974. 154 pp.

       Seventeen-year old Graham, who smokes pot and uses other drugs
       with his friends, gets arrested for dealing. After spending a
       night in jail, Graham vows to stay away from drugs. Graham is
       put on five years of probation and given a strict set of rules to
       follow. His parents appear to lose all faith in Graham and watch
       his every move. A friend is supportive of Graham, but she is
       more interested in telling him about her own family problems. When
       Graham finds his probation and home situation to be too much, he
       begins drinking alcohol to forget about his problems. After Gra-
       ham runs away and is almost killed when hitchhiking, he promises
       his parents that he will shape up. Yet he returns to drinking as
       an outlet once again.

       IL: Ages 11-18   RL: 4.0

2.40   White, Wallace. *One Dark Night.* New York: Franklin Watts, 1979.
       90 pp.

       When fifteen-year old Greg gets in trouble with his crowd of
       friends, Greg's parents decide to have him spend the summer with
       his Uncle Roy, a small-town sheriff. Uncle Roy's wife died a
       year ago and Greg senses a change in his uncle's behavior. Greg
       also notices that his uncle drinks heavily and that certain people
       in the town have turned against his uncle. When Uncle Roy, in a
       drunken state, and some of his friends try to take the law into
       their own hands, they are arrested. Greg tries to be supportive
       when his uncle later loses his position as sheriff. When Greg
       leaves at the end of the summer, he is saddened that his uncle
       has let alcohol influence his life so much.

       IL: Ages 11-18   RL: 3.0

2.41   Windsor. *Diving for Roses.* see Ch. 7.

2.42   Wojciechowska, Maia Rodman. *Tuned Out.* New York: Harper and
       Row, 1968. 125 pp. Dell, 1969 pap.

       Sixteen-year old Jim anxiously awaits his older brother, Kevin's,
       return from college for summer vacation. However, when Kevin
       arrives, Jim is shocked at the changes in his brother. Kevin, who
       has turned against the Establishment, has a haggard look and ad-
       mits to smoking pot and taking LSD. Kevin urges Jim to smoke
       pot as well, but Jim doesn't like the experience. When Kevin has
       a "bad trip" on acid, he must be hospitalized and can have no
       visitors. Jim plans to help Kevin escape from the hospital, but
       Kevin doesn't want to see him. At the end of the summer, the
       brothers finally talk and Kevin explains the expectations he has
       always their parents have imposed on him. Jim is happy about
       Kevin's recovery and release from the hospital, but he feels the
       relationship between him and his brother will never again be the
       same.

       IL: Ages 14-18.   RL: 7.5

3.
Divorce and Separation of Parents

Rising divorce rates reflect one of the more serious issues affecting many young people in modern society. Throughout the last several decades, there has been a trend toward an ever increasing number of children to be confronted with the divorce of their parents. Currently, it is estimated that there are over 1 million children under the age of eighteen living in one-parent homes after the divorce of their parents.[1]

Divorce as a process normally involves an initial separation of parents; this separation is typically accompanied by anger and a sense of failure for the parents, and ultimately conflicting loyalties, among other things, for the children after the divorce. What scientific evidence there is suggests that divorce is often better (or at least less harmful) for children than an unhappy, conflict-ridden marriage. But this is a scant consolation for children who have to navigate the emotional transition from a two-parent to a one-parent family. Many of these same children will in time experience the remarriage of their parents resulting in another major emotional transition into a reconstituted family.[2]

The impact of divorce on children can be better understood by viewing it as a two stage process, the predivorce stage and the postdivorce stage. Divorce as a process differs from other kinds of family breakdown, such as the death of one parent, in that both parents often continue to have contact with the child after the family has been dissolved. The death of a parent, one form of family breakdown, means a clearly broken relationship with that parent. However, if we look at divorce, the child's relationship with the parent who leaves, usually the father, is greatly altered but not ended. Such a relationship is not only difficult for the child, but also for the absent parent.

Predivorce

The problems associated with the pre- and post- stages of divorce are not necessarily mutually exclusive; however, some problems are likely to be more pronounced in one stage than the other. During the predivorce stage, it is not unusual for the child to experience the emotional trauma of heated arguments and fighting between parents. Parents also

often separate for a trial period of time, thus giving the child an introduction to living in a single-parent family, usually with the mother.
During the separation stage, children will often experience conflicting
loyalties between their mother and father. This conflicting loyalty will
many times continue after the parents are divorced. Unfortunately, some
parents heighten this conflicting loyalty by trying to "outdo" the other
parent to win the child's favor.

Many children of divorce are relieved when their parents separate
for the first time because their home life becomes more peaceful once the
parents aren't constantly in turmoil. However, the child may also feel
abandoned by the parent who has left the home. Consequently, the
child is likely to be hostile toward that parent. Hostility may also be
directed against the parent who remains. This hostility toward the parents may be expressed in a variety of ways, resulting in both school
and home behavioral problems. For example, children may deprive themselves of food by refusing to eat, or of pleasure, by refusing to play.
At school, children whose parents are separated may act out in many
ways such as fighting with other children or not doing homework. The
child may simply behave in a general negative way, thus making an all-
around nuisance of itself in many different social settings.

Other common reactions in children during the predivorce stage that
are also likely to carry over after the divorce is finalized are such reactions as denial, depression and regression, and guilt.[3] For example, a
child may express denial by fantasizing that the daddy is simply on a
trip and will return within a matter of days. Regression of the child
may be expressed by resorting back to behaviors of a previous developmental stage, such as bedwetting. Children, as well as their parents,
are likely for a time period to feel guilty about the breakdown of their
family. Through steps mysterious to the parents but quite logical to
the child, children whose parents are separated may arrive at the con-
clusion that they are responsible for the separation and divorce of their
parents. The younger child may remember, for example, being naughty
in the past, behavior which was probably trivial in the eyes of an adult,
however of major proportions to the child. The child might say, "Daddy
went away because I was noisy in the morning and he couldn't sleep."
Older children naturally have more insight into their social surroundings
and are not likely to feel guilty in this form, but instead may express
it in different ways.

Postdivorce

Looking at the postdivorce stage, some children appear to experience
particular kinds of problems. One common reaction found in certain children during this stage is the fear that the parent who remains with the
child will also leave. This fear appears to be more pronounced in younger children. Some children during the postdivorce stage may develop a
fear that since their parents don't love each other anymore, the parents
may stop loving the child as well.

Other different types of problems confronting many children during
the postdivorce stage center on the child's home and school. There is
a high probability that the child will be expected to perform additional
household chores which may be resented. The house the child has lived
in may need to be sold, involving a move to a new neighborhood and

attendance at a different school. Even the child who remains in the same neighborhood and attends the same school may avoid certain friends or friends may avoid this child because of the stigma attached to divorce. These school and home behavioral problems may be shortlived but are quite troublesome to the child at the time they occur.

Recent work by Wallerstein and Kelly has found that age differences of children and their psychosocial development have an important impact on the capacity of the child to integrate and understand the divorce process. Their preliminary findings suggest that the intensity and duration of a child's response to separation and divorce is related to such factors as a child's age, developmental needs, and personality structure.[4] This kind of important work will help to more precisely define divorce-related treatment strategies. However, until this occurs, the general reactions of children to separation and divorce appear fairly predictable and can be dealt with by being keenly aware of the many mixed feelings children experience about the process and by allowing the child time to work these feelings through.

Criteria for Book Selection

Books selected for this chapter have as main characters young people whose parents are either separated or divorced. Books were chosen which seem to hold out hope for children whose parents are separated or divorced without being unrealistic. An effort was made to select books that would help young people understand and deal with the feelings and emotions associated with this time in their lives. A very few books also mention another important aspect, the child's awareness of the parent's pain and trauma following separation or divorce. Problems of the predivorce stage, including separation of the parents, as well as adjustments associated with the postdivorce stage are focused on in the books selected for this chapter.

Books in this chapter dealing with the predivorce stage describe the breaking up process, or separation, of parents. They tend to focus on the child's bewilderment and unhappiness at this time. Certain children who were characters in these books denied the separation of their parents by telling their peers that the absent parent was away on a trip. One child even claimed her mother was dead. Although most of the books stress the difficulty of the child in adjusting to living with one parent only, several also mention the relief some children felt that the tense unhappy climate in their home was finally gone. Books selected which illustrate the predivorce stage do not point to any specific character in the family as being to blame for the situation.[5] Frequently children in these books erroneously felt as if the separation of their parents was somehow their fault and even promised to make changes in their behavior to bring the absent parent back. However, this idea on the child's part was always cleared up by one of the child's parents.

Other books selected for this chapter deal with the postdivorce stage. Books were generally avoided which had a "happy ending" where parents reunited as this situation rarely happens.[6] Rather most of the books deal with the problems of coping with everyday life once the divorce is final. Various books mention problems children of divorce have to deal with such as changes in the financial situation, a possible move from a house to an apartment, and added household responsibilities for the child.

The adjustment of the child to only occasional visits with the non-custody parent rather than the daily contact experienced in the past is focused on in many of the books. A few children in these books began having school problems and/or behavior problems at home after the divorce of their parents.

Possible solutions for children dealing with the separation and divorce of their parents were subtly woven into the plot of most of these books. Some of the children who were characters in the books annotated in this chapter found comfort in peers who also had divorced parents and had been through the same situation. Several of the young people in these books turned to understanding teachers or other professional helpers after the separation or divorce of their parents. Still other children simply accepted their parents' breakup and adjusted to their new familial situation as time passed.

NOTES

1. John T. Pardeck, "Supporting American Families Through a National Social Policy," *Family Therapy* (Volume VI, No. 1, 1979): 13.
2. Robert R. Bell, *Marriage and Family Interaction* (Homewood, Illinois: The Dorsey Press, 1975), p. 571.
3. J. Louise Despert, *Children of Divorce* (Garden City, New York: Dolphin Books, 1962), pp. 14-19.
4. Judith S. Wallerstein and Joan B. Kelly, "The Effects of Parental Divorce: Experiences of the Child in Early Latency," *American Journal of Orthopsychiatry* (Volume XLVI, No. 1, 1976): 33-42; see also Wallerstein and Kelly, "The Effects of Parental Divorce: Experiences in Later Latency," *American Journal of Orthopsychiatry* (Volume XLVI, No. 2, 1976): 256-269.
5. Marsha Kabakow Rudman, *Children's Literature: An Issues Approach* (Lexington, Massachusetts: D.C. Heath and Company, 1976), p. 47.
6. Rudman, p. 46.

BOOKS

3.1   Adler, C.S. *The Silver Coach*. New York: Coward, McCann, and
      Geoghegan, 1979. 122 pp.

      When their mother goes back to school following her divorce,
      twelve-year old Chris and her seven-year old sister, Jackie, go
      to spend the summer with a grandmother they hardly know. Chris,
      who hates her mother and idolizes her father, is sure that her
      paternal grandmother will share these feelings. Jackie is quite
      immature and believes her parents will eventually reunite. The
      girls eagerly await a visit from their father. However, when he
      arrives with a woman he is dating and her children along, Chris
      and Jackie are shattered. Chris begins to see that her father is
      not without faults. She is also better able to understand the many
      pressures and demands placed on her mother as a single parent.
      With their grandmother's insight and understanding, both girls
      mature during the course of the summer and are anxious to start
      over with their mother.

      IL: Ages 11-14   RL: 6.5

3.2   Alexander, Anne. *To Live a Lie*. New York: Atheneum, 1975.
      165 pp.

      When eleven-year old Jennifer's parents get a divorce, she and her
      younger brother and sister move with their father to another city.
      Jennifer has many responsibilities thrust upon her at home, doing
      most of the housework and caring for her siblings. Blaming her
      mother for the divorce, Jennifer tells her new friends at school
      that her mother is dead. Jennifer's twelfth birthday is bleak be-
      cause her younger sister becomes ill. Jennifer angrily sends back
      unopened a package from her mother. When Jennifer's mother ar-
      rives two days later, Jennifer pours out all her feelings - that her
      mother never wanted children and that Jennifer feels to blame for
      the divorce. After much discussion, Jennifer and her mother are
      able to clear up some of the misunderstandings and Jennifer de-
      cides to tell her friends the truth about her parents.

      IL: Ages 8-11   RL: 4.0

3.3   Ames, Mildred. *What Are Friends For?* New York: Charles Scrib-
      ner's Sons, 1978. 145 pp.

      Two eleven-year old girls, Amy and Michelle, develop a friendship
      when they discover that they both live with divorced mothers.
      They both feel rejected by their fathers and Michelle, whose father
      is a psychiatrist, "counsels" Amy and helps her over some rough
      times. Amy finds, however, that other girls at her school dislike
      Michelle and will not play with Amy if Michelle is with her. Be-
      cause of this and a fight they have, Amy avoids Michelle for a
      while, but they reunite when Michelle confides in Amy the devas-
      tating news that her father plans to remarry. The girls' friend-
      ship once more is in jeopardy when Amy discovers that Michelle is
      a shoplifter. When Michelle goes to live with her father, Amy feels

(Ames, Mildred)

happier away from her friend and she begins to better understand
her parents' inability to live together.

IL: Ages 11-14   RL: 7.0

3.4   Berger, Terry. *How Does it Feel When Your Parents get Divorced?*
New York: Julian Messner, 1977. 62 pp.

Two years after her parents' divorce, a young girl describes their
stormy relationship when they were together and her pain when her
father left. For a while, she pretended her parents would get
back together. When she realized that was unlikely, she started
to misbehave and didn't go around her friends at school. She felt
better once she saw that her parents were both happier apart, but
she still became angry if her dad canceled a visit with her. Now
she and her mother live in an apartment and her mother works and
has begun dating men. The girl knows that both parents love her
and she finds herself thinking less about her parents' divorce now
and more about things she is interested in.

IL: Ages 8-11   RL: 2.5

3.5   Berger. *Stepchild.* see Ch. 11.

3.6   Blue, Rose. *A Month of Sundays.* New York: Franklin Watts, 1972.
60 pp.

Ten-year old Jeff is confused when he comes home from summer
camp to find his parents planning to get a divorce. For a while,
Jeff even thinks the divorce may be his fault. His mother moves
out of their house into a city apartment. Jeff feels lonely with his
mother working longer hours and he finds it difficult to adjust to
his new school. He misses his father and eagerly anticipates Sundays, which are spent with his dad. However, instead of always
doing special activities with his dad on Sundays, Jeff longs to
just talk to his dad. Jeff has an argument with his mother and
runs out of the house, but upon his return, they talk over their
new life and the changes for both of them and for Jeff's father.
Jeff eventually begins to make new friends at his school and grows
accustomed to his parents' divorce.

IL: Ages 8-11   RL: 4.0

3.7   Blume, Judy. *It's Not the End of the World.* New York: Bradbury Press, 1972. 169 pp. Bantam, 1973 pap. LC, braille and
talking book.

When her father doesn't come home one night, eleven-year old
Karen is hurt and confused. Karen wonders if it has anything to
do with her parents' frequent arguments. She has no one to talk
to - her older brother is moody and seldom at home and her little
sister doesn't understand the situation. Karen's mother eventually
tells the children that she and their father have decided to separate, but she is vague about the possibility of divorce. Karen

(Blume, Judy)

promises her grandfather that she will try to get her parents back together, but it doesn't work. Karen's older brother becomes more and more uncommunicative and runs away from home; Karen's parents have still another fight over that. With little help from their parents, Karen and her brother and sister finally come to the realization that their father will never live with them again. They also find that they must face many changes - their house must be sold, their mother must take a job, and they may have to move to a different city.

IL: Ages 11-14   RL: 4.0

3.8   Bridgers. *Notes for Another Life*. see Ch. 4.

3.9   Cleaver. *Me Too*. see Ch. 10.

3.10   Colman, Hila. *What's the Matter with the Dobsons?* New York: Crown Publishers, 1980. 113 pp.

Thirteen-year old Amanda and her younger sister, Lisa, become concerned when their parents' arguments become more frequent and intense. Feeling that her father is unreasonable, Amanda sides with her mother while Lisa moves closer to her father. When Amanda disobeys her father and her parents disagree over her punishment, Amanda's father decides to leave home. Lisa goes to live with him at his hotel room but finding that she is homesick for her mother and sister, Lisa soon moves back home. The girls' father and mother eventually become reconciled, but each member of the family is aware that there must be more understanding and flexibility for their family to stay intact.

IL: Ages 11-14   RL: 7.0

3.11   Cone, Molly. *The Amazing Memory of Harvey Bean*. Boston: Houghton Mifflin Company, 1980. 83 pp.

When Harvey's parents separate and leave him with the decision of which parent to live with, Harvey feels that neither parent really wants him. After telling each of his parents that he will live with the other one, Harvey takes off on his own. Harvey meets an eccentric older couple, Mr. and Mrs. Katz, and decides to stay with them for the summer. Once Harvey's parents locate him, he realizes that they really do care about him. Harvey plans to spend weekdays with his mother and weekends with his father, with occasional visits to Mr. and Mrs. Katz.

IL: Ages 8-11   RL: 6.0

3.12   Corcoran, Barbara. *Hey, That's My Soul You're Stomping On*. New York: Atheneum, 1978. 122 pp.

Sixteen-year old Rachel goes to spend the summer with her grandparents while her parents decide whether they will get divorced. Rachel enjoys most of the older people at the Palm Springs motel,

(Corcoran, Barbara)

but is relieved to meet two young people, Ariadne and her younger brother. Rachel is angry with her mother when she finds out that her parents definitely are getting a divorce and she decides to stay with her grandparents to finish school. However, when Rachel discovers that Ariadne is suicidal and that her brother has been beaten by their father, she begins to feel that lots of families have problems, maybe worse than hers. After hearing about her mother's earlier years from her grandparents, Rachel begins to better understand some of her mother's problems. Believing she is lucky to have parents who both at least love her if not each other, Rachel decides to return to live with her mother and try to help her through this difficult time.

IL: Ages 11-18   RL: 7.5

3.13 Danziger, Paula. *The Divorce Express*. New York: Delacorte Press, 1982. 148 pp.

Phoebe, who is fourteen, has problems adjusting to her parents' divorce. She feels that her parents took everything into account during their divorce settlement except her feelings. Phoebe must shuttle back and forth between her father's home in the country where she stays all week and her mother's city apartment where she spends weekends. Her parents' lifestyles greatly differ which is also an adjustment Phoebe must make. She grows accustomed to her parents both dating other people and her mother's eventual decision to remarry. Through the help of her understanding father and a friend whose parents are also divorced, Phoebe tries to find a place for herself within the lives of her two parents.

IL: Ages 11-18   RL: 6.5

3.14 Danziger, Paula. *The Pistachio Prescription*. New York: Delacorte Press, 1978. 154 pp. Dell, 1978 pap.

Cassie, thirteen years old and the middle child in her family, finds herself having an asthma attack whenever there's a disagreement between her parents. Having a beautiful older sister that she is constantly in battle with only adds to Cassie's problems. When their parents' arguments increase, Cassie and her older sister call a truce to share their fears about what's going on in their family. The night that Cassie's parents announce their plans to divorce, Cassie has a very severe asthma attack. She and her sister and brother have a hard time adjusting to seeing their father only on weekends and watching their mother date other men. When Cassie's younger brother is involved in an accident, he hopes that his parents will reunite out of concern for him, but Cassie realizes that will never be possible.

IL: Ages 11-14   RL: 7.0

3.15 Gerson, Corinne. *How I Put My Mother Through College*. New York: Atheneum, 1981. 136 pp.

(Gerson, Corinne)

When thirteen-year old Jess's parents get divorced, her mother becomes withdrawn and moody, seldom leaving her room. Therefore Jess and her younger brother, Ben, are delighted when their mother announces she is enrolling at a college. With their mother in school, there are many adjustments for the children to make with Jess taking over most of the household chores. In addition, the children find it difficult when their mother, as well as their father, begin dating other people. The role reversal of Jess's mother becoming a college cheerleader and confiding in Jess about her dates leaves Jess confused and sometimes angry. Eventually Jess's father remarries and the two children grow fond of their new stepmother. However, Ben runs away in an attempt to get his mother to break up with a man he does not like. The two children and their mother see a therapist and things begin to change - Jess's mother becomes more responsible for her children and for part of the housework while Jess and Ben feel they have an adult figure to confide in about their problems.

IL: Ages 11-14 RL: 7.5

3.16 Goff, Beth. *Where is Daddy? The Story of a Divorce.* Boston: Beacon Press, 1969. 27 pp. Beacon Press, Large Print.

A small girl, Janey, wakes up one morning to find that her father has left home. When Daddy returns and tells Janey that he and her mother are getting divorced, Janey blames herself for it. Janey and Mommy go to live with her grandmother, who watches Janey when Mommy takes a job. Afraid that her mother may leave her too, Janey becomes very quiet and tries to never show any negative feelings. Only when Janey takes out her angry feelings on her dog, does her mother realize how unhappy Janey is. Mommy takes Janey to see her workplace and her grandmother tries to be more patient with Janey. Daddy also tries to visit Janey more often.

IL: Ages 5-8 RL: 3.0

3.17 Goldman, Katie. *In the Wings.* New York: The Dial Press, 1982. 166 pp.

Fifteen-year old Jessie is thrilled when she gets a lead part in a school play and she throws herself into rehearsals to avoid being at home. Jessie's parents are fighting more and more and her younger brother is convinced that they're getting a divorce. When Jessie's father moves out of the house, Jessie tries to convince herself that she likes it because the house is so quiet. However, she is depressed when she visits her father's tiny apartment and he insists on doing activities all day on Saturdays. Jessie begins to have problems concentrating at school and during her play rehearsals. Although initially Jessie's mother seems younger and more energetic, when she and Jessie's father make the final decision to divorce, the financial and legal implications of the situation overwhelm her. Jessie becomes defiant toward her mother and has a disagreement with her best friend. However, on opening night

(Goldman, Katie)

of her play, Jessie is happy to see that both parents are in the
audience giving her support.

IL: Ages 11-18   RL: 7.0

3.18 Green. *Ice River*. see Ch. 11.

3.19 Greenfield, Eloise. *Talk About a Family*. New York: J.B. Lippincott, 1978. 60 pp. Scholastic, 1980 pap.

When her oldest brother returns from the Army, Genny is convinced that he can make everything right in her family once again,
particularly the arguments between her parents which are becoming
more frequent. On the day of her brother's surprise party, Genny
sees her parents have another dispute but they cover it up in
their efforts to make it an enjoyable day for everyone. When her
father announces the next morning that he is moving out of the
house, Genny is angry at her parents and also at her older brother for not being able to "fix" everything. A friend helps Genny
to understand how people and families change sometimes and she
decides to talk to her brothers and sisters about ways to face
their new situation.

IL: Ages 8-11   RL: 3.5

3.20 Heide, Florence Parry. *When the Sad One Comes to Stay*. New
York: J.B. Lippincott, 1975. 74 pp. Bantam, 1976 pap.

Young Sara is lonely after she and her mother move to a different
part of the city following her parents' separation. Sara likes their
beautiful new apartment and nice neighborhood, but she misses her
fun-loving father and finds herself wandering in older deteriorating
neighborhoods similar to the one where she used to live. Lacking
any friends her age, Sara becomes acquainted with an eccentric
old woman with whom she can share her troubles. Sara's father
tries to get in touch with her to her mother's chagrin and Sara
is torn apart by hearing his voice once again. Although Sara
loses contact with the old woman, she finally begins making friends
her own age.

IL: Ages 8-11   RL: 5.5

3.21 Helmering, Doris Wild. *I Have Two Families*. Nashville: Abingdon,
1981. 43 pp.

Eight-year old Patty describes her feelings when she discovers
that her parents are getting a divorce and her worries about which
parent she will live with. Because of her mother's irregular working hours, it is decided that Patty and her younger brother will
live with their father. Time is scheduled with their mother each
week as well. Although the children have adjustments to make -
their father's meals are different, their mother asks them to help
more with chores, their father begins dating - the children's new
life soon develops a pattern. Patty tells her friends that it's

(Helmering, Doris Wild)

sometimes a pain for her parents to be divorced, but mostly it's OK having two families.

IL: Ages 8-11   RL: 4.0

3.22   Holland. *Heads You Win, Tails I Lose*. see Ch. 2.

3.23   Holland. *The Man Without a Face*. see Ch. 9.

3.24   Hunter. *Me and Mr. Stenner*. see Ch. 11.

3.25   Irwin, Hadley. *Bring to a Boil and Separate*. New York: Atheneum, 1980.   123 pp.

When thirteen-year old Katie returns from summer camp, she is devastated when she learns that her parents' growing differences have caused them to separate. Katie's best friend, Marti, is away so Katie must cope by herself with the anger she feels toward her parents. She also tries to hide her parents' separation from friends and neighbors. When Katie's parents actually sign their divorce papers and her grandfather unexpectedly finds out, the divorce becomes a reality for all of Katie's family. Katie is finally able to confide in her best friend Marti. Marti reveals her suspicion that her own parents, who seem unhappy, are probably only staying together for Marti's sake - an act which Marti disagrees with. After an act of rebellion, Katie finds herself preoccupied with a new school year and therefore not thinking about her parents' divorce so much.

IL: Ages 11-14   RL: 6.5

3.26   Klein, Norma. *It's Not What You Expect*. New York: Pantheon Books, 1973.   128 pp.   Avon, 1974 pap.

Fourteen-year old Carla is upset when her father decides to spend the summer in New York "finding himself," but her twin brother Oliver takes it in stride. When the twins visit their father's apartment overnight, Carla suspects that her father is having an affair. Their mother begins inviting male friends over to their house as well. Late in the summer, Carla and Oliver discover that their older brother's girlfriend is pregnant and plans to get an abortion. Carla hesitantly tells her mother about the abortion only to find out that her mother once had an abortion before she was married. The children's father returns at the end of the summer, but Carla feels her family will never be quite the same.

IL: Ages 11-18   RL: 6.5

3.27   Lexau, Joan M. *Emily and the Klunky Baby and the Next-Door Dog*. New York: The Dial Press, 1972.   41 pp.   LC, talking book.

Emily, a preschooler, resents it when her mother asks her to watch her baby brother. Since her parents' divorce, Emily feels as if her mother is always busy and doesn't want Emily and the baby

(Lexau, Joan M.)

around. Emily decides to run away to her father's apartment with her baby brother. She soon becomes lost and is frightened. After circling the block, Emily sees her mother in front of her house and runs to her. Later Emily explains her feelings and is comforted by her mother, who decides to spend more time with her children.

IL: Ages 5-8   RL: 2.5

3.28   Lexau, Joan M. *Me Day*. New York: The Dial Press, 1971.   27 pp.

Rafer, a young black person, wakes up excited about his birthday but is very disappointed when he doesn't get even a card from his father. Rafer's parents divorced two years ago shortly after his dad lost his job. Rafer's mother sends him to the store, but he still doesn't feel any better. He walks along thinking about how much he misses his father. When Rafer finds his father waiting for him down the block, he is delighted and they make plans to spend the whole day together.

IL: Ages 5-8   RL: 2.5

3.29   Mann, Peggy. *My Dad Lives in a Downtown Hotel*. Garden City, NY: Doubleday and Company, 1973. 92 pp. Avon, 1974 pap. LC, talking book.

Joey, a young boy in elementary school, is accustomed to his parents' frequent disagreements. Therefore, he can not understand why his father walks out of the house one night after a heated argument with Joey's mother. Joey visits his father's office with a list of behaviors that he promises to change in an attempt to get his father to return home. When his plans fail, Joey feels anger toward both parents. Joey is shocked when he sees his father's barren hotel room and he resents his father packing and taking away his personal belongings from Joey's home. Only when he meets a friend whose father also isn't living at home, does Joey begin to adjust to his parents' separation.

IL: Ages 8-11   RL: 3.5

3.30   Mazer. *Guy Lenny*. see Ch. 11.

3.31   Mazer, Norma Fox. *I, Trissy*. New York: Delacorte Press, 1971. 150 pp. Dell, 1977 pap.

Trissy, who is eleven years old, has difficulty accepting her parents' divorce and uses her typewriter to vent all her frustrations. Trissy blames her mother for the divorce and misbehaves in an effort to get back at her mother. She writes on the walls of her father's apartment and accidentally starts a fire in her brother's room. Trissy also provokes her best friend until they are no longer speaking. When Trissy learns that her mother is planning to remarry, she begins to better understand her parents' needs. With her parents' support and understanding, Trissy decides to

(Mazer, Norma Fox)

change her behavior and become more responsible for her own actions.

IL: Ages 11-14   RL: 5.5

3.32   Miles. *The Trouble with Thirteen.* see Ch. 9.

3.33   Moore, Emily. *Something to Count On.* New York: E.P. Dutton, 1980. 103 pp.

When their parents decide to separate, ten-year old Lorraine and her younger brother, Jason, are very upset. Lorraine, who has always been a class clown, seems to have more behavior problems than ever at school. Her mother begins taking college courses and seems to have no time to talk to Lorraine at home. Lorraine and Jason become very excited when their father announces he is buying his own business, but they are disillusioned when he keeps canceling their weekend visits with him. With her father absent and her mother becoming more aloof, Lorraine continues misbehaving at school. She finally finds a friend in her new teacher, who is aware of Lorraine's home situation and wisely overlooks most of Lorraine's misbehavior at school.

IL: Ages 8-11   RL: 6.0

3.34   Newfield, Marcia. *A Book for Jodan.* New York: Atheneum, 1975. 41 pp.

Nine-year old Jodan feels happy and secure with her parents and they share many activities together. When her parents start to argue over little things, Jodan is confused and surprised when they announce their plans to divorce. Jodan is excited about moving to California with her mother, but she really misses her father and still can't understand her mother's explanation for their divorce. When Jodan visits her father for a holiday, they do many things together and her father also tries to make Jodan understand why he and her mother need to live apart. Wanting to show Jodan how important she is to him even when they're apart, Jodan's father gives her a scrapbook he has made which recalls their happy times together.

IL: Ages 8-11   RL: 3.0

3.35   Okimoto. *My Mother is not Married to my Father.* see Ch. 11.

3.36   Park, Barbara. *Don't Make Me Smile.* New York: Alfred A. Knopf, 1981. 114 pp.

Ten-year old Charles has difficulty accepting his parents' decision to divorce. He resents his mother always telling him to cheer up and he refuses to go to school because he feels everyone will stare at him. Charles decides to run away and live in a tree at the park until his mother persuades him to return home. He is incredulous when his father arrives on Saturday to take him to the zoo. When

(Park, Barbara)

his grades fall and he starts misbehaving at school, Charles' father takes him to see a child psychologist. Charles finds that talking things over with someone helps and that eventually his world will fall back into place.

IL: Ages 8-11   RL: 3.0

3.37 Peck. *Father Figure: A Novel.* see Ch. 8.

3.38 Perry, Patricia and Marietta Lynch. *Mommy and Daddy are Divorced.* New York: The Dial Press, 1978. 26 pp.

Ned and his little brother, whose parents are divorced, are eager to spend a Wednesday morning with their father. They have fun with their father but are both upset when he must leave. Ned questions his mother about their divorce; she asks him to remember all the arguments she and his father used to have and explains how they are both happier apart. The days pass slowly but Saturday finally comes and the two brothers once again see their father. Again it is hard to say good-bye, but they know they will see their father soon.

IL: Ages 5-8   RL: 3.5

3.39 Pevsner. *A Smart Kid Like You.* see Ch. 11.

3.40 Pfeffer, Susan Beth. *Starting with Melodie.* New York: Four Winds Press, 1982. 122 pp.

Fifteen-year old Elaine sympathizes with her best friend Melodie when Melodie's parents divorce. Although Melodie's parents are very involved in their careers, they both want custody of Melodie and her younger sister. Elaine is surprised when Melodie's mother changes their phone number and guards her daughters' movements in attempting to keep them away from their father. Melodie is often upset and makes demands on Elaine's time almost to the exclusion of Elaine's other friends. When their mother plots to send her daughters to a different city to stay with an aunt, Melodie's younger sister runs away and both parents finally realize the emotional strain they are putting their daughters through. After Melodie's family starts to settle their differences, Elaine realizes how much she appreciates the stability of her own family.

IL: Ages 11-18   RL: 8.0

3.41 Platt. *Chloris and the Freaks.* see Ch. 11.

3.42 Platt, Kin. *Chloris and the Wierdos.* Scarsdale, NY: Bradbury Press, 1978. 230 pp. LC, braille.

Thirteen-year old Jenny still misses her stepfather a year after her mother's divorce from him. When Jenny begins to date Harold, who also has a divorced mother, they both agree that their mothers have a right to a social life. Yet Jenny seems to dislike most of

(Platt, Kin)

the men her mother dates. Jenny's older sister, Chloris, even threatens to run away if their mother dates. Jenny feels better after she and her mother have a talk about this issue, but Chloris is still adamant in her insistence that their mother not date. When their mother decides nevertheless to go on a weekend trip with a male friend, Chloris runs away in an attempt to ruin her mother's plans. Jenny begins to realize how Chloris has always managed to control other's lives and upon Chloris's return, many of the family's conflicts are still left unresolved.

IL: Ages 11-18   RL: 7.0

3.43 Schwartz, Sheila. *Like Mother, Like Me*. New York: Pantheon Books, 1978. 166 pp. LC, talking book.

When her college professor father runs away with one of his students, sixteen-year old Jen must help her mother adjust to being separated. Jen's mother dates a variety of men but never develops a lasting relationship with any of them. Sympathetic and understanding, Jen is always there for her mother to confide in. Eventually, however, Jen finds herself taking on more of the household responsibilities as her mother falls into a depression. Jen is resentful as she has started to date herself. Jen's mother finally becomes involved with a women's self-help group and when Jen's father returns and wants to reconcile, Jen's mother has the confidence to tell him no.

IL: Ages 11-18   RL: 6.5

3.44 Shyer. *Welcome Home, Jellybean*. see Ch. 10.

3.45 Smith. *Kick a Stone Home*. see Ch. 9.

3.46 Stolz, Mary. *Leap Before You Look*. New York: Harper and Row, 1972. 259 pp. Dell, 1973 pap.

Fourteen-year old Jimmie worries about the increased tension between her parents, especially after she meets her father's pretty new dental assistant. She also is concerned that she has not yet begun to menstruate and she isn't interested in boys. Jimmie senses that her parents are growing farther apart, but she is still shocked when they announce their plans to divorce. Her mother goes to Mexico for a quickie divorce and puts their house up for sale. After the divorce, Jimmie's mother becomes more and more withdrawn and takes her children to live with her own mother. Unable to confide in her mother, Jimmie turns to her grandmother with her anxieties about her parents and her emerging sexuality. Even though her mother and grandmother try to celebrate Christmas that year as usual, Jimmie is overcome with memories of her absent father.

IL: Ages 11-18   RL: 9.5

3.47   Stolz, Mary. *What Time of Night is It?* New York: Harper and
       Row, 1981. 209 pp. LC, talking book. also published by Harper
       and Row in 1979 as *Go and Catch a Flying Fish.*

       When her parents have an argument and her mother leaves home,
       thirteen-year old Taylor feels lost and betrayed. Taylor's father
       seems to withdraw from everyone. Taylor's ten-year old brother
       Jem believes his mother will return at any time and her four-year
       old brother B.J. starts regressing developmentally and having be-
       havioral problems. Taylor is at least able to turn to her best
       friend Sandy with her concerns. When Taylor's grandmother ar-
       rives, Taylor is relieved of the responsibility of taking care of her
       siblings, but she is unhappy with her grandmother's strict morals
       and her obsession with housecleaning. Taylor worries about Jem
       and B.J. losing their interest in nature and the spontaneity they
       once had when her mother was at home. When Taylor's mother un-
       expectedly returns home and her grandmother leaves, Taylor real-
       izes that everyone in her family may need to make some changes for
       her family to stay intact.

       IL: Ages 11-18   RL: 7.5

3.48   Tolan, Stephanie S. *The Liberation of Tansy Warner.* New York:
       Charles Scribner's Sons, 1980. 137 pp.

       Tired of being taken for granted by her husband and children,
       fourteen-year old Tansy's mother leaves home in an attempt to
       "find herself." Tansy's father withdraws from everyone, becoming
       careless about his appearance and staying home from work. Tansy
       and her older siblings struggle to keep the household running
       and begin to realize the important role Tansy's mother played in
       their family. Although Tansy's father and siblings want her moth-
       er to return for selfish reasons, only Tansy appears to understand
       her mother's unfulfilled needs. When Tansy eventually locates and
       visits her mother, Tansy's mother tells her that she can never come
       back home. Returning to her father and siblings, Tansy feels she
       has become more self-sufficient and she is proud of it.

       IL: Ages 11-18   RL: 8.0

3.49   Wolitzer. *Out of Love.* see Ch. 11.

3.50   Wolkoff. *Happily Ever After . . . Almost.* see Ch. 11.

4.
Emotional and Behavioral Problems

The number of children in the United States having moderate to severe emotional or behavioral problems, as reported by the 1970 White House Conference on Children, consisted of approximately ten percent of the 50 million children who were then of school age. The Conference also reported that one out of three children of poverty-stricken homes had serious emotional problems requiring treatment. A small number of those children needing mental health services actually receive such care.[1]

Emotional problems also confront many members of the adult population.[2] It is estimated that nearly one in three adults needs mental health care. Of those adults having emotional problems who are parents, much has been written about the effects of these troubled parents on their children.

Troubled Children

The research literature suggests that some common characteristics are likely to be found among children confronted with emotional or behavioral problems. It must be remembered, however, that not all of these characteristics are found in troubled children, and in varying degrees, these characteristics can be found in most "normal" populations of children as well. The intent of the discussion on the following characteristics is not to identify discrete syndromes, but instead to provide a general conceptual framework for describing children who may be in need of mental health services.

Numerous clinicians have noted low frustration tolerance and limited ability to postpone gratification in many children having emotional and behavioral problems.[3] Among clinical populations of these children, this low frustration level results in outbursts at home and in school, and the lashing out at persons and other objects in the child's social environment.

A low self-image has also been found in many children confronted with behavioral and emotional problems. Children with emotional problems have a tendency to have higher failure rates in school and often have problems developing meaningful relationships with others; children with behavioral problems are confronted with similar difficulties. This failure in turn impacts the way the child sees himself - this view is likely to be negative. The child may have a tendency to view the self as "bad" or "stupid." In the Ericksonian sense, this low self-image in a troubled child such as a juvenile delinquent is reflected in such things as a tatoo etched in the forearm with the words "Born to lose" or through the child's dress, posture, and demeanor.

Relationship deficits with other people are also a major problem of troubled children. There may be a tendency for the child to be fearful of forming close relationships with others and to "con" or manipulate those with whom a relationship has formed. Such children may have difficulty in joining peer groups, and generally, simply lack social skills that "normal" individuals possess. The child will resort to inappropriate behavior as a way of handling discomfort. Some common relationship problems of troubled children include isolation, manipulation, bizarre behavior, overdependency, and intimidation.

Troubled children have a tendency to *isolate* themselves from others. These children spend much of their time in private activity - such as sitting alone and daydreaming. Peer relationships are sparse and the child develops avoidance reactions for dealing with potentially difficult social encounters. The isolated child usually knows how to stay out of trouble and generally is a passive individual. The child exists in isolation because of deficits in normal social interaction skills.

The *manipulation* of others is another characteristic found among certain troubled children. These children typically have a low level of trust in peers and others. Manipulative children are skilled at "conning" others and often play one individual off against the other. Since these children have difficulty in forming close relationships, they often manipulate others to make up for deficits in their interactional skills.

Bizarre behaviors are at times characteristic of some troubled children. Abnormal behaviors such as grimacing, hand flapping, an obsession with rituals, and other unusual behaviors are often exhibited in these children. These behaviors serve as a mechanism to keep others at bay. The behaviors are repulsive at times and often frightening. Generally other children will not play with these children because they never really know what to expect from them.

Overdependence seems to be a trait found among certain groups of children with emotional or behavioral problems. Overdependent children demand excessive time and emotional support from others. These children will nearly always check with an adult or authority figure before engaging in activities with others. Adult approval and support are constantly sought and demanded by this child.

A final characteristic among troubled children is a tendency to *intimidate* others. Intimidating children assume a position of dominance in most social situations. This bully behavior gets the child in trouble in the school, home, and other places. Such a child is a prime candidate to lead and participate in the juvenile delinquent gang. The dominant behaviors elicited by the intimidating child insure that the child will not have to form close or meaningful relationships with others.

It must be noted that the above relationship deficits are found in varying degrees in most children; however, for the troubled child these deficits are more pronounced and prevent close relationships with other people. Such relationship deficits can also be found in the adult world and may be characteristic of the troubled parent with "normal" children.

Troubled Parents

Up until the mid-sixties, the mental health literature often implied that pathological conditions of parents contributed to emotional and behavioral problems in their children. More recent literature suggests that troubled parents sometimes can bring about emotional problems in their children; however, there are many children who are not necessarily damaged by their parents' emotional or behavioral problems. Even though children with troubled parents do not always develop emotional or behavioral problems themselves, these children must create mechanisms that will help them to cope with the problems of their parents - professional help is often needed to assist them in developing these coping mechanisms.

One common problem associated with troubled parents is child abuse and neglect. Parents, for example, who have a low frustration level may have a tendency to be abusive with their child or children.[4] If other factors are present with this low frustration level such as poverty, unemployment, etc. the chance of abuse increases. Parents having problems with alcoholism or drug addiction may well be prime candidates to not only abuse their children but also to neglect them as well. An example of neglect would be the alcoholic mother who drinks all day and fails to properly clothe, feed, and generally care for her children. The alcoholic parent may also be violent during the time drinking occurs. One final problem which is a form of abuse is sexual abuse. Countless children have to face this problem, not only from their parents, but also from other adults as well. Sexual abuse traumatizes the child emotionally and often has long term effects that remain with the child into adulthood.

Troubled parents at times have relationship problems not only with their own children, but with others as well. The troubled parent may, for example, live in isolation from others including immediate family members. Such a relationship deficit not only contributes to such mental health problems as depression, but also has been found to be a variable associated with child abuse.

The troubled parent may also exhibit unusual behaviors such as ritualistic behavior that the child does not understand, but must develop coping mechanisms to deal with. Parents with emotional or behavioral problems also in some cases become overdependent on their children thus providing the stage for role reversal. In this situation, the child is forced to become the parent; such a relationship is emotionally unhealthy for the child and the adult alike.

Like the troubled child, the parent confronted with emotional or behavioral problems must deal with problems ranging from a low self-image to relationship deficits. It is again emphasized that such characteristics are found in most "normal" populations; however, the severity of such characteristics seems to be greater among troubled individuals.

Criteria for Book Selection

This chapter includes books where the main character is a child with varying degrees of emotional or behavioral problems. The difficulties faced by this troubled child are focused on, as well as the effects of his emotional or behavioral problem on siblings and parents. Books were also selected which deal with troubled parents. The troubled parent's effect on the family, especially the children, is emphasized in certain books annotated in this section.

Various types of emotional problems of children are illustrated in the books in this chapter. A few books depict children who have a low self-image; they often feel isolated and may experience difficulty in making friends. Other books portray children who are having more than the usual amount of difficulties in their relationships with parents, teachers, or siblings. Still other books deal with young people who have more pro-nounced emotional problems. Some of these young people suffer from delusions; others are obsessed with rituals; and a few even attempt suicide.

Books in this chapter dealing with behavioral problems of young peo-ple tend to focus on the child's behavior at school or with friends. A few young people who are characters in these books vandalized property; others were often truant from school. Teen-age runaways are described in a few of the books. Some youth became involved with shoplifting. Gang behavior, including physical violence, is illustrated in certain books. Some of the adolescents who were characters in these books are put on probation or put in juvenile detention centers.

Parents who are troubled are the focus of other books in this chap-ter. The effects of the parent's problems on the children in the family are emphasized in these books. Books were selected where parents were involved with child neglect or abuse. Often these parents had problems such as alcoholism and unemployment. The feelings of instability and frustration experienced by the neglected child, as well as the fear and distrust suffered by the physically or sexually abused child, are men-tioned. Other books deal with parents who become depressed and with-drawn; a few require hospitalization due to their mental problems. The children of these mentally ill parents experience emotions ranging from disgust and hate to pity. In some books, the child is given the over-whelming task of taking on the parental role in caring for siblings and the household.

For bibliotherapy purposes, troubled children should be able to iden-tify with characters in these books whose problems are similar to their own. Young people whose parents are troubled may see themselves in the characters of the books dealing with this issue as well. The most helpful books in this chapter offer children a way to cope with or even-tually overcome their problems. Possible solutions for minor problems facing children included sharing their problems with a parent or teacher. The majority of the books dealing with more serious problems of both children and parents mentioned professional counseling. This professional help was usually in the form of school counselors, psychologists, social workers, or psychiatrists.

NOTES

1. *Profiles of Children - 1970 White House Conference on Children* (Washington, D.C.: U.S. Government Printing Office, 1972).
2. Paul B. Horton and Gerald R. Leslie, *The Sociology of Social Problems* 5th ed. (Englewood Cliffs, New Jersey: Prentice-Hall, 1974), p. 528.
3. Luciano L'Abate and Leonard T. Curtis, *Teaching the Exceptional Child* (Philadelphia: W.B. Saunders Company, 1975), p. 261.
4. Ray E. Helfer and C. Henry Kempe (eds.), *Child Abuse and Neglect: The Family and the Community* (Cambridge, Massachusetts: Ballinger, 1976).

BOOKS

4.1   Addy, Sharon. *We Didn't Mean To.* Milwaukee: Raintree Children's
      Books, 1981. 31 pp.

      Tommy and his friends thoughtlessly commit minor acts of vanda-
      lism, such as writing graffiti on walls. Tommy and a friend ran-
      sack what they believe is a rival basketball team's clothing and e-
      quipment; they are shocked to discover it is actually their own
      team's locker room. When the coach finds out who vandalized his
      team's property, he demands that the boys think of a way they
      can make up for the consequences of their actions.

      IL: Ages 8-11   RL: 3.0

4.2   Ames. *What Are Friends For?* see Ch. 3.

4.3   Anderson, Mary. *Step on a Crack.* New York: Atheneum, 1978.
      180 pp. LC, talking book.

      Sarah, who is fifteen, is disturbed about her frequent nightmares
      during which she kills her mother. Even more disturbing is her
      shoplifting that always follows the nightmare. When Aunt Kat
      comes to visit for the summer, Sarah's strange behaviors increase
      and she finds herself sleepwalking at night in her mother's room.
      Sarah cries out for help to a friend and together they try to find
      an explanation for Sarah's behavior. A visit to a clairvoyant and
      a search through some historical records help Sarah to dredge up
      some early childhood memories of her mother abandoning and abus-
      ing her. Then Sarah recalls that the abusive mother was actually
      Aunt Kat. Sarah's mother explains to her that Aunt Kat, unable
      to handle the emotional strain of being a single parent, gave up
      Sarah to her older sister to raise. Feeling unforgiving toward
      Aunt Kat, Sarah is hopeful that professional counseling will help
      her to deal with her problem behaviors.

      IL: Ages 11-18   RL: 6.5

4.4   Anonymous. *Go Ask Alice.* see Ch. 2.

4.5   Arrick, Fran. *Steffie Can't Come Out to Play.* Scarsdale, NY:
      Bradbury Press, 1978. 196 pp. LC, braille.

      Sick of the drudgery of her home life in a Pennsylvania mining
      town, fourteen-year old Stephanie runs away to New York City
      to be a model. Soon after her arrival in New York, Steffie meets
      a man called Favor who gives her expensive gifts and asks Steffie
      to share his luxurious apartment. Steffie is very homesick but she
      falls in love with Favor and is willing to work the streets as a
      prostitute for him. Steffie is soon one of Favor's top earners.
      Favor's other girls, jealous of Steffie's youth and beauty, create
      problems for Steffie and she is beaten by Favor. Steffie is fright-
      ened by some of the requests of her customers and is even slipped
      a drug by one man. Two policemen start to hassle Favor about
      using Steffie and deciding that she is more trouble than she's

(Arrick, Fran)

worth, Favor throws Steffie out. Steffie has nowhere to go until
one of the policemen convinces her to go to a shelter for runaways.
Steffie eventually returns home.

IL: Ages 11-18   RL: 6.5

4.6 Ashley. *Break in the Sun.* see Ch. 11.

4.7 Ashley, Bernard. *Terry on the Fence.* New York: S.G. Phillips,
     1977. 196 pp.

Terry, an eleven-year old English boy, runs away from home after
a heated argument with his mother and older sister. Terry is ac-
costed by a gang and threatened with a knife by the gang's fifteen-year old leader, Les. The gang forces Terry to aid them in
burglarizing his own school before they will release him. When the
school headmaster links Terry with the burglary, Terry seeks out
Les to try to persuade the gang to return the stolen goods. After
Terry witnesses Les being physically abused by his mother, Terry
begins to understand Les's gang involvement. Terry also senses
the security of his own home as compared to Les's. The two boys
are taken to a juvenile court where Terry is discharged due to his
forced involvement in the crime and Les is sent to a community
home.

IL: Ages 11-18   RL: 8.0

4.8 Barness. *Listen to Me!* see Ch. 2.

4.9 Bauer, Marion Dane. *Tangled Butterfly*. New York: Houghton
     Mifflin, 1980. 162 pp.

Seventeen-year old Michelle has an outburst at her older brother's
wedding and he tells her she is "crazy." Michelle can not tell anyone that she was not responsible for her behavior, but that an
inner voice she calls grandmother directed her actions. Michelle's
mother, who has denied for years that there is anything wrong
with her daughter, will not agree to take her for professional help
as Michelle's father suggests. Instead Michelle and her mother
take a trip to an island where a former teacher, Paul, saves Michelle from taking her own life. Paul quit teaching because of a
painful experience with a psychotic student, yet he can not keep
himself from befriending Michelle. When Paul tries to talk Michelle
into seeing a psychiatrist, she runs away with his infant daughter.
Finally Michelle's family comes to the realization that she desperately needs help.

IL: Ages 11-18   RL: 6.0

4.10 Blume, Judy. *Blubber*. Scarsdale, NY: Bradbury Press, 1974.
     153 pp. Dell, 1981 pap. LC, braille and talking book.

Jill, who is a fifth-grader, becomes involved in her classmates'
teasing of an obese girl named Linda. Jill and her friends trip

(Blume, Judy)

Linda in class, partially strip her in the bathroom, and think up
other ways to make Linda's life miserable. When Jill and her friend
play a prank on Halloween, they blame Linda for tattling and hold
a mock trial for her at school. Jill's mother forces her to sit by
Linda during a bar mitzvah which makes her even more resentful
toward the girl. When Linda becomes one of the gang, Jill is suddenly the object of everyone's teasing. Jill puts a stop to her
classmates' teasing her and a stalemate is reached; however, Linda
finds herself friendless once again.

IL: Ages 8-11   RL: 3.0

4.11 Blume, Judy. *Then again, maybe I won't*. Scarsdale, NY: Bradbury
Press, 1971. 164 pp. Dell, 1973 pap. Bradbury Press, Large
Print. LC, talking book.

When his father makes a good business deal, twelve-year old Tony
and his parents make a move to a suburb on Long Island. Tony
misses his old neighborhood, especially his paper route and old
friends. Tony's family is caught up in a new lifestyle with a plush
home and a maid. Tony's mother is eager for him to make friends
with Joel, the boy next door, but Tony is upset by some of Joel's
activities such as drinking and shoplifting. Tony is also worried
about the wet dreams he is having. His many anxieties eventually
lead to a "nervous stomach." When Tony ends up in the hospital
with severe stomach pains, he is referred to a psychiatrist to help
him sort out his troubling emotions.

IL: Ages 11-18   RL: 3.5

4.12 Bosse, Malcolm J. *The 79 Squares*. New York: Thomas Y. Crowell,
1979. 185 pp. Dell, 1982 pap.

Fourteen-year old Eric is involved with a gang and has been put
on probation for vandalizing his school. When Eric meets and
starts spending time with an old man, Mr. Beck, he finds he is
spending less time with his gang. Eric's probation officer and his
parents warn Eric to stay away from Mr. Beck when it is discovered
that he has just been released from prison. But Eric continues to
see the old man, who criticizes Eric for his excessive drinking
and delinquent behavior. When people in the neighborhood become
upset over Mr. Beck's prison record and Eric's gang comes to
harass the old man, Eric defends Mr. Beck. Eric and Mr. Beck
are both hospitalized for injuries. When Mr. Beck dies soon afterward, Eric feels that he has lost his closest friend.

IL: Ages 11-18   RL: 7.0

4.13 Bridgers, Sue Ellen. *Notes for Another Life*. New York: Alfred
A. Knopf, 1981. 250 pp.

Sixteen-year old Kevin and his thirteen-year old sister, Wren,
have lived with their grandparents since their father was committed to a mental hospital several years earlier. It is painful for the

(Bridgers, Sue Ellen)

children to visit their father and their mother, who is busy with a life of her own, only sees them infrequently. Kevin tends to be moody and sometimes worries that he may have inherited his father's condition. Happy that their father has improved enough to return home, Kevin and Wren are shocked when their mother arrives and announces that she is seeking a divorce. The children's mother is also taking a new job much farther away and when she rejects Kevin's offer to move in with her, Kevin takes an overdose of pills. Kevin recovers but his father falls into another deep depression and must be returned to the hospital. When his mother leaves as well, Kevin tries to put his life back together without the support of his parents.

IL: Ages 11-18   RL: 8.5

4.14 Byars, Betsy. *The Pinballs*. New York: Harper and Row, 1977. 136 pp. LC, talking book.

Three foster children come to live with the Mason family: fifteen-year old Carlie, who has been physically abused by her stepfather; Harvey, thirteen, whose drunken father drove an automobile over both his legs; and eight-year old Thomas J., an orphan who has lived with two elderly women for several years. Carlie is bossy and insulting in her new foster home, while Harvey seems withdrawn and Thomas J. suffers from loneliness. The Masons offer encouragement to each child and gradually the three children begin to feel like a family. When Harvey becomes depressed after a visit with his father and his legs later develop a serious infection, Carlie is determined to improve his physical and mental health. Mr. Mason helps Thomas J. overcome his grief when the two women who cared for him both die. Feeling secure in their foster home, the three children share their feelings of rejection and begin to care about each other.

IL: Ages 11-14   RL: 5.5

4.15 Clymer, Eleanor. *Luke Was There*. New York: Holt, Rinehart, and Winston, 1973. 74 pp. Archway, 1976 pap. LC, braille.

Julius, who has been abandoned by his father, his uncle, and his stepfather, grows frightened when his mother becomes ill and needs to be hospitalized. Julius and his little brother are sent to a children's home where Julius meets a counselor named Luke. Julius becomes attached to Luke and develops trust in him; therefore, Julius is shattered when Luke leaves the home to take another job. Not believing Luke's promise to return, Julius begins stealing and even runs away from the home. However, when Julius finds Ricky, an abandoned youngster even more frightened than he is, the two return to the children's home. Luke indeed comes to see Julius and when Julius and his brother return home to their mother, Julius in turn promises to come see Ricky at the home.

IL: Ages 8-11   RL: 3.5

4.16   Colman. *Diary of a Frantic Kid Sister*. see Ch. 10.

4.17   Cormier, Robert. *The Chocolate War*. New York: Pantheon Books,
       1974. 253 pp. Dell, 1975 pap. LC, braille and talking book.

Jerry, a high school freshman, is stunned by his mother's death
and his father's subsequent depression. He tries to bury himself
in schoolwork and football practice and is surprised when he is
approached to become a member of his school's secret society. Archie, the ruthless leader of the society, gives Jerry the tough assignment of refusing to participate in the school's annual chocolate
sale. A teacher tries to intimidate Jerry into joining the chocolate
sale, but he steadfastly refuses. Even when given the go-ahead
by Archie to sell chocolates, Jerry still refuses in defiance of the
society. The angry teacher and the secret society join in their
efforts to teach Jerry a lesson, resulting in a gang fight that seriously injures Jerry.

IL: Ages 14-18   RL: 8.5

4.18   Danziger, Paula. *The Cat Ate My Gymsuit*. New York: Delacorte
       Press, 1974. 147 pp. Dell, 1975 pap. LC, talking book.

Thirteen-year old Marcy has a poor self concept and is particularly
concerned about being overweight and not doing well in gym class.
Marcy's father constantly yells at her at home, calling Marcy a
failure and demanding strict obedience, while Marcy's mother hides
from the situation by taking tranquilizers. Marcy gets a replace-
ment English teacher at her school, Ms. Finney, who encourages
students to express themselves in after-school group sessions.
Marcy begins to gain confidence in herself at school and home.
When Ms. Finney is dismissed because of her unconventional teaching methods, Marcy helps to organize a student protest to get
Ms. Finney reinstated. Marcy's father is furious when she is suspended from school because of the protest, but Marcy's mother
tells Marcy in private how proud she is of her daughter's behavior.
Although Ms. Finney is reinstated, she feels it is best to resign
anyway; yet she leaves behind many good things - Marcy's mother
shows more independence and begins taking night classes and Marcy
decides to diet and starts seeing a psychologist.

IL: Ages 11-14   RL: 5.0

4.19   Donovan. *Remove Protective Coating a Little at a Time*. see Ch. 9.

4.20   Gold, Sharlya. *Amelia Quackenbush*. New York: The Seabury
       Press, 1973. 153 pp. LC, braille.

Twelve-year old Amelia is apprehensive about starting junior high
school with her underdeveloped figure and hand-me-down clothes.
She is surprised when Donna, a pretty girl popular with the boys,
befriends her and starts giving her expensive gifts. Amelia is
elected to the student council but when she excitedly tells her family about it, Amelia's older sister, Courtney, makes an announcement
as well - that she is pregnant and doesn't want to get married but
will have the baby. Amelia's family is in turmoil with Amelia and

(Gold, Sharlya)

her parents supporting Courtney's decision but another sister feeling that Courtney should have an abortion. Amelia is in desperate need of a new dress to wear to her first student council meeting, so she goes along with her friend Donna's idea to shoplift a new dress. Amelia is filled with guilt afterwards and plans to return the dress, but Donna blackmails her into hiding a stolen bike as well. After being questioned about the stolen items by their principal and making plans to return everything, Amelia drops her friendship with Donna and feels she has matured.

IL: Ages 11-14   RL: 6.0

4.21 Green, Phyllis. *Walkie-Talkie*. Reading, MA: Addison-Wesley, 1978. 96 pp.

Fourteen-year old Richie is hyperactive, friendless, and constantly in trouble at home and school. He has failed two years of elementary school. Although Richie's father feels he will outgrow his current problems, Richie's mother has no faith in her son and totally rejects him. When Richie meets Norman, a boy in a wheelchair with a severe speech problem, the two become friends. Richie spends the summer involved in different activities with Norman and feels that he is better able to control his behavior. However, Richie's control falls apart one day and he cruelly teases his friend Norman. Unable to regain his relationship with Norman, Richie wonders how long he will continue to be friendless and disruptive.

IL: Ages 11-14   RL: 3.0

4.22 Greene. *Getting Nowhere*. see Ch. 11.

4.23 Hanlon, Emily. *It's Too Late for Sorry*. Scarsdale, NY: Bradbury Press, 1978. 222 pp. LC, talking book.

High school sophomores Kenny and Phil have been best friends for years. However, their friendship falls apart when Kenny makes the football team and Phil begins using marijuana. Always tending to be obnoxious, Phil starts a campaign to make life totally miserable for Harold, a retarded teenage boy who moves into Kenny's neighborhood. Kenny starts dating Rachel, who enjoys working with retarded youth, and the two begin including Harold in their activities. When Kenny finds himself becoming more and more attracted to Rachel, he grows jealous of Rachel's attention to Harold and breaks up with her. Kenny and Phil spend some time together once again. Stoned on marijuana one day, Kenny verbally abuses Rachel and Harold when he sees them together and even punches Harold. A bewildered Harold runs away and is not found for several days. Feeling guilty, Kenny makes several attempts to regain his friendship with Harold. Kenny realizes, however, that his relationship with Rachel is over.

IL: Ages 11-18   RL: 6.5

4.24   Harris, Marilyn. *The Runaway's Diary*. New York: Four Winds
        Press, 1971. 222 pp. Archway, 1974 pap.

        Because of her parents' frequent quarrels, fifteen-year old Cat de-
        cides to run away. While hitchhiking, Cat encounters many differ-
        ent people - some helpful and others which are disturbing to Cat.
        Cat spends some time with a seriously ill woman who chooses not
        to seek medical attention. Eventually Cat camps on a mountainside
        where she tries to sort out her feelings about her parents, other
        people, and life and death. She becomes ill and is nursed back to
        health in a cave by a mysterious man Cat later discovers has fled
        from a mental hospital. Cat finally decides to return home and
        face her parents. However, she is struck by a car and dies while
        hitchhiking back home.

        IL: Ages 11-18   RL: 5.0

4.25   Hautzig, Deborah. *Second Star to the Right*. New York: Green-
        willow Books, 1981. 151 pp.

        Feeling that she is imperfect and not in control of her life, four-
        teen-year old Leslie begins dieting. Leslie is urged on by compli-
        ments from her parents and peers and starts eating less and less
        while undertaking more physical exercise. Eventually Leslie stops
        menstruating and she vomits whenever her parents force her to
        eat. She also feels as if a dictator in her mind controls her eating
        habits. Leslie's mother, blaming herself for what is happening to
        her daughter, starts seeing a psychiatrist. When Leslie's body
        weight falls to 76 pounds and her blood pressure falls, she is hos-
        pitalized and given tranquilizers. Leslie's parents seek out a spe-
        cialist in anorexia nervosa and Leslie is eventually placed in resi-
        dential treatment with several other girls afflicted by the same con-
        dition. There Leslie finally begins taking in small amounts of nu-
        trients and talking out some of her problems with a therapist.

        IL: Ages 11-18   RL: 6.5

4.26   Heide, Florence. *Growing Anyway Up*. New York: J.B. Lippincott,
        1976. 127 pp.

        Florence is very nervous about her mother's decision to move to a
        different state. Florence's widowed mother is very uncommunica-
        tive and watches television all the time, leaving Florence lonely and
        unable to form relationships with other people. In her new envir-
        onment, Florence tries to make people and objects she encounters
        "safe" by going through a ritual of looking at four different points
        a certain number of times. However, Florence is worried when her
        ritual does not work on George, a man her mother begins to date.
        Florence's aunt arrives, making Florence feel alive with her con-
        stant chattering, but Florence feels more lonely than ever when her
        aunt leaves once again. When Florence discovers that her mother
        plans to marry George, she feels abandoned and decides to run
        away. Florence's aunt finds her and together they figure out what
        has always made Florence so compulsive and nervous - she feels
        responsible for her father's death because she refused to kiss his
        suitcase and make it "safe" the day her father was killed on a

(Heide, Florence)

business trip. After her aunt convinces Florence that the death was not her fault, Florence is relaxed and calm for the first time in years.

IL: Ages 11-18   RL: 6.0

4.27   Hunt, Irene. *The Lottery Rose: A Novel*. New York: Charles Scribner's Sons, 1976. 185 pp. Grosset and Dunlap, 1981 pap.

After being physically abused frequently by his alcoholic mother and her boyfriend, seven-year old Georgie is fearful and distrustful of adults and has behavior problems at school. His only interest is a library book about beautiful flowers; therefore, Georgie is thrilled when he wins a rosebush in a lottery. When his mother's boyfriend brutally beats Georgie, he must be hospitalized and is sent to a boys' home afterward. Georgie plants his rosebush in a neighboring garden and befriends a five-year old retarded boy, Robin, and Robin's grandfather; however, Georgie will have nothing to do with Robin's mother. Over the summer Georgie spends much time with Robin and Robin's grandfather teaches Georgie to read. When Robin wanders away to a lake and drowns, Georgie is overcome with grief and digs up his rosebush to plant on Robin's grave. In sharing their sadness over Robin's death, Georgie turns to Robin's mother and she asks if Georgie will belong to her now.

IL: Ages 11-14   RL: 8.5

4.28   Kellogg, Marjorie. *Like the Lion's Tooth*. New York: Farrar, Straus, and Giroux, 1972. 148 pp. LC, braille.

Eleven-year old Ben, who has been physically and sexually abused by his father, is sent to a school for "problem children" mainly for his own protection. There he is befriended by Julie, whose mother is in a mental institution and whose father deserted her family. He also meets Madeline, who was sexually abused like himself, and Odie, who constantly shoplifts. Although Ben feels protected at this school, he frequently runs away to see his mother. Ben's younger brother, also at the school but separated from his older brother, commits suicide. A frightened and lonely Ben tries to locate his mother but failing to do so, resigns himself to coping with life at the school.

IL: Ages 11-14   RL: 7.0

4.29   Kerr, M.E. *Dinky Hocker Shoots Smack*. New York: Harper and Row, 1972. 198 pp. Dell, 1973 pap. G.K. Hall, Large Print. LC, talking book.

Fifteen-year old Tucker becomes friends with an overweight, sloppily dressed fourteen-year old girl, Dinky. Dinky's parents are very involved in charities and her mother works with ex-drug addicts, leaving Dinky alone much of the time. Tucker begins to date Dinky's attractive cousin, Natalia, and he sets up a date for

(Kerr, M.E.)

Dinky with P. John, who is also overweight. P. John and Dinky
join Weight Watchers together, giving each other encouragement
to diet, and Dinky seems to thrive under P. John's influence.
Meanwhile Tucker finds his relationship with Natalia rather disturbing and he discovers that Natalia has received treatment for mental
problems in the past. Dinky's parents dislike P. John and when
Dinky is forbidden to see him, she begins to eat constantly and
becomes a recluse. Dinky's parents try to solve her problems with
a prescription for diet pills and then are annoyed when Dinky develops some problem behaviors. Finally, a grossly overweight
Dinky acts out in such a way that her parents become aware that
in their efforts to help others with problems, they have totally ignored the needs of their own daughter.

IL: Ages 11-18.   RL: 7.5

4.30   Luger, Harriet. *The Elephant Tree*. New York: The Viking Press,
       1978.   115 pp.   LC, talking book.

Dave, a ninth grader with a stepfather who beats him and a mother who drinks heavily, is frequently truant from school. He finds
himself enrolled in a program for delinquent boys. Chaperoned by
two adult leaders, the group of boys goes on a desert camp-out.
There Dave and Louie, who attends a rival high school, immediately
become enemies and threaten each other with knives. When Louie
steals a jeep from the campsite and Dave goes along with him on a
dare, the two become hopelessly lost in the desert. They wander
aimlessly for two days without food or water, each blaming the
other for their predicament. Only when Louie saves Dave's life,
do the two boys realize how much they need each other. Talking
out their feelings with each other, Louie and Dave become friends
and remain on good terms after they are rescued.

IL: Ages 11-18   RL: 6.5

4.31   MacLachlan, Patricia. *Mama One, Mama Two*. New York: Harper and
       Row, 1982.   25 pp.

Maudie's foster mother, Mama Two, tells young Maudie the story of
how she came to stay with them. Maudie's mother, Mama One, was
quite poor but she used to have good times with Maudie. Then
Mama One became depressed and stayed in her room all the time,
leaving Maudie to take care of herself. A social worker talked to
Mama One and assisted her in getting help with her problems. The
social worker also told Maudie about the "for-a-while" home he was
taking her to. Maudie was sad and cried for Mama One at first,
but she feels secure in her foster home now and hopes to eventually return home with Mama One.

IL: Ages 5-8   RL: 2.0

4.32   McLendon. *My Brother Joey Died*. see Ch. 8.

4.33   Mazer. *The War on Villa Street*. see Ch. 2.

4.34   Mazer. *I, Trissy*. see Ch. 3.

4.35   Miklowitz. *Did You Hear What Happened to Andrea?* see Ch. 9.

4.36   Moore. *Something to Count On*. see Ch. 3.

4.37   Morgan, Alison. *All Kinds of Prickles*. New York: Elsevier/Nelson Books, 1980. 175 pp.

Abandoned by his parents as a baby, Paul has been raised on his grandfather's isolated farm. When the grandfather dies, a bewildered Paul goes to live with his aunt and uncle and cousin Joanna, who is a sixth grader like himself. Since Paul has never met these relatives before, he feels strange and unwelcome in their home. His aunt and Joanna make an effort to communicate with Paul, but he says little to anyone except a pet goat he brought with him from the farm. When Paul's mother contacts his aunt and expresses a desire to see him eventually, Paul is even more distressed. After Paul's goat causes trouble in the neighborhood, Paul's uncle tries to find a new home for it but failing to do so, has the goat put to sleep. Upon discovering his goat's death, Paul vandalizes his uncle's garden and runs away. However, a talk with a kindly old man persuades Paul to return. Paul finally begins to feel more secure living with his aunt and uncle when they let him have a new pet and he even agrees to a short visit with his mother.

IL: Ages 11-14   RL: 7.5

4.38   Myers. *It Ain't All for Nothin'*. see Ch. 2.

4.39   Neufeld, John. *Lisa, Bright and Dark*. New York: S.G. Phillips, 1969. 125 pp. New American Library, 1970 pap. LC, braille.

Sixteen-year old Lisa believes she is losing her mind. She hears voices in her mind and has bad days when she stays isolated in her home. When Lisa's parents ignore her pleas for help, three of Lisa's friends, one of whom has suffered from emotional problems, try to persuade a school counselor to help Lisa. Without the go-ahead from Lisa's parents, the counselor can only give Lisa's friends advice. The friends begin their own therapy sessions with Lisa which seem to help her slightly. However, Lisa once again slips into a depression and withdraws from reality; she almost dies after walking through a glass door. While hospitalized, Lisa also takes a drug overdose. Lisa's father is finally persuaded to send Lisa to a private hospital for psychiatric help. A psychiatrist gives Lisa's friends encouragement and advice on how to respond to Lisa once she returns.

IL: Ages 11-18   RL: 7.0

4.40   Neville. *Garden of Broken Glass*. see Ch. 2.

4.41   Norris. *Take My Waking Slow*. see Ch. 2.

4.42   Orr, Rebecca. *Gunner's Run*. New York: Harper and Row, 1980. 150 pp.

(Orr, Rebecca)

Nine-year old Gunner, whose mother died after his birth, lives
with his father and older sister. Gunner's father, who is an alcoholic, frequently beats Gunner, sometimes to the point of uncon-
sciousness. When Gunner's older sister runs away to California,
Gunner decides he must escape his father as well. An old man
takes Gunner in and the two become close friends. When Gunner
tries to get in contact with his father, he is only beaten once a-
gain. The older man who Gunner stays with becomes increasingly
ill and Gunner feels a great sadness when the man dies. Gunner,
who has developed a better self-concept through his friendship
with the old man, doesn't know what he will do now but hopes for
his sister's return.

IL: Ages 8-11.   RL: 3.5

4.43 Park. *Don't Make Me Smile*. see Ch. 3.

4.44 Paterson, Katherine Womeldorf. *The Great Gilly Hopkins*. New
      York: Thomas Y. Crowell, 1978. 148 pp. Avon, 1979 pap. LC,
      talking book.

Abandoned by her mother eight years ago, eleven-year old Gilly
is now in her third foster home. Bright and very independent,
Gilly sets out to create trouble in her newest foster home where
she will live with Trotter, her foster parent, and another foster
child who is younger and believed to be retarded, W.E. Gilly ter-
rorizes W.E. and is extremely rude to Trotter, who is the first
adult who has ever really cared about Gilly. When Gilly receives
an impersonal postcard from her real mother, she steals money from
a neighbor for a bus ticket but her efforts to run away fail. Then
Gilly's maternal grandmother comes to take Gilly home with her.
Gilly finally sees her mother who doesn't want her. Heartbroken,
Gilly begs Trotter to let her return but Trotter, although she desperately misses Gilly, encourages Gilly to stay with her grandmother where she is needed the most.

IL: Ages 11-14   RL: 7.5

4.45 Petersen, P.J. *Would You Settle for Improbable?* New York: Del-
      acorte Press, 1981. 185 pp. Dell, 1983 pap.

Fourteen-year old Michael and his classmates are in awe of Arnold,
a new student at their school who has spent most of his life in juvenile detention centers. Arnold puts up a tough front and is an
expert at stealing, lying, and conning people. Michael begins to
understand Arnold better when he goes to Arnold's home, which is
a shack, and meets Arnold's alcoholic mother. When Arnold takes
the rap for an act of vandalism he didn't commit to protect another
student, everyone is amazed. Even the teachers think Arnold is
turning over a new leaf when he studies hard to pass an important
test which will allow him to graduate from junior high. Eventually,
however, Arnold's mother is arrested by the police for drunk and
disorderly conduct and disappears upon her release. Arnold takes
a friend's money and steals a car, putting him once again back in
the juvenile center.

(Petersen, P.J.)

IL: Ages 11-14   RL: 7.0

4.46   Pevsner. *And You Give Me a Pain, Elaine.* see Ch. 10.

4.47   Philips, Barbara. *Don't Call Me Fatso.* Milwaukee: Raintree Children's Books, 1980. 31 pp.

Tired of being teased by classmates at school, Rita complains to her parents because she's overweight. Rita's stepfather suggests that the whole family change their eating habits and her mother encourages Rita to join her in exercise. It is difficult for Rita to give up her favorite treats and she becomes frustrated when she takes a swimming class. However, with her parent's encouragement, Rita eventually begins to show a weight loss and decides to keep up the good habits of eating wisely and exercising.

IL: Ages 8-11   RL: 3.0

4.48   Platt. *Chloris and the Wierdos.* see Ch. 3.

4.49   Platt, Kin. *Headman.* New York: Greenwillow Books, 1975. 186 pp. Dell, 1977 pap. LC, talking book.

Fifteen-year old Owen, whose widowed mother is an alcoholic, has been convicted for several offenses including theft and assault with a dangerous weapon. He is sent to a two-year youth correction center whose goal is to help teenage boys straighten up their lives. Owen is cooperative and has a good relationship with a counselor at the center. However, Owen plans to eventually join a gang for survival in his tough neighborhood. Owen is released from the center after only eight months to help out his mother, whose drinking has become worse. Reluctant to return to his old neighborhood, Owen is robbed during his first venture out onto the streets. Owen and two other boys form their own gang with Owen the headman of the gang. In an attack on the gang which robbed him, Owen is stabbed and loses consciousness, wondering what is the sense of it all.

IL: Ages 14-18   RL: 6.0

4.50   Rinkoff, Barbara Jean Rich. *Member of the Gang.* New York: Crown Publishers, 1968. 127 pp.

Woodie, a thirteen-year old black, does poorly in school and feels unimportant despite his parents' interest in him. Therefore, Woodie is happy to become a member of a gang, feeling that he will achieve recognition this way. Woodie becomes involved with shoplifting through his gang. He also reluctantly joins in a fight against a rival gang. When one of the gang members is stabbed, the other boys scatter but Woodie stays with the injured boy until the police come. Woodie's parents are hurt when he is put on probation, but Woodie feels he has learned something. He decides to "buckle down at school" and be known for something other than gang involvement.

(Rinkoff, Barbara Jean Rich)

IL: Ages 11-14   RL: 4.0

4.51   Roberts, Willo Davis. *Don't Hurt Laurie!* New York: Atheneum,
       1978. 166 pp.

Eleven-year old Laurie, who lives with her mother, stepfather, and
two stepsiblings, has been physically abused by her mother since
she was three. Laurie's mother insists to neighbors and hospital
staff that Laurie is "clumsy" and the family frequently moves.
Therefore, Laurie is unable to make friends except for her younger
stepbrother, Tim, who knows the truth about Laurie's being abused.
Laurie feels unable to confide in her stepfather since he is never
home when her mother abuses her and she fantasizes about her
real father coming to rescue her. In a rage one day, her mother
threatens to kill Laurie because she is so much like her father who
deserted Laurie and her mother long ago. Only when her mother
attacks a pet dog, does Laurie finally turn on her mother. Laurie
is beaten unconscious by her mother and when she comes to, she
and her stepsiblings flee to their grandmother's house. To Laurie's
relief, the grandmother believes the children's story, as does Laurie's stepfather. Laurie's mother, who had been abused herself as
a child, receives treatment and Laurie feels safe and secure at the
grandmother's house for the first time ever.

IL: Ages 11-14   RL: 6.0

4.52   Ruby, Lois. "Faces at a Dark Window" in *Arriving at a Place
       You've Never Left.* New York: The Dial Press, 1977. 149 pp.
       Dell, 1980 pap.

Sixteen-year old Ellen describes her disbelief and embarrassment
when her mother has a mental breakdown. Ellen's mother has no
interests outside the home and there has always been very poor
communication between Ellen's parents. Ellen's mother is institutionalized and the family dutifully visits her each week. Ellen begins to lose some of her anger toward her mother during these visits and realizes she can help her mother to recover.

IL: Ages 11-18   RL: 8.0

4.53   Ruby, Lois. "Justice" in *Arriving at a Place You've Never Left.*
       New York: The Dial Press, 1977. 149 pp. Dell, 1980 pap.

Jonah, who is fifteen, is arrested for the murder of his father.
Jonah shot his father after seeing him beat his younger brother.
Jonah respects and trusts his attorney during the murder trial but
his mother, trying to protect her dead husband's reputation, denies
that her husband ever beat her youngest son. With Jonah on the
verge of being convicted, his mother finally reveals the truth about
the years of beatings. Jonah feels that his mother is a stranger
and is reluctant to leave the jail in her custody.

IL: Ages 11-18   RL: 8.0

4.54 Ruby, Lois. "Like a Toy on the End of a String" in *Arriving at a Place You've Never Left*. New York: The Dial Press, 1977. 149 pp. Dell, 1980 pap.

A girl's dormitory is plagued by repeated thefts of personal belongings. The residence advisor feels that one of the dorm residents is doing the stealing and that the girl may not be aware of doing it. When Marcia, a very popular and friendly girl, is caught in the act, she becomes hysterical and begs for help with her illness. Upon Marcia's expulsion from school, her mother is advised to seek psychiatric help for her daughter, but she denies the need for it.

IL: Ages 11-18   RL: 8.0

4.55 Ruby. *What Do You Do in Quicksand?* see Ch. 7.

4.56 Sallis, Susan. *An Open Mind*. New York: Harper and Row, 1978. 139 pp.

Fifteen-year old David, who is still bitter about his parents' divorce several years ago, is angry when his father introduces him to a woman he is dating. David is also having some problems at school and in an effort to please his counselor, he agrees to do volunteer work at a school for the handicapped. There David meets and becomes friends with Bruce, a spastic boy. When David learns that Bruce's mother is the woman his father is dating, David stops going to the school. David becomes greatly concerned when his mother announces she needs to have a hysterectomy over Christmas vacation. During this time, David encounters Bruce, who has run away from his school, and the two hide out at David's house. There Bruce tells David that he no longer wants to burden his mother so she will be free to remarry. Able to see his father's situation in a new light, David tells Bruce they would be brothers if his father and Bruce's mother marry. David tries to care for Bruce, but worried about Bruce's need of medication, he insures that his father and Bruce's mother are able to locate the two boys.

IL: Ages 11-18   RL: 7.5

4.57 Samuels. *Run, Shelley, Run!* see Ch. 2.

4.58 Scoppettone. *Happy Endings Are All Alike*. see Ch. 9.

4.59 Scoppettone. *The Late Great Me*. see Ch. 2.

4.60 Shyer, Marlene Fanta. *My Brother, The Thief*. New York: Scribner's Sons, 1980. 138 pp. Scholastic, 1983 pap.

When twelve-year old Carolyn realizes that her sixteen-year old half-brother Richard is involved with shoplifting and stealing, she tries to protect him. Richard, who feels worthless because his father abandoned him at the age of two, is trying to get enough money together so that he can search for his real father. Carolyn's parents are unaware of Richard's activities even when the police warn them of Richard's friend's police record. When Carolyn's parents arrange for Richard's father to come visit and he

(Shyer, Marlene Fanta)

doesn't show up, Richard's self-esteem lowers and his relationship
with his stepfather becomes more strained. Only after Carolyn is
falsely accused of theft during her attempt to return some of Richard's stolen items, does Richard come forward and confess to the
police. Richard is released and he comes to realize that his "real"
father is the stepfather who raised him and loves him.

IL: Ages 11-18   RL: 7.0

4.61 Smith, Doris Buchanan. *Last Was Lloyd*. New York: The Viking
      Press, 1981. 124 pp. Dell, 1982 pap.

Twelve-year old Lloyd is ridiculed by his classmates for being overweight and is unfairly blamed by his teacher for disrupting the
classroom. Lloyd's mother, who gave birth to Lloyd at the age of
fourteen and has been married three times, adds to her son's problems by fixing huge amounts of his favorite foods to make Lloyd
happy. Overprotective of Lloyd, his mother also lets Lloyd frequently miss school. When a new girl at school is harassed by
classmates, she and Lloyd become allies. Lloyd eventually realizes
that he must make an effort to eat better and to exercise if he
wants to change the monotonous pattern of his life.

IL: Ages 11-14   RL: 6.0

4.62 Smith, Doris Buchanan. *Tough Chauncey*. New York: William Mor-
      row and Company, 1974. 222 pp.

Thirteen-year old Chauncey tries to prove he is "tough" by beating
up his classmates, creating trouble in the neighborhood, and performing daring acts which physically injure him. Neglected by his
mother who drinks excessively and can't even take care of herself,
Chauncey lives with his grandparents. Chauncey's grandfather
abuses him, locking Chauncey in a closet for hours and beating
him for the slightest offense, and his grandmother gives silent approval. Chauncey pleads with his mother to live with her, but she
decides to give his grandparents legal custody of Chauncey. When
Chauncey's grandfather deliberately and cruelly kills Chauncey's
kittens, Chauncey runs away. Another boy aids Chauncey in finding a hiding place and this boy tells Chauncey about several years
he spent in a foster home. Thinking that foster care may be the
answer for him, Chauncey decides to tell his story to a social worker.

IL: Ages 11-14   RL: 5.0

4.63 Smith, Nancy Covert. *The Falling-Apart Winter*. New York: Walk-
      er and Company, 1982. 112 pp.

Addam, a seventh grader, feels his world is falling apart when his
parents move from a small town to an urban area. Addam has
problems adjusting to his new school and his parents seem to always be arguing since the move. Addam's mother becomes more
and more depressed and spends some time in a mental hospital.

(Smith, Nancy Covert)

Once she returns home, Addam is ashamed to invite anyone over
to his house. Addam's mother becomes an outpatient at a mental
health clinic where Addam and his father attend sessions with a
psychiatrist as well. Addam begins meeting in a group with other
new students and feels more comfortable in his new school. He
also writes a paper on mental illness showing that he understands
his mother's problems. Through the family's sessions with the psychiatrist, the reasons for Addam's mother's depression are revealed
and Addam and his parents decide to make some changes in their
lives.

IL: Ages 11-14   RL: 5.5

4.64   Voigt. *Dicey's Song*. see Ch. 10.

4.65   Wolitzer, Hilma. *Toby Lived Here*. New York: Farrar, Strauss,
and Giroux, 1978. 147 pp.

After her widowed mother is sent to a mental hospital, twelve-year
old Toby and her little sister, Anne, are placed in a foster home.
Although Toby is reluctant to settle into life with her new foster
parents, little Anne feels happy and secure there. When Toby's
father died several years before, her mother didn't grieve but
plunged ahead with life cheerfully; Toby also finds herself bottling
up emotions and concealing the truth from her friends about her
mother's condition. Toby writes many letters to her mother which
are unanswered and on Toby's birthday, she blurts out to her foster parents that she hates her mother. When the two sisters visit
their mother, Toby realizes that her mother has finally come to
terms with her emotions much like Toby has started to do. When
their mother is released and wants her daughters back once again,
Toby feels sad to leave her foster home and plans to keep in touch.

IL: Ages 11-14   RL: 6.0

5.
Moving to a New Home

An astounding 5,529,000 families with children, more than 18 percent of the total number of families in the United States, move each year according to the Census Bureau. This kind of mobility of families and children is typical of most industrialized societies throughout the world.[1]

Moving creates special adjustment problems for children who must deal with a new social environment. When children move to a new neighborhood, they must make new friends, attend new schools, and learn to adjust to many new social situations. For many children, this adjustment is not always easy and can be extremely anxiety-producing.

It is helpful to let children know that it is OK to worry about their upcoming move. Many children make little or no fuss when their families announce that they are moving; it is a mistake to think that they are not anxious. Even if the change promises is some ways a better life for the family, these advantages are often overlooked by a child whose main interest centers on lost companions, new teachers, and strange school buildings. When a move is talked about to a child, it is best to avoid cliche's such as "everything will work out all right." When a child loses a best friend because of moving, everything is not all right. When children move to a new house and neighborhood, it may well be the worst thing that has ever happened to them.[2]

Naturally younger children who are moving experience adjustment problems that differ somewhat from older children. Preschoolers, for example, may regress in such ways as refusing to use the commode in the new house or wanting to sleep in their parent(s)' bed instead of in their new room. The school age child, among other things, must make a whole new set of friends who may not want this new child as part of their peer group. Adolescents must give up boyfriends or girlfriends as well as other important ties related to school or other organizations.

Children, like adults, prefer stability in their social environment. This stability gives the person a reference point which they can rely upon each day. This stability allows one to know generally what is expected in most social encounters. Moving disrupts familiarity of one's environment and forces the individual to learn whole new sets of responses for dealing effectively with new situations.

Moving is generally easier for adults because they have more control over the changes taking place during and after the move. However, children generally have little to say about the move and must make the best of a very difficult transition for them. As society becomes more complex, mobility of children and their families will increase. The problems of children associated with this movement must be dealt with by parents and at times by professionals skilled in the area of counseling.

Criteria for Book Selection

Books which involve the moving of a child's family are the focus of this chapter. The difficulties children experience when they move, as well as the positive aspects related to moving, are illustrated in these books. Although most of the children who are characters in these books moved because of a parent's job, a few of the children experienced moves related to a parent's death, separation or divorce of their parents, or other family issues.

Because a move can be quite traumatic for younger children, many of the books included in this chapter depict small children or even animals. Most of the characters have negative feelings before their family's move. They worry about such things as losing friends, leaving behind a well-known backyard, or missing their old bedroom. However, the majority of these younger characters are able to find new friends easily and discover advantages to their new homes and neighborhoods.

Older children who are characters in the books in this chapter have their worries too. With peer groups more established in older children, those characters who moved usually had a period of loneliness when they began attending a new school. Most of these older children had to make an effort to establish new peers by joining an organization or becoming involved in an interesting activity. The most helpful books illustrate the child's parents as having adjustments to make in their new surroundings, with new and different job responsibilities and new friends to make as well.

Children who are facing a move can benefit from reading about others who have made this transition. They will probably share some of the apprehension felt by characters of the books in this chapter. However, children who are moving, much like the characters in this chapter, should experience some of the benefits of moving as well - sharing the moving experience with family members, making new friends, and exploring a new neighborhood. A parent, teacher, or other significant adult, as illustrated in many of this chapter's books, can help to make a child's adjustment to moving an easier transition.

NOTES

1. Alvin Toffler, *Future Shock* (New York: Random House, 1970), p. 78.
2. Francis Roberts, "When Your Child Changes Schools," *Parents* (July 1983): 32-35.

BOOKS

5.1   Alexander. *To Live a Lie.* see Ch. 3.

5.2   Amdur, Nikki. *One of Us.* New York: The Dial Press, 1981.
       133 pp.

       When her father gets transferred, Nora and her parents move to
       a new town. It is difficult for Nora to make new friends, so she
       plays alone and is comforted by her pet rabbit. Nora's parents
       seem too busy for her; her father is often irritable as he adjusts
       to his new job and Nora's mother is busy setting up their new
       household. Nora finally becomes friends with a blind boy, Jerry,
       who encourages her to enter an essay contest. After Nora wins
       the essay contest, some girls at school ask her to eat lunch with
       them, but Nora insists that Jerry be included in the group as well.

       IL: Ages 8-11   RL: 5.0

5.3   Bates. *Bugs in Your Ears.* see Ch. 11.

5.4   Blue. *A Month of Sundays.* see Ch. 3.

5.5   Blume. *Superfudge.* see Ch. 10.

5.6   Blume. *Then again, maybe I won't.* see Ch. 4.

5.7   Brandenberg, Franz. *Nice New Neighbors.* New York: Greenwillow
       Books, 1977. 56 pp. Scholastic, 1980 pap.

       The six Fieldmouse children have just moved into a new neighbor-
       hood and want to make new friends. However, when they approach
       different groups of children playing, no one wants the Fieldmouse
       children to join in. Their mother tells them it will just take time
       to make new friends and their father suggests that the Fieldmouse
       children find something interesting to play themselves. Curious to
       see what the new children are doing, the other children in the
       neighborhood soon find themselves all in the Fieldmouse's backyard.

       IL: Ages 5-8   RL: 3.0

5.8   Chaikin, Miriam. *I Should Worry, I Should Care.* New York: Harper
       and Row, 1979. 103 pp. Dell, 1982 pap.

       Molly is upset over her family's move to a new neighborhood. She
       had to leave good friends behind, and although her younger broth-
       ers and sisters seem to make new friends easily, it is harder for
       Molly to meet anyone. Molly and her parents are also disheartened
       by reports on the radio of Hitler's rise to power and the persecu-
       tion of the Jews. Molly finally makes some new friends, but is up-
       set over their teasing of an obese woman who sits on her steps all
       day. School is almost to start and Molly mourns the fact that there
       is no money for any new school clothes. Finally, Molly meets some
       friendly boys who move into the neighborhood and is delighted when
       her aunt brings new clothes for all the family.

(Chaikin, Miriam)

IL: Ages 11-14   RL: 7.0

5.9   Clifton, Lucille.   *Good, Says Jerome*.   New York: E.P. Dutton,
        1973.   25 pp.

Jerome, a young black child, worries about moving to a new house.
He is afraid that once he moves into a new place, he'll get lost and
he thinks his new teacher won't like him.   He is also sure he'll
find a monster in his new house.   However, his wise older sister,
Janice Marie, reassures Jerome that there is nothing to worry a-
bout - only good things will happen.

IL: Ages 5-8   RL: 3.0

5.10   Haywood, Carolyn.   *Eddie's Valuable Property*.   New York: William
        Morrow and Company, 1975.   192 pp.

Ten-year old Eddie is worried over his family's need to move because of his father's job transfer.   He is especially upset when
his father says that Eddie can't take all his valuable property
along, which is a collection of junk he has found.   However, when
Eddie's father sees some antique toys in the valuable property collection, he decides that Eddie can bring everything.   The new
house is in the country and has a barn, much to the delight of
Eddie and his three brothers.   Eddie gets a new sheepdog and
makes many friends at his new school.   His best friend even likes
to collect valuable property just as much as Eddie does.

IL: Ages 8-11   RL: 3.5

5.11   Hoff, Sydney.   *Irving and Me*.   New York: Harper and Row, 1967.
        226 pp.   Dell, 1972 pap.

Thirteen-year old Artie tries to adjust to living in Florida after his
parents' move from Brooklyn because of his mother's arthritis.   He
leaves good friends and a dog behind that he feels he can never
replace.   After the move, Artie quickly makes a friend of fourteen-
year old Irving, whom he convinces to quit smoking.   Artie becomes
involved with a community center and gets a part in a play.   However, Artie has problems with Charlie, an older youth with a police
record, when they both try to impress the same girl.   When things
fall apart at the community center and Charlie gets the girl, Artie
tries to hitchhike and run away from home.   Irving and a stray
dog, however, convince him to give Florida another try.

IL: Ages 11-14   RL: 6.5

5.12   Hughes, Shirley.   *Moving Molly*.   Englewood Cliffs, NJ: Prentice-
        Hall, 1978.   30 pp.   Prentice-Hall, 1982 pap.   LC, talking book.

When Molly's parents announce the family's move from a city apart-
ment to a home in the country, everyone anticipates the move.
However, once their furniture is moved and the boxes are unpacked,
Molly feels lonely and bewildered in her new home.   Molly begins

(Hughes, Shirley)

playing at the unoccupied house next door, caring for some stray cats and plants in the yard. When a family with twins moves in next door, Molly finds herself just as busy and happy as the rest of her family.

IL: Ages 5-8   RL: 3.0

5.13   Hurwitz, Johanna. *New Neighbors for Nora*. New York: William Morrow and Company, 1979. 78 pp. Dell, 1982 pap. LC, braille and talking book.

Seven-year old Nora is excited when a new family moves into their apartment building. Hoping for a new playmate, she discovers instead eight-year old Eugene who is a showoff and replaces her as oldest child in the building. Eugene has bunkbeds, drinks soft drinks all the time, and gets to watch lots of television, all things Nora is denied. Nora gains new respect for Eugene, however, when he teaches her to blow bubbles with bubblegum and the two eventually become good friends.

IL: Ages 8-11   RL: 3.5

5.14   Jones, Penelope. *I'm Not Moving*. Scarsdale, NY: Bradbury Press, 1980. 29 pp.

Not wanting to leave her digging hole in the backyard, five-year old Emmy refuses to move to a different house with her parents and brothers. She visits different houses in her present neighborhood, trying to find a place to stay, but none of them suit her. After Emmy's father promises to help her dig an even better hole in her new yard, Emmy decides the best place to be is with her parents.

IL: Ages 5-8   RL: 2.5

5.15   Lowry, Lois. *Anastasia Again*. Boston: Houghton Mifflin, 1981. 145 pp. Dell, 1982 pap.

Twelve-year old Anastasia is horrified at her parents' decision to move to the suburbs. She likes their small, cluttered city apartment and tries to get her toddler brother to join in the protest with her. The family makes a list of things they want their new home in the suburbs to have; Anastasia asks for a tower where her bedroom could be. When they find a house with a tower, everyone instantly falls in love with it. There are many tears during the packing as the family say good-bye to their familiar rooms and their friends. Once her family moves into their house in the suburbs, however, Anastasia befriends an elderly lady who lives next door and a boy who likes to ride bikes like herself.

IL: Ages 8-11   RL: 6.0

5.16   Manley, Deborah. *A New House*. Milwaukee: Raintree Children's Books, 1979. 31 pp.

(Manley, Deborah)

A family moves into a new house in a different neighborhood. The
construction of their new house is described. The family meets
new friends and everyone helps with the many chores in their new
house. They explore the neighborhood, looking for familiar buildings such as the library and hospital, and try to find the stores
they will need to use.

IL: Ages 5-8   RL: 2.5

5.17   Milford, Sue and Jerry. *Maggie and the Good-bye Gift*. New York:
       Lothrop, Lee, and Shepard, 1979.   31 pp.

Wondering what "transferred" means, young Maggie soon discovers
that she and her family are going to leave their friends behind and
move to a different city.   Maggie enjoys the trip to their new home,
but once there, everyone in Maggie's family is sad because there
are only strangers on their street.   Remembering an unopened gift
an old friend gave them, Maggie finds that it is an electric can
opener.   She opens up so many cans of food that her family must
invite all their neighbors over to get rid of the food.   Several
months later, Maggie passes the good-bye gift on to a boy who is
moving away.

IL: Ages 5-8   RL: 3.0

5.18   Rabin. *Changes*. see Ch. 8.

5.19   Schulman, Janet. *The Big Hello*. New York: Greenwillow Books,
       1976. 32 pp. Dell, 1980 pap.

A little girl is apprehensive about her family's move to California.
She reassures her doll, Sara, that the plane ride will be fun and
that California will be wonderful.   When Sara gets lost soon after
their arrival, the little girl's father gets her a dog so she will have
someone to sleep with.   The little girl and her dog find a new
friend the next day and she is feeding the doll Sara.   That night,
the little girl falls asleep telling Sara and her dog about the fun
they will all have tomorrow.

IL: Ages 5-8   RL: 2.0

5.20   Sharmat, Marjorie Weinman. *Gila Monsters Meet You at the Airport*.
       New York: Macmillan Publishing Company, 1980.   28 pp.

A young boy from New York City worries about his parents' move
to the West. He thinks that everyone out West rides a horse and
wears a cowboy hat and he is convinced that there are cactus and
gila monsters everywhere.   Upon his arrival at an airport out West,
the boy meets Tex, who has similar worries about moving to New
York City. Tex thinks it snows all the time, it's so crowded that
people sit on top of each other, and that alligators live in the
sewers in the city. While riding to his new house, the boy from
New York sees many things that remind him of his former home
and he decides that it won't be so bad living out West after all.

(Sharmat, Marjorie Weinman)

IL: Ages 5-8   RL: 3.0

5.21   Sharmat, Marjorie Weinman. *Mitchell is Moving*. New York: Mac-
       millan Publishing Company, 1978. 46 pp. Scholastic, 1980 pap.

Mitchell the dinosaur wants a change in surroundings and decides
to walk for two weeks and make a new home. His neighbor, Marge,
wants Mitchell to stay and comes up with different ways to imprison
him in his old home, but Mitchell says he will only escape. He reassures Marge that he still likes her and that they will always be
friends. Mitchell takes along his favorite belongings and builds a
new home after his two-week journey, but he is lonely. Marge
comes to visit him and they decide to build her a new home next
to Mitchell's.

IL: Ages 5-8   RL: 3.0

5.22   Shecter, Ben. *Someplace Else*. New York: Harper and Row, 1971.
       167 pp.

Eleven-year old Arnie is upset over his parents' move to a new
neighborhood. The new apartment is smaller and his father, who
once owned a store, is now forced to work long hours in a factory.
At Arnie's new school, all the other children seem to know each
other and he gets into trouble with his new teacher the first day.
Arnie also has problems getting along with his rabbi during lessons
leading to his bar mitzvah. In addition, Arnie's mother has to be
hospitalized for an operation and his grandmother dies. A stray
dog Arnie finds, a new younger more understanding rabbi, and a
part in the school play all help to make Arnie feel better in his
new neighborhood.

IL: Ages 11-14   RL: 7.5

5.23   Shura, Mary Francis. *Chester*. New York: Dodd, Mead, and Com-
       pany, 1980. 92 pp.

When Chester moves into the neighborhood, a group of five friends
is upset. Chester has more freckles than Jamie and more brothers
and sisters than Amy. He alienates the other three children by
taking away each of their distinctions as well. The five friends
start quarreling with each other as their dislike for Chester grows.
He even charms their teacher at school with a story about why he
was tardy. However, Chester is pulled into the circle of friends
when they all join to hunt for his missing pet goat.

IL: Ages 8-11   RL: 4.0

5.24   Smith. *The Monster in the Third Dresser Drawer*. see Ch. 10.

5.25   Smith. *The Falling-Apart Winter*. see Ch. 4.

5.26   Thompson, Vivian L. *Sad Day, Glad Day*. New York: Holiday
       House, 1962. 38 pp. Scholastic, 1974 pap.

(Thompson, Vivian L.)

Kathy is sad about her family's move from a home in the country to a city apartment. She feels that the new place will never feel like home, but her mother explains that "home" is anywhere that Mother, Daddy, and Kathy are together. Kathy is particularly distressed when she finds that she has left her favorite doll behind; however, Kathy finds a doll in her new bedroom closet left with instructions for someone to care for it. By the end of moving day, Kathy feels much better after she spots a playground across the street and discovers she can run the apartment elevator herself.

IL: Ages 5-8   RL: 2.0

5.27   Wallace-Brodeur. *The Kenton Year*. see Ch. 8.

5.28   Watson, Wendy. *Moving*. New York: Thomas Y. Crowell, 1978. 23 pp.

Muffin does not want to move to a new house. When her parents start packing, Muffin does not want any of her belongings to be included as she plans to continue living in her old house. Muffin's parents confess they will be sad to leave the old house and may feel lonely at first in their new house. When Muffin's parents are ready to leave, they urge Muffin to come with them to the new house for just a while. Muffin decides to give the new house a try.

IL: Ages 5-8   RL: 2.5

5.29   Wood, Phyllis Anderson. *Pass Me a Pine Cone*. Philadelphia: The Westminster Press, 1982. 160 pp.

When his father gets a job as a high school principal, tenth grader Sam and his parents make a move to a town in the Sierra Mountains. Sam helps his parents unpack and anxiously waits for school to begin. Wondering how the other students will react to the new principal's son, Sam is relieved when he makes friends with a girl his age before school begins. Once school starts, Sam runs into difficulties with one of his teachers and must transfer to another class. Sam's stand against the unfair teacher makes many friends for him in his new town.

IL: Ages 11-14   RL: 6.5

6.
Physical Handicaps

Individual differences in people are universal. No two people are exactly alike, and the differences between the extremes of human variability are tremendous. Differences in weight, height, and physique among children and adults often vary greatly. People range intellectually from the extremely gifted to the totally custodial. The sensory acuity of individuals varies from the totally deaf and blind at one extreme to the other extreme of people with hyperacute sensitivity. In all dimensions of human development, aptitude, and physical characteristics, the extent of differences is tremendous.

These extreme differences found among individuals essentially mean that it is difficult to define what is "normal." We typically define "normal" as being average, ordinary, or commonplace. We often define those things we don't understand or that are unusual as being "abnormal." Often "normal" is translated into other terms such as good, pure, true, right, and hence, praiseworthy. To be "abnormal" often means to be the opposite of these terms, such as unclean, wrong, and worthy of only scorn. Unfortunately for those who are handicapped, the label "abnormal" is often used to describe them, resulting in treatment that is less than fair. The handicapped adult as well as the handicapped child is often stigmatized and treated as "abnormal."

Handicapped Children

In this section, the kinds of handicaps dealt with are those that are physical. The population group focused on are children of all ages. The handicapped parent raising children is not dealt with.

Among children, the most common physical handicaps are visual handicaps, deafness, and various orthopedic handicaps such as epilepsy, cerebral palsy, multiple sclerosis, and muscular dystrophy. Other well-known physical handicaps are asthma, diabetes, etc. All of these kinds of handicaps create unique problems for children confronted with them. At times, these problems may require professional help.

Visual handicaps. The sighted often consider blindness to be one of the most severe handicaps imaginable for children.[1] If we try to imagine what a loss of vision would be like for a child, most sighted think in negative terms - total dependency, profound unhappiness, and helplessness. Children who lose their sight do not necessarily experience extreme misfortune. Many sightless children lead relatively normal and independent lives. Our false perception about them is often one of their major problems.

The inherent limitations of blind children are relative to the extent that current technology is available to them to help compensate for their blindness. Blindness (a) prevents direct access to the printed word, (b) deprives the child of important social cues, (c) restricts mobility in unfamiliar surroundings, and (d) limits the child's direct perception of distant environment, as well as objects too large to be apprehended tactually. The many new technologies help blind children overcome these inherent limitations.

It is estimated that one in three thousand school-age children meet the medico-legal criterion for blindness, and that one in five hundred have vision in the 20/70 to 20/200 range commonly designated as the partially sighted.[2] These estimates suggest that many children are visually handicapped.

The problems facing the visually handicapped child are numerous - many of these problems are reinforced by the sighted. Since the popular stereotype of helplessness and dependency is a dominant belief about visually handicapped children, our treatment of them often results in social practices which prevent the development and exercising of skills leading to independence. In essence, the visually handicapped learn dependence from their social environment.

Communication is another problem of the visually handicapped. The child who is visually handicapped is deprived of important social cues needed for interpersonal communication. Such cues as facial expressions, gestures, and movement are not perceived by the blind child.

Another major problem facing visually handicapped children is the development of a positive self-esteem. Since the cultural stereotype of the visually handicapped is often negative, visually impaired children may begin to see themselves in negative terms. It is important that the sighted working with these children make special efforts to reinforce positive feelings among the visually handicapped.

These are but a few of the many problems facing the visually handicapped child. It is important to remember that these problems are not necessarily inherent in the nature of being visually handicapped, but are relative to the extent that current technologies are available to help the blind person deal with them.

Deafness. It is estimated that 300,000 children are sufficiently aurally impaired to warrant special care and treatment.[3] These children are very special in that they are a misunderstood, disadvantaged minority group. They are at times labeled as unmotivated, inattentive, and even mentally retarded. They are also unable to acquire speech in the ordinary way, resulting in a denial of full access to the community and broader society for many of them.

Children who are aurally handicapped are typically classified as hard-of-hearing or deaf. How they are classified depends on the degree of hearing loss. Like other handicapped children, the aurally handicapped are often stigmatized by society, thus resulting in a negative labeling process that complicates the lives of these children.

Aurally impaired children, also much like other handicapped groups, have a tendency to limit their levels of aspiration to avoid failure.[4] However, there is little evidence to suggest that these low levels of aspiration are due to the child's social or emotional adjustment.[5] Given the low level of access into mainstream society available to the handicapped, a tendency to limit one's aspirations would appear to be created more by society than by this special child.

Orthopedic and other physical handicaps. It is generally considered that about 1 percent of school-age children are afflicted with crippling conditions or health impairments.[6] The impairment of such children may be due to accidents, disease, or congenital anomalies. Children with cerebral palsy are usually classified among those with orthopedic difficulties for educational purposes because of the severe nature of the physical involvement resulting from cerebral palsy.[7]

As found among other handicapped children, a major problem of orthopedically handicapped children is often a low self-esteem. This low self-esteem may be a result of the condescending attitudes on the part of society toward these children.

Most of the adjustment differences between the orthopedically handicapped child and the "normal" child are related to the child's fear of participation; this often creates a degree of anxiety for the child. Much of this fear can be overcome if parents and other significant people in the child's life have positive attitudes toward the orthopedically handicapped child; such attitudes help the child compensate for its orthopedic problems.

Some of the better known orthopedic handicaps are epilepsy and cerebral palsy. Of these, epilepsy is one of the older afflictions known to man. The generally accepted figure of the incidence of epilepsy is one-half of 1 percent of school-age children.[8] It is estimated that between three to six infants per 1,000 have cerebral palsy.[9]

Other well-known physical handicaps that are not orthopedic in nature are asthma, speech problems, and diabetes. Even though these kinds of handicaps may not be as severe in nature as orthopedically based problems, they nonetheless can impact a child's self-esteem and social and emotional well-being.

Criteria for Book Selection

Books selected for this chapter depict young people who are confronted with various types of physical handicaps. Many of the books deal with children who are blind or hearing impaired; other books have characters who are orthopedically handicapped due to cerebral palsy, spina bifida, or other causes. A few books illustrate children who are faced with epilepsy, speech problems, diabetes, and asthma. Several of the books are available in forms such as cassettes or in braille to facilitate their use with the handicapped.

The most helpful books on physical handicaps deal with the problem realistically. Through the use of realistic characters and situations, these books help to dispel myths about particular disabilities, reveal the inner feelings of children with handicapping conditions, and describe the involvement of family members and other significant others.[10] More so than any other chapter, books portraying actual children, as well as fictional characters, are included.

Books selected for this chapter explore the problems faced by children with physical handicaps. Many of these problems involve the handicapped child's relationship with other nonhandicapped individuals. The reactions of other people to the handicapped child's condition cannot be ignored. The reactions illustrated in the books in this chapter range from a parent's or teacher's overprotectiveness of the handicapped child to staring or pity expressed by strangers. Some of the characters who are blind resent the well-meaning but unneeded help given to them by other people in crossing streets, going up steps, etc. Those characters with hearing impairments often felt self-conscious about wearing a hearing aid or using sign language around others who were not handicapped. Children in these books who are confined to wheelchairs because of an orthopedic handicap sometimes felt left out when other children participated in certain games on the playground.

In addition to the problems faced by the handicapped child, the books in this chapter also stress the many activities and accomplishments these young people are capable of. Certain children in these books who are hearing impaired are involved with dancing, playing a musical instrument, and swimming. Other children in this chapter with orthopedic handicaps ride specially designed bicycles, help with household chores, and participate in family activities such as camping. A blind girl in one of the books jumps rope and rides a horse. Skills associated with compensating for one's handicap such as use of a brailler or typewriter, learning sign language or lip reading, or learning how to give insulin injections to oneself are all illustrated.

Children faced with physical handicaps should be able to identify with characters in this chapter which share the same handicap. There are no easy solutions to the everyday problems encountered by physically handicapped children. Reading or hearing about other handicapped children's accomplishments, however, may inspire a child to try some previously avoided activity. The knowledge that they are capable of certain skills - coupled with the support of parents, teachers, and other significant adults - can aid in the development of a much-needed positive self-image in the handicapped child.

NOTES

1. William D. David, "Your Health: Eye Care," *Today's Education* (Volume 59, No. 3, 1970): 40.
2. Charles W. Telford and James M. Sawrey, *The Exceptional Individual* 4th ed. (Englewood Cliffs, New Jersey: Prentice-Hall, 1981), p. 369.
3. Telford and Sawrey, p. 409.

    4. M.S. Stinson, "Relations Between Maternal Reinforcement and
Help and the Achievement Motive in Normal Hearing and Hearing-Impaired
Sons," *Developmental Psychology* (Volume 10, 1974): 348-53.
    5. L.R. Bowyer and J. Gillies, "The Social and Emotional Adjustment
of Deaf and Partially Deaf Children," *British Journal of Educational Psychology* (Volume 42, 1972): 305-8.
    6. Telford and Sawrey, p. 421.
    7. Telford and Sawrey, p. 420.
    8. United States Office of Education, *Better Education for the Handicapped: An Annual Report, Fiscal Year, 1969* (Washington, D.C.: U.S.
Government Printing Office, 1970).
    9. V. Apgar and J. Beck, *Is My Baby All Right?* (New York: Pocket
Books, 1974).
    10. Jeanne Bracken and Sharon Wigutoff with Ilene Baker, "Children
with Special Needs" in *Books for Today's Young Readers* (Old Westbury,
New York: The Feminist Press, 1981).

BOOKS

6.1   Allen, Marjorie N. *One, Two, Three - AH-CHOO!* New York: Coward, McCann, and Geoghegan, 1980. 63 pp.

A young boy, Wally, is allergic to dust, fur, and feathers. Despite his allergy shots and medicine, he is unable to keep a dog as a pet. Wally tries a frog and a snake as pets, but finally finds a hermit crab to be the perfect pet. All the other animals at a pet show make Wally sneeze, but his hermit crab wins a prize.

IL: Ages 5-8   RL: 3.0

6.2   Amdur. *One of Us*. see Ch. 5.

6.3   Blume, Judy. *Deenie*. Scarsdale, NY: Bradbury Press, 1973. 159 pp. Dell, 1974 pap. LC, talking book.

Twelve-year old Deenie isn't interested in her mother's dreams of having her become a model. Her mother is always complaining about Deenie's posture, saying that she slouches. When Deenie's gym teacher also notices her bad posture, the teacher recommends that Deenie see a physician. It is discovered that Deenie has adolescent idiopathic scoliosis. Deenie, who has always felt uneasy around handicapped people, is horrified when she finds out that she will need to wear a back brace for four years. She fears that her condition may have been caused by her masturbating, but Deenie's gym teacher reassures her otherwise. Deenie is fitted with her brace, which is formed from a plaster mold, and she's given a body stocking to wear under it to prevent irritation, all of which seems repulsive to her. Deenie tries to hide her brace with certain types of clothing and finds it difficult to adjust to wearing it. Deenie's decision to not remove her brace at a party she attends shows her gradual acceptance of her condition.

IL: Ages 11-14   RL: 3.5

6.4   Branfield, John. *Why Me?* New York: Harper and Row, 1973. 233 pp. LC, talking book.

Twelve-year old Sarah, an English girl, hates the urine tests, injections, and strict diet that accompany her diabetic condition. She envies her healthy older sister, Jane; Jane, who feels that her parents favor Sarah, is also jealous. The two sisters are constantly bickering and Jane is even injured in a fight with Sarah. When Sarah begins neglecting her diet and refusing to give herself injections, her physician suggests that Sarah see a psychiatrist. Sarah finds a stray dog at this time and trying to convince her parents to let her keep it, she starts to show more responsibility for her diabetic condition. When Sarah suspects that her dog has diabetes too, she begins to share her insulin with the dog. Through her psychiatrist, Sarah is able to talk out her feelings about having diabetes and is better able to cope with the inconveniences it creates. A boy Sarah meets also makes her feel more comfortable about her condition. Sarah begins to always feel tired and must

(Branfield, John)

have her insulin amount increased; she must also cope with the
death of her dog, whose diabetic condition was too far advanced to
treat. Sarah continues to progress with her psychiatrist and she
and her sister Jane begin to improve their relationship with each
other.

IL: Ages 11-18   RL: 8.0

6.5   Corcoran, Barbara. *A Dance to Still Music*. New York: Atheneum,
        1976. 180 pp. Atheneum, 1977 pap. LC, braille.

Fourteen-year old Margaret, deaf for more than a year due to a
serious ear infection, has a difficult time adjusting to a move with
her mother from Maine to Florida. Margaret's father left right after
she was born and her mother has always been unhappy and rest-
less, leaving Margaret alone much of the time. Afraid that she may
yell at people due to her deafness, Margaret stops talking completely and communicates only by writing messages on paper. When Margaret's mother announces her plans to remarry and send Margaret
to a private school for the handicapped, Margaret runs away in-
tending to return to Maine. However, Margaret meets a kind woman
named Josie who lives on a houseboat and invites Margaret to stay
with her. Margaret begins to talk once again to Josie and to feel
more optimistic about her condition. Her mother and stepfather
eventually find Margaret, but she persuades them to let her continue to live with Josie and to begin attending classes for the hearing impaired at a nearby university.

IL: Ages 11-18   RL: 7.5

6.6   Dacquino, V.T. *Kiss the Candy Days Good-Bye*. New York: Dela-
        corte Press, 1982. 129 pp.

Jimmy, a seventh-grader trying to make the wrestling team, becomes
concerned when he starts to lose weight. He also can't understand
why he is always so thirsty and irritable. When Jimmy passes out
in front of his home, his parents rush him to the hospital and he
is diagnosed as having diabetes. Jimmy must stay in the hospital
for a week giving urine samples and receiving insulin injections.
He and his parents are given advice about his diet. Jimmy learns
how to test his own urine and give himself injections before he
leaves the hospital. Back at home, Jimmy must adjust to always
being on time for meals and being more cautious about some of his
physical activities. However, with the help of his family and
friends, Jimmy feels that he can live comfortably with his diabetes.

IL: Ages 11-14   RL: 5.5

6.7   Danziger. *The Pistachio Prescription*. see Ch. 3.

6.8   Fanshawe, Elizabeth. *Rachel*. Scarsdale, NY: Bradbury Press,
        1975. 27 pp.

(Fanshawe, Elizabeth)

Young Rachel, who is confined to a wheelchair, participates in many activities at her school and is a member of a Brownie troop. Her friends like to push her in her wheelchair, but Rachel prefers that they do not. Rachel camps with her family, is learning to swim, and plans to learn to ride a horse soon. She likes to talk to her father about the many things she can be when she grows up.

IL: Ages 5-8   RL: 2.5

6.9   Gerson. *Passing Through.* see Ch. 8.

6.10 Green. *Walkie-Talkie.* see Ch. 4.

6.11 Hallman, Ruth. *Breakaway.* Philadelphia: The Westminster Press, 1981. 92 pp. Dell, 1983 pap.

After losing his hearing through an accident at a high-school swimming meet, Rob is shut off from the world by his overprotective mother. Rob's girlfriend Kate encourages him to run away with her and make a life for himself. Rob and Kate get rooms at a boardinghouse where they work on sign language and lip reading. Rob acquires a dog that is trained to "hear" for a deaf person as well. Through coaching a group of younger boys, Rob discovers that he can be useful and perhaps find a suitable career. When Rob's mother eventually finds him, she is pleased with his independence and is willing to learn how to communicate with her son.

IL: Ages 11-18   RL: 4.5

6.12 Hanlon. *The Swing.* see Ch. 11.

6.13 Hermes, Patricia. *What if They Knew?* New York: Harcourt, Brace, Jovanovich, 1980. 121 pp. Dell, 1981 pap.

Worried that someone will discover that she has epilepsy, ten-year old Jeremy is hesitant to make new friends and attend a new school when she lives temporarily with her grandparents. Jeremy's grandmother doesn't like to talk about Jeremy's condition, but her grandfather has several helpful discussions about it with Jeremy. A classmate who knows about Jeremy's "secret" even threatens to tell everyone at school if Jeremy isn't friendly to her. When Jeremy does have a seizure at school after becoming lax about taking her medication, she is embarrassed and wants to hide. However, two friends and the school principal are all concerned about and very supportive of Jeremy. Jeremy is relieved that she is finally able to talk openly about her epilepsy with other people.

IL: Ages 8-11   RL: 5.5

6.14 Hlibok, Bruce. *Silent Dancer.* New York: Julian Messner, 1981. 63 pp. Wanderer, 1982 pap.

Ten-year old Nancy, who is deaf, is eager to wake up on Fridays because that is the day she attends ballet class. Nancy's parents

(Hlibok, Bruce)

and brother are also deaf and the family communicates in sign language at breakfast. A day at the School for the Deaf is illustrated
as Nancy checks her hearing aids, works with a speech teacher,
and participates in her classes. Then she and several of her classmates go to the Ballet School where an interpreter uses sign language to facilitate communication between the ballet instructor and
the deaf students. Nancy works very hard on her stretching ex-
ercises and at correcting mistakes in some of her dance movements.
She recalls the time she danced at Lincoln Center as part of a benefit for handicapped children. As Nancy's class finishes, she
looks forward to next Friday's ballet class.

IL: Ages 8-11   RL: 4.0

6.15   Howe. *A Night Without Stars*. see Ch. 8.

6.16   Kelley, Sally. *Trouble with Explosives*. Scarsdale, NY: Bradbury
       Press, 1976. 117 pp.

Twelve-year old Polly is worried about attending a new school because she stutters. Polly's new teacher, who is very strict, is not
very understanding of Polly's problem and forces Polly to recite
before the class. A new friend, Sis, comes to Polly's rescue and
gives her support at school. But Polly is not able to confide in
Sis about her visits to a psychiatrist concerning her stuttering.
When Sis is unfairly punished by their teacher, Polly uses her newly gained self-confidence to lead a group of students in protest.
She discovers that other students have received therapy for various
reasons as well. Polly's speech problem begins to occur less frequently and her psychiatrist helps Polly to understand the situations that lead to her stuttering.

IL: Ages 11-14   RL: 6.0

6.17   Kent, Deborah. *Belonging: A Novel*. New York: The Dial Press,
       1978. 200 pp. Grossett and Dunlap, 1979 pap. LC, braille and
       talking book.

Fifteen-year old Meg, who was born blind, chooses to attend public
high school rather than a special school for the blind. On her first
day at school, Meg is pleased at the way she manages to negotiate
the hallways and classrooms, although she is annoyed at the well-
meaning but unneeded help some of her fellow students offer. Meg
joins the staff of the school paper where she meets Lindy and Keith,
both serious students who tend to be loners. Meg is pleased when
she becomes friends with some members of the "right" crowd and
is invited to one of their parties. After cancelling previous plans
with Lindy and Keith to attend the party, Meg is disappointed when
she finds people drinking alcohol, smoking pot, and engaging in
petting. Meg turns once more to Lindy and Keith and the three
publish an editorial supporting an eccentric teacher who is unfairly
being forced to resign. When Meg and her two friends are suspended because of the editorial, Meg is glad that she has not been
given special treatment because of her blindness. With the support

(Kent, Deborah)

of her understanding parents, Meg realizes that she values her in-
dividualism over the need to be popular.

IL: Ages 11-18   RL: 7.0

6.18 Kingman, Lee. *Head Over Wheels*. Boston: Houghton Mifflin, 1978.
186 pp. Dell, 1981 pap. LC, braille and talking book.

Identical seventeen-year old twins Kerry and Terry are involved
in an automobile accident that leaves Terry a quadriplegic. Feeling
guilty because his brother will never walk again, Kerry visits his
twin at the hospital as much as possible. However, Kerry finds
that Terry is becoming withdrawn and he misses the closeness they
have always shared. Terry's girlfriend recoils from his condition
while Kerry's girlfriend is friendly and supportive. Terry's family
struggles to pay their mounting hospital bills as Terry spends weeks
in physical therapy. Eventually Terry returns home where his family has adapted the basement to his needs. Terry is able to take
care of his personal needs and spends much time with friends. Although the twins regain their closeness, they realize that with Kerry
making plans for what to do after high-school graduation, their
lives will be very different.

IL: Ages 11-18   RL: 7.5

6.19 Lasker, Joe. *Nick Joins In*. Chicago: Albert Whitman and Company, 1980. 29 pp.

Nick, who is confined to a wheelchair, is apprehensive about attending a public elementary school. His parents try to prepare Nick
for his new experience by answering his numerous questions and
the school prepares for him by building a ramp for his wheelchair
and obtaining a special desk. The students in Nick's room ask him
many questions about his handicap and he is curious about their
activities at school as well. Gradually, Nick and the other children
grow accustomed to each other in the classroom. Nick even shows
himself to be able to perform an activity no one else can do on the
playground.

IL: Ages 8-11   RL: 3.0

6.20 Levine, Edna S. *Lisa and her Soundless World*. New York: Human
Sciences Press, 1974. 29 pp.

The five senses, which most children have full use of, are discussed
before Lisa is introduced, who does not have the sense of hearing.
Lisa, deaf since birth, experienced much turmoil before her parents
realized her problem. Her deafness is compared to a television with
the sound turned off. Once Lisa's deafness was diagnosed, she
started to wear a hearing aid and learned about lip-reading. The
way in which she began to learn to speak by feeling the vibrations
when her teacher spoke and her use of finger-spelling are both
illustrated. Lisa is depicted as having to make more of an effort
than most children to learn things, yet she is capable of doing almost anything she wants.

(Levine, Edna S.)

IL: Ages 8-11   RL: 2.5

6.21 Mack, Nancy. *Tracy*. Milwaukee: Raintree Children's Books, 1976.
      31 pp.

      Tracy, a young girl with cerebral palsy, attends a public elemen-
      tary school where she uses a wheelchair and crutches. She is some-
      times disappointed that she cannot jump rope or run around, but
      she does participate in games and plays on some of the playground
      equipment. The other children at Tracy's school are quite accept-
      ing of her and offer help if she needs it. Tracy goes to a physical
      therapist twice a week and is learning to type since she has diffi-
      culty in writing. At home, Tracy is depicted as needing minimal
      help from her family and is shown playing in the yard with siblings
      and riding a special type of bicycle.

      IL: Ages 8-11   RL: 3.0

6.22 Madison. *Growing Up in a Hurry*. see Ch. 7.

6.23 Mathis, Sharon Bell. *Listen for the Fig Tree*. New York: The Vi-
      king Press, 1974. 175 pp. LC, talking book.

      Muffin, a sixteen-year old black girl, is blind but she takes care
      of the house and looks after her mother. Muffin's father was mur-
      dered a year ago and as the holidays approach, her grief-stricken
      mother starts drinking heavily. Muffin gets tired of going out to
      find her mother when she's drunk and of cleaning up after her
      mother when she gets sick later. Muffin's boyfriend helps her with
      errands and takes her to school and a neighbor, Mr. Dale, gives
      Muffin emotional support. Muffin makes plans for a big Christmas
      celebration with Mr. Dale helping her make a new dress. When
      Muffin is attacked in a hallway and her new dress is ruined, it is
      Mr. Dale, instead of her mother, who takes command of the situa-
      tion and gets Muffin to a hospital. With her mother sinking in de-
      spair and declaring that there will be no Christmas this year, Muf-
      fin shows her great strength by proceeding with her holiday plans.

      IL: Ages 11-18   RL: 8.0

6.24 Milton, Hilary. *Blind Flight*. New York: Franklin Watts, 1980.
      138 pp.

      Thirteen-year old Debbie, who has been blind for a year, takes a
      plane trip with her uncle. He is trying to get Debbie's mind off
      an upcoming operation which will attempt to restore her sight. When
      their plane is hit and the windshield shatters, Debbie's uncle loses
      consciousness. Debbie, on the verge of freezing, is forced to radio
      for help. It takes the efforts of many people to calm Debbie down
      and get her to steady the plane. With the gas tank nearly empty,
      Debbie bravely brings the plane down safely and feels she can eas-
      ily face the operation after this experience.

      IL: Ages 11-14   RL: 7.5

6.25   Peter, Diana. *Claire and Emma*. New York: The John Day Company, 1976. 28 pp.

Claire, who is four years old, and her sister Emma, a two-year old, are both deaf. They are shown playing with friends and joining in activities at home with their mother and older brother. A picture and explanation of hearing aids, which both sisters wear, is included. Claire and Emma are receiving training in lip-reading and Claire attends a school where she works with a speech trainer. Problems the girls face, such as inability to understand all the words on television and difficulty in climbing a tree because of a poor sense of balance, are explained. However, activities the sisters can do well, such as swimming at the pool and playing games with friends, are also stressed.

IL: Ages 5-8   RL: 3.5

6.26   Petersen, Palle. *Sally Can't See*. New York: The John Day Company, 1974. 23 pp.

Twelve-year old Sally, who was born blind, is shown at her home and at the special school she attends. All the things Sally has learned to do, such as reading braille and using her white cane for walking, are mentioned. However, it is also explained that it has taken much time for Sally to learn these things. Sally's use of her other four senses to compensate for her lack of sight is stressed. Sally has accomplished many things - swimming, jumping rope, and riding a horse.

IL: Ages 8-11   RL: 3.5

6.27   Peterson. *I Have a Sister - My Sister is Deaf*. see Ch. 10.

6.28   Rabe, Berniece. *The Balancing Girl*. New York: E.P. Dutton, 1981. 28 pp.

Margaret, a first-grader, is very good at balancing objects while in her wheelchair or on her crutches. A boy in her class, Tommy, belittles Margaret's efforts and even knocks down a castle she makes out of classroom objects. When the teacher announces a school carnival, Margaret has the idea of setting up an intricate chain of dominoes and selling chances on who will get to set off the chain reaction at the carnival. Tommy unsuccessfully attempts to ruin Margaret's creation a couple of times. The night of the carnival, Tommy's name is drawn to push the first domino and Margaret is surprised when Tommy joins in to cheer her for raising the most money.

IL: Ages 5-8   RL: 4.0

6.29   Rosenberg, Maxine B. *My Friend Leslie: The Story of a Handicapped Child*. New York: Lothrop, Lee, and Shepard, 1983. 42 pp.

A kindergarten girl tells of her friendship with Leslie, a multi-handicapped child who has been mainstreamed into a public school classroom. Although Leslie wears two hearing aids, has a vision impairment, and also has mobility problems, she is an outstanding reader

(Rosenberg, Maxine B.)

and is able to participate in many school activities. Leslie is well accepted by her classmates who are eager to do things for her, but Leslie's friend explains that Leslie doesn't need help most of the time.

IL: Ages 5-8   RL: 3.5

6.30 Sallis. *An Open Mind.* see Ch. 4.

6.31 Scoppetone, Sandra. *Long Time Between Kisses.* New York: Harper and Row, 1982. 207 pp.

Billie feels that she should make some changes in her life during her sixteenth summer or she'll go crazy, so she crops her hair and dyes it purple. She also breaks up with her boyfriend when she meets and becomes infatuated with Mitch, who is five years older than her and has multiple sclerosis. Billie visits Mitch in his lonely apartment as often as possible and they discuss his condition. Billie is thrilled when Mitch gives her a key to his apartment. Confused by her strong feelings for Mitch, Billie and Mitch eventually have an argument and stop seeing each other. Only then is Billie made aware of certain things - that Mitch is using an assumed name and that he ran away from his family and fiance'. Billie tries to forget her feelings for Mitch and makes an effort to reunite him with his fiance' who still loves him.

IL: Ages 11-18   RL: 7.0

6.32 Southall, Ivan. *Let the Balloon Go.* New York: St. Martin's Press, 1968. 141 pp. LC, talking book.

John, who is twelve years old and lives in Australia, finds it difficult to be "like other kids" because he has cerebral palsy. John's parents, especially his mother, are very overprotective of him, not letting him ride a bike, run, or use hand tools. When John finally convinces his mother to leave him at home alone for the first time, he is excited about his sudden freedom. John uses a forbidden ladder to get up in a tree and climbs very high by his own effort. A crowd gathers below the tree shouting advice to him and a policeman attempts to reach John, but becomes caught between two branches. John climbs down and rescues the policeman, but then falls the rest of the way to the ground. Later, shaken but unhurt, John faces his parents; they agree to stop overprotecting him and to start treating him more like other boys his age.

IL: Ages 11-14   RL: 5.0

6.33 Stein, Sara. *About Handicaps: An Open Family Book for Parents and Children Together.* New York: Walker and Company, 1974. 46 pp.

Matthew and Joe, two young boys, are good friends but Matthew is sometimes frightened about Joe's physical deformity. Joe has cerebral palsy which creates problems when he walks. Matthew sometimes imitates Joe's walk. He also jumps and runs very fast

(Stein, Sara)

whenever he's around Joe as if he fears his legs will become crippled like Joe's. When Matthew does not want to enter a store because he sees a man with a hook for a hand going in, his father talks to him about people with handicaps. Matthew's father reassures him that he doesn't have to worry so much about becoming handicapped himself. Matthew seems to develop an even closer relationship with Joe after this. An adult text is included to guide discussions with children about the material in this book.

IL: Ages 5-8   RL: 2.5

6.34 Thomas, William E. *The New Boy is Blind*. New York: Julian Messner, 1980. 62 pp.

Ricky, who is blind, starts attending a public elementary school. The boy who sits next to Ricky befriends him, helping him find his way around the school building and playing with him at recess. The other children in the classroom are fascinated by Ricky's use of a brailler and they are all eager to participate in mobility training along with Ricky. Ricky does have some problems at school - he rocks and sings sometimes during class and some older children laugh at him on the playground. Ricky's mother is also very overprotective of him, making him come home for lunch. Gradually, Ricky adjusts to his classroom and his mother gives him more freedom, allowing him to ride a bus and go on a field trip with the rest of his class.

IL: Ages 8-11   RL: 3.0

6.35 Wahl, Jan. *Jamie's Tiger*. New York: Harcourt, Brace, Jovanovich, 1978. 45 pp.

After recovering from German measles, young Jamie first notices at his birthday party that he cannot hear. Jamie's parents and his teacher do not suspect what is wrong, but his grandmother notices Jamie's sudden inattentiveness and suggests that he be evaluated by a physician. Jamie's parents explain to him about his deafness as best they can and they assure him they still love him. Jamie learns lip-reading and finger spelling and begins wearing a hearing aid. Although it is difficult for Jamie to return to school, he soon finds that his friends accept him and are interested in the special skills he has acquired.

IL: Ages 5-8   RL: 3.5

6.36 White, Paul. *Janet at School*. New York: Thomas Y. Crowell, 1978. 23 pp.

Janet, who has spina bifida, is shown doing many activities at her school. Her participation on the playground and in a gymnastics class are portrayed, as well as problems she experiences with her wheelchair and walker. Janet is also seen at home eating, playing a game, and helping with household chores. Spina bifida is explained, complete with a diagram of the body. Janet is portrayed as a friendly child, willing to talk to others about her disability.

(White, Paul)

IL: Ages 8-11   RL: 4.0

6.37 Winthrop. *A Little Demonstration of Affection*. see Ch. 10.

6.38 Winthrop, Elizabeth. *Marathon Miranda*. New York: Holiday House,
      1979. 155 pp.

      Twelve-year old Miranda, who has asthma, is embarrassed by her
      attacks and feels left out when she has problems participating in
      group sports at her school. When Miranda meets a new girl Phoebe,
      she is appalled at Phoebe's suggestion that they jog together. How-
      ever, with Phoebe's encouragement and support, Miranda finds that
      she is capable of running. When Miranda has an asthma attack af-
      ter running one day, she decides to be more cautious but still plans
      to enter a six mile marathon with Phoebe. Appreciative of her
      friend, Miranda is able to help Phoebe through a crisis as well when
      Phoebe discovers she is adopted.

      IL: Ages 11-14   RL: 6.5

6.39 Wolf, Bernard. *Anna's Silent World*. New York: J.B. Lippincott,
      1977. 48 pp.

      Six-year old Anna, who was born deaf, receives special training
      with a speech pathologist so that she can read, write, and talk like
      other children. Although she sometimes feels self-conscious about
      her two hearing aids, Anna participates in many activities at the
      elementary school she attends and she takes ballet classes. When
      a hearing friend cannot understand Anna while the two are playing,
      Anna's mother explains lip-reading and shows Anna's hearing aids
      to the friend. Anna is especially pleased when she receives a re-
      corder for a present as she will be able to make her own music.

      IL: Ages 5-8   RL: 5.0

6.40 Wolf, Bernard. *Connie's New Eyes*. New York: J.B. Lippincott,
      1976. 96 pp. Archway, 1978 pap. LC, talking book.

      Alison, who is fifteen years old, makes a request to Seeing Eye,
      Inc. for a puppy to raise and train to be a guide dog. She spends
      over a year patiently training the pup, Blythe, in obedience before
      returning Blythe to the agency. Connie, who has been blind from
      birth, comes to Seeing Eye, Inc. to train intensively for a month
      with Blythe. Hesitant with each other at first, Connie and Blythe
      gradually develop trust in each other and become a team. Connie
      returns home with Blythe and the dog accompanies her each day to
      her job as a teacher of handicapped children. With Blythe's help,
      Connie has a successful year of teaching and many new opportuni-
      ties open up for her.

      IL: Ages 11-18   RL: 6.0

6.41 Wolf, Bernard. *Don't Feel Sorry for Paul*. New York: J.B. Lip-
      pincott, 1974. 96 pp. LC, talking book.

(Wolf, Bernard)

Paul, who is seven years old, has difficulties due to his hands and
feet being incompletely formed at birth. Paul wears a prosthesis
and is shown being fitted for a new prosthesis during one of his
visits to an amputee clinic. Yet Paul is involved in horseback riding, biking, and football and he participates in many activities at
his school. He helps his mother with tasks in the kitchen and
roughhouses with his dad. Some of Paul's classmates make unkind
remarks to him and adults often look at him with pity, but Paul's
mother very realistically declares, "Don't feel sorry for Paul. He
doesn't need it."

IL: Ages 8-11   RL: 6.0

6.42   Young, Helen.   *What Difference Does it Make, Danny?* Great Brit-
       ain: Andre' Deutsch, 1980.   93 pp.

Danny is quite good at sports and is encouraged by his parents
and classroom teacher to do his best. Known to have epilepsy
since the age of two, Danny has been able to lead a normal life with
the help of medication. He has only had one epileptic attack at
school which his teacher handled quite calmly. However, a new
physical education teacher at his school is frightened of Danny's
epilepsy and refuses to let Danny participate in certain sports such
as swimming. Danny becomes a behavior problem at home and school
due to his frustration at being unable to participate in gym period.
When Danny is truant one day and swims across a canal to save a
drowning child, he becomes a hero and his physical education teacher realizes his wrong judgement of Danny.

IL: Ages 11-14   RL: 7.0

6.43   Zelonsky, Joy.   *I Can't Always Hear You.* Milwaukee: Raintree
       Children's Books, 1980.   31 pp.

Kim, who has a hearing impairment, feels strange when she starts
attending a public elementary school after having always been in a
special school. She feels self-conscious because of her hearing aid
and the kids in her classroom laugh when she gives a wrong answer
in class. Kim's mother and teacher are supportive, but Kim feels
like not going back to the school. Then Kim meets the school principal who also wears a hearing aid and the principal helps Kim to
see her strong points. Kim and her classmates finally discover
that they all have individual differences - one boy wears braces,
a girl is very tall, and one is adopted.

IL: Ages 8-11   RL: 3.0

7.

Pregnancy and Abortion

The number of babies born to adolescents outside of marriage has steadily increased since the mid-1960s.[1] Among unmarried women aged fifteen to nineteen, the birth rate increased from approximately 16 per 1000 in 1960 to nearly 25 per 1000 in 1975.[2] The Supreme Court decisions, however, legalizing abortion in the early 1970s have had a major impact on curbing the number of babies born to both black and white teenagers.[3] Approximately 360,000 women under the age of nineteen have abortions each year.[4]

Teenage Pregnancy

The so called sexual revolution of the late 1960s brought about enormous changes among youth in the United States. This revolution was characterized by a sharp increase in premarital intercourse among adolescents, especially females. Presently about half of today's young people are sexually active by the time they reach the age of eighteen.[5]

The increasing number of youth becoming sexually active is not only due to the changing social climate; several other variables have been identified that appear to contribute to this trend as well. Factors associated with participation in coitus, particularly for certain females, include strong dependency needs, a desire for affection, and the need to develop self-esteem. Other variables found to be related to this change in sexual behavior for females are a belief in equality between sexes, attitudes deviating from the norms, criticism of society, and alienation.[6] Sexually active males seem to be affected more by peer group pressures and generally show behaviors that are more aggressive.[7]

Unfortunately, many sexually active teenagers do not use birth control. Those who do not have been identified as often having one or more of the following characteristics: (a) under eighteen years of age, (b) low socio-economic status, (c) membership in a minority group, (d) no plans to attend college, and (e) fundamentalist protestants. Several psychological variables have also been identified in sexually active teenagers not using birth control. These, among others, are a desire to get pregnant, an ignorance of risks of pregnancy, feelings of fatalism, high levels of anxiety, and low ego strengths. It has been reported that many teenage girls who do use birth control are sexually active for a year or more before they seek help in obtaining contraceptives.[8]

Teenage pregnancy clearly has long-term effects on the young person. A number of studies have reported that young women who have their first child before they are eighteen are more likely to be confronted with a variety of problems. There is a high probability that these young women will work at low paying jobs and will not achieve a high level of education.[9] They also will have a tendency to be dependent on public assistance, have a large family, and be more prone to separation and divorce.[10]

The children of teenage mothers also are confronted with certain problems. There is limited evidence suggesting that these children have greater health problems. Much of this is thought to be due to poverty and not necessarily directly related to the fact that the mother is young.[11] Other studies have found that adolescent parents have difficulty in providing adequate childcare for their offspring.[12]

Little research has been done on the effects of teenage pregnancy on the male. There is some evidence reporting that teenage fathers have different psychological needs from their counterparts who do not become parents.[13] Most of these adolescent fathers are unprepared psychologically to assume parenthood.[14] In essence, the teenage father is an individual about whom little is known, thus making counseling and therapy very difficult.

Abortion

The number of pregnant teenagers who get abortions continues to increase each year. There is little to imply that this trend will change in the near future.

Only a few studies are available on the effects of abortion on the teenage mother. Girls who were good students before their pregnancy and who came from intact, non-Catholic families have been found to experience fewer psychological problems following an abortion.[15] Those who had abortions and were likely to regret their actions tended to be Catholic, from lower socio-economic origins, poor students, and had felt the abortion was forced on them.[16] Most pregnant teenagers have been found to be relieved after their abortion; those who do experience adverse psychological effects have been found to have a history of anxiety and depression.[17] Evidence reports that adolescents who are reluctant to abort and decide to keep their babies have a tendency to be alienated. These adolescents see having a baby as being the only positive action they can take to contribute to society.[18]

The long-term effect of abortion on the adolescent mother or father is clearly an area that demands much more research. Given the limited amount of information on this problem and the controversy surrounding it, those who work with the adolescent in this area of practice must use great caution in recommending what the adolescent parent should do. It is clearly a choice that the adolescent parent, rather than the helping professional, must make.

Criteria for Book Selection

Books where a young person is facing pregnancy and/or abortion are
the focus of this chapter. Most of the books have a teenage female as
the main character; however, a few of the books concern the teenage
male perspective. The most helpful books on this issue explore the many
varying emotions experienced by the pregnant teenager, as well as the
important decision-making process concerning what to do about the pregnancy.

The majority of teenage girls who are characters in these books felt
panicky and worried when they first suspected they were pregnant. A
trip to a doctor or clinic to confirm their pregnancy was an ordeal for
most of these girls. It was usually difficult for the pregnant girls to inform their boyfriends and/or parents about the pregnancy. However,
books where the pregnant female was overcome with guilt or shame were
generally avoided. It should also be noted that certain pregnant girls in
the books in this chapter felt happiness and a sense of fulfillment at being
pregnant.

The teenage father played a minor role in most of the books concerning pregnancy and abortion in this chapter. Some of the teenage males
were quite concerned for their girlfriends once they were informed of
the pregnancy and made efforts to be supportive of them. Other males
withdrew from the situation and did not accept any responsibility for their
girlfriend's condition. A few of the books in this chapter explored the
great turmoil a teenage father experiences; one male even takes on the
rearing of his baby once it is born.

The portrayal of parental involvement concerning a teenage pregnancy
greatly varied in this chapter. Most of the pregnant girls were reluctant
but did go ahead and inform their parents of the pregnancy; a few of
the girls did not involve their parents at all. Involvement of the male's
parents was not generally stressed. Most of the parents were helpful
and supportive of their pregnant daughters; however, a few of the parents tried to dictate how the situation should be handled.

For bibliotherapy purposes, there are a wide range of solutions mentioned in this chapter. A teenager faced with pregnancy can identify
with the emotions and decision-making process the characters in these
books experienced. The majority of the girls in this chapter at least
considered abortion and discussed it with their boyfriend or parents.
The girls who did indeed choose to have an abortion were usually accompanied on their visit to the abortion clinic by someone who cared for them.
Other girls decided to continue with their pregnancy and either keep the
baby or place it for adoption. Their pregnancies were generally continued
at home with their parents; however, a few girls went to an unwed mother's home. In addition, a few of the pregnant teenage females miscarried
before they had made a decision concerning their pregnancy. Although
marriage is mentioned as an alternative in several of the books, none of
the teen-age girls portrayed actually married the fathers of their babies.

NOTES

1.   June Sklar and Beth Berkov, "Teenage Family Formation in Post-war America," *Family Planning Perspective* (Volume 6, Spring 1974): 80-90.
2.   Ibid.
3.   Catherine S. Chilman, "Teenage Pregnancy: A Research Review," *Social Work* (Volume 24, No. 6, 1979): 492-498.
4.   Charles Zastrow, *Introduction to Social Welfare Institutions* (Homewood, Illinois: The Dorsey Press, 1982), p. 186.
5.   Chilman.
6.   Ibid.
7.   Ibid.
8.   Ibid.
9.   Kristin Moore and S. Hofferth, *The Consequences of Age of First Birth* (Washington, D.C.: Urban Institute, 1978).
10. Ibid.
11. Chilman.
12. Ibid.
13. Robert L. Barret and Bryan E. Robinson, "Teenage Fathers: Neglected Too Long," *Social Work* (Volume 26, No. 6, 1982): 486.
14. Ibid.
15. Chilman.
16. Ibid.
17. Ibid.
18. Sylvia B. Perlman, "Pregnancy and Parenting Among Runaway Girls," *Journal of Family Issues* (Volume 1, No. 2, 1980): 262-273.

BOOKS

7.1   Beckman, Gunnel. *Mia Alone*. New York: The Viking Press, 1975.
       124 pp. Dell, 1978 pap. LC, talking book.

       Mia, a seventeen-year old Swedish girl, fears that she is pregnant.
       Hesitant to confide in her parents who are having marital problems,
       Mia finally tells her boyfriend, Jan, about her suspicions. Although
       Jan is not overly happy about the situation, he asks Mia to marry
       him if she is indeed pregnant. Mia is in turmoil as she awaits the
       results of her pregnancy test, which must be done twice. Mia also
       is disturbed when she learns from her grandmother that her parents
       decided to marry because her mother was pregnant with Mia. When
       Mia's father tells her that he and her mother have decided to sepa-
       rate, Mia confesses to her father about her possible pregnancy.
       Mia's father is very supportive and helps her to explore the moral
       and psychological issues of her decision. When Mia later discovers
       that she is not really pregnant, her boyfriend is greatly relieved
       but Mia feels confused and lonely.

       IL: Ages 14-18   RL: 9.5

7.2   Blume. *Forever*. see Ch. 9.

7.3   Christman, Elizabeth. *A Nice Italian Girl*. New York: Dodd, Mead,
       and Company, 1976. 139 pp.

       After the sheltered life she has led due to her very strict widowed
       father, Anne is amazed when a handsome, popular boy starts dating
       her during her junior year of college. Anne can not help falling in
       love and soon she and Steve are regularly making love. When Anne
       becomes pregnant and tells Steve about it, he declares he cannot
       marry Anne because he needs all his money for law school. Because
       of her Roman Catholic background, Anne won't even consider abor-
       tion. Therefore she is relieved when Steve sets up an adoption
       through a lawyer in St. Louis. The couple wishing to adopt Anne's
       baby will pay all her hospital and living expenses in return for the
       baby. However, after Anne arrives in St. Louis, she discovers
       that she has been the victim of an adoption plot and that Steve
       planned to get Anne pregnant for a fee. Hurt and full of shame,
       Anne is determined to keep the baby. When Anne finds she cannot
       make it financially on her own, she is forced to receive help from
       the adopting couple but is determined to pay it back. Although a
       priest and Anne's two older brothers try to persuade her to give
       up her baby, Anne demands her son immediately after delivery.

       IL: Ages 14-18   RL: 7.5

7.4   Dizenzo, Patricia. *Phoebe*. New York: McGraw-Hill, 1970. 120 pp.
       Bantam Books, 1970 pap.

       A sixteen-year old girl, Phoebe, thinks that she might be pregnant.
       Phoebe has had little information on sex so she looks up facts about
       pregnancy in library books which convince her that she is pregnant.
       Unable to turn to her mother and father who frequently argue with

(Dizenzo, Patricia)

each other, Phoebe hesitates to tell her boyfriend as well. Finally Phoebe confides in her closest friend who convinces Phoebe to see a doctor. When Phoebe's pregnancy is confirmed by the doctor, she agonizes over whether to get an abortion or to have the baby and place it for adoption. Phoebe visits another high-school girl who was pregnant a couple of years before, but the older girl can give her no advice. Phoebe finally faces up to the fact that she cannot deal with the situation alone and that she must tell her parents and her boyfriend about her pregnancy.

IL: Ages 11-18   RL: 6.5

7.5   Elfman, Blossom. *A House for Jonnie O.* Boston: Houghton Mifflin, 1976. 175 pp. LC, braille.

Sixteen-year old Jonnie, who is pregnant, constantly argues with her divorced mother and yearns to see her father who has not contacted her for years. Jonnie's boyfriend, Billy, urges her to get an abortion and then leaves town for several months. Jonnie attends a special school for pregnant girls and she and her classmates become enmeshed in the problems each of them faces. When Jonnie's mother announces her plans to remarry, Jonnie is determined to rent a house where she and three of her classmates could live with their babies. The four girls pool their welfare checks to rent a house, but circumstances force the group to break up and give up their short-lived independence. Billy returns and wants Jonnie to sell their infant so that they can have money to start a new life. This and an impersonal letter with money, rather than a visit, from Jonnie's father cause Jonnie to consider suicide. However, she decides that she wants to live for the sake of her unborn child. After the baby is born, Jonnie makes a painful decision to reject Billy and turn to her mother and soon-to-be stepfather for help.

IL: Ages 11-18   RL: 6.0

7.6   Eyerly, Jeanette. *Bonnie Jo, Go Home.* New York: J.B. Lippincott, 1972. 141 pp. Bantam, 1972 pap.

Bonnie, a lonely seventeen-year old girl, faces the ordeal of seeking an abortion. Bonnie decides on an abortion because she feels she could not have given the baby away once it was born and if she had kept it, she could not have given it much of a life. With no emotional support from her mother and stepfather, Bonnie's father simply provides her with a plane ticket and money for the abortion. Bonnie makes the trip to New York thinking that everyone knows her secret. At the abortion clinic, Bonnie must fill out a questionnaire that stirs up painful memories. She is forced to seek another doctor because her pregnancy is too far advanced for a simple abortion from the clinic. Bonnie's stay in New York is eleven days long as the hospital waits for her father to give written permission due to the legal difficulties of performing an advanced abortion. Bonnie is greatly relieved once the abortion is over. As she leaves New York, Bonnie feels that she has aged considerably.

IL: Ages 14-18   RL: 8.0

7.7   Eyerly, Jeanette. *He's My Baby Now.* New York: J.B. Lippincott, 1977. 156 pp. Archway, 1980 pap.

Sixteen-year old Charles is shocked when he discovers that he is an unwed father. After being sexually involved with Daisy the summer before, Charles had given her money for an abortion when she told him she was pregnant. Charles visits the hospital to see the baby and feels an instant affection for it which makes him wonder if he made the right decision last summer when he refused to marry Daisy. When Charles is asked by a social worker to sign a release form along with Daisy so the baby can be adopted, he refuses to do so. Charles feels unable to confide in his divorced mother about his fatherhood as she has started to date and is seldom at home. He begins to wonder what his own father was like whom his mother divorced shortly after Charles was born. Charles finally decides to kidnap his baby from its foster home, but after a clumsy attempt to care for it himself, he returns the baby. After signing the adoption release forms, Charles tries to talk to Daisy with no success. He finds that he cannot completely forget his son but looks for him in every baby he sees.

IL: Ages 11-18   RL: 8.0

7.8   Gold. *Amelia Quackenbush.* see Ch. 4.

7.9   Hinton, Nigel. *Getting Free.* Nashville: Thomas Nelson, 1978. 189 pp.

Johanna, who is fifteen and lives in England, feels happiness as well as worry when she tells her boyfriend, Pete, that she is pregnant. Pete can't bring himself to tell his mother about the pregnancy and when Johanna tells her parents, they are outraged. Johanna's father, who is a clergyman, won't even discuss the situation with Pete, banning him from their house. When her father makes plans for Johanna to get an abortion against her wishes, she and Pete decide to run away. Pete and Johanna must live in several uncomfortable places and Pete must take a low-paying job. When the police begin to search for them, Pete steals a car and the two decide to head for a commune. Caught in a snowstorm, Pete goes for supplies in the car and nearly freezes to death while Johanna stays at an abandoned house and suffers a miscarriage. Even with the loss of the baby, the two are determined to reach the commune together. The police eventually catch up with them, but Johanna and Pete feel they will be back together at some time.

IL: Ages 11-18   RL: 7.5

7.10   Klein. *It's Not What You Expect.* see Ch. 3.

7.11   Lee, Mildred. *Sycamore Year.* New York: Lothrop, Lee, and Shepard, 1974. 190 pp. New American Library, 1976 pap.

Thirteen-year old Wren, who is lonely after moving to a new town, becomes friends with Anna, who is fourteen. Neither of the girls is interested in the opposite sex until Anna meets Tony, a handsome older boy. Wren dislikes Tony but Anna, unknown to her mother,

(Lee, Mildred)

starts meeting him secretly and becomes pregnant. Fearing that
news of her pregnancy may affect her mother's plans to remarry,
Anna confides only in Wren. The two girls devise an immature
plan to spend the summer at a grandparent's farm where Anna's
baby could be born and given to a childless aunt to raise. When
Wren's parents discover the girls' plan, Anna's mother takes her
to a doctor where her pregnancy is confirmed. Because her pregnancy is too far advanced to consider an abortion, it is decided
that Anna will be sent to a home for unwed mothers.

IL: Ages 11-14   RL: 8.0

7.12 Luger, Harriett. *Lauren: A Novel*. New York: The Viking Press,
      1979. 157 pp. Dell, 1981 pap.

Seventeen-year old Lauren suspects that she is pregnant but she
tries to delay facing the possibility as long as possible. When two
friends take Lauren to a clinic and her pregnancy is confirmed,
she tells her boyfriend about it. Lauren's boyfriend and his parents confront Lauren and her parents. Everyone agrees that Laur-
en should get an abortion, except Lauren. Lauren runs away from
home and stays with two young women who are unmarried and have
children. A neighboring married couple who are unable to conceive
a child warn Lauren to take the welfare of her baby seriously.
Lauren works a low-paying job, tries to get on public assistance,
and even considers suicide before deciding to return home to her
parents. They are shocked when Lauren announces her plans to
have the baby and keep it. Lauren even resumes her relationship
with her boyfriend but he tells her he will not marry her. Finally
Lauren decides she must do what is best for her unborn child; she
will let the childless couple who so desperately wanted a baby adopt
her baby once it is born.

IL: Ages 11-18   RL: 8.0

7.13 Lyle, Katie Letcher. *Fair Day, and Another Step Begun*. New York:
      J.B. Lippincott, 1974. 160 pp. Dell, 1975 pap.

Ellen, who is sixteen and lives with her father, falls hopelessly in
love with John, who is older and is a recent college graduate. She
becomes pregnant after a brief encounter with John. When Ellen
tells John about her pregnancy, he laughs at her and offers her
money for an abortion which Ellen refuses. John finds himself
dwelling on thoughts about Ellen and the unborn baby and he goes
to live at a commune to escape the situation. Ellen, who believes
that the power of her love will eventually win over John, follows
him to the commune. John ignores Ellen and turns to another girl
for companionship. When Ellen finally gives up hope of reaching
John, she prepares to leave the commune. However, Ellen's labor
begins before she can leave and John witnesses the birth of the
baby which he finally claims to be his own.

IL: Ages 11-18   RL: 7.0

7.14   Madison, Winifred. *Growing Up in a Hurry*. Boston: Little, Brown,
       and Company, 1973. 168 pp. Archway, 1975 pap. LC, braille.

       With two pretty, popular sisters and parents who are mainly con-
       cerned with their social status, sixteen-year old Karen feels like an
       outcast. Karen has always felt friendless and unattractive and is
       embarrassed by her stuttering, which is at its worst around her
       parents. When Karen falls in love with Steve, she finally feels
       wanted and loved. Karen and Steve become lovers and eventually
       Karen becomes pregnant. Because of his future plans, Steve claims
       that marriage is out of the question and insists that Karen get an
       abortion. Karen is once again left alone. When Karen finally tells
       her parents about her pregnancy, they are quite concerned about
       their friends finding out and immediately make arrangements for an
       abortion. During the stressful time period before and immediately
       after Karen's abortion, she and her mother grow closer.

       IL: Ages 11-18   RL: 7.0

7.15   Minshull, Evelyn. *But I Thought You Really Loved Me*. Philadelphia:
       The Westminster Press, 1976. 154 pp.

       Teenage Koral can't understand her boyfriend's rejection when she
       tells him about her pregnancy. Koral's parents won't allow her to
       get an abortion, so she goes to Haven House, a home for unwed
       mothers. There Koral meets other girls who are putting their ba-
       bies up for adoption or taking their babies home after they are
       born. One girl has been raped and another insists that she is
       still a virgin. Although Koral's older married sister wants to adopt
       her baby, Koral decides against it. Through Koral's experiences
       at Haven House, she grows less bitter toward her former boyfriend
       and her parents as she becomes involved with other teenage girls
       in her situation.

       IL: Ages 11-18   RL: 8.0

7.16   O'Dell. *Kathleen, Please Come Home*. see Ch. 2.

7.17   Powers, Bill. *A Test of Love*. New York: Franklin Watts, 1979.
       90 pp. Dell, 1980 pap. LC, braille and talking book.

       Sixteen-year old Patricia is frightened when she goes to a clinic
       and discovers she is six weeks pregnant. Unable to confide in her
       parents, Patricia tells her best friend about her pregnancy and then
       goes to see her college-age boyfriend Tommy. Tommy does not
       want to marry Patricia at this time and he insists that she have an
       abortion. Confused about what to do and feeling nauseous, Patricia
       spends the next few days in a panic. After another argument with
       Tommy about getting an abortion, Patricia runs from him and is in-
       volved in an accident which causes her to have a miscarriage. Tom-
       my tells Patricia's parents about her pregnancy and miscarriage
       when they arrive at the hospital. Patricia's parents express their
       concern for Patricia without placing blame.

       IL: Ages 11-18   RL: 3.5

7.18   Prince, Alison. *The Turkey's Nest*. New York: William Morrow
       and Company, 1980. 223 pp.

       Seventeen-year old Kate is involved with an older divorced man,
       Laurie. When Kate discovers that she is pregnant, she cannot ac-
       cept Laurie's wish for her to have an abortion. At the suggestion
       of her very understanding mother, Kate decides to spend some time
       with her aunt who lives on a farm outside London. There Kate be-
       comes busy with activities on the farm. She has many helpful talks
       with a young neighbor Alec. Although she receives many letters
       from Laurie, Kate finds that her feelings for Laurie have diminished.
       During an unexpected visit from Laurie, he asks Kate to return to
       London with him but she declines. Kate begins to grow closer to
       Alec; he drives her to childbirth classes and teaches her how to
       drive. Once Kate's son is born, her father shows up and wants
       Kate to live with him and Kate's stepmother. Kate decides to accept
       her father's offer, but she really longs to stay on the farm she has
       grown to love. When Kate tells Alec of her plans, he asks Kate to
       marry him, having fallen in love with Kate and her baby.

       IL: Ages 14-18   RL: 6.0

7.19   Ruby, Lois. "Found by a Lost Child" in *Arriving at a Place You've
       Never Left*. New York: The Dial Press, 1977. 149 pp. Dell, 1980
       pap.

       Shana, who is sixteen and pregnant, is hurt when her boyfriend
       will not accept any responsibility for the unborn baby. However,
       her mother is quite supportive of Shana's decision to have the baby
       placed for adoption. When the baby's father visits Shana in the
       hospital, Shana realizes that she never really loved him. Her former
       boyfriend, however, feels much turmoil after seeing his child at the
       hospital nursery. Too late, the baby's father finds he cannot deny
       his involvement with the mother and baby.

       IL: Ages 11-18   RL: 8.0

7.20   Ruby, Lois. *What Do You Do in Quicksand?* New York: The Viking
       Press, 1979. 199 pp. Fawcett, 1981 pap.

       Sixteen-year old Matt and his family move next door to Leah, a de-
       fensive fifteen-year old girl who lies and behaves strangely. Matt
       is in a dilemma because a girl he once dated is pregnant and claims
       that Matt is the father of her baby. Unable to think of the girl
       getting an abortion, Matt makes arrangements to take over the
       baby's care once it is born. Leah has problems of her own as
       well - she never knew her own father and her mother's second hus-
       band made sexual advances toward Leah as a child. Leah's mother
       died shortly after marrying her third husband, so Leah now lives
       with her elderly stepfather. Once the baby arrives at Matt's house,
       his family is in turmoil due to the baby's demands and irregular
       schedule. Matt's grades fall at school and he has no social life.
       Leah begins helping with the baby's care and soon grows very fond
       of the baby, pretending that the baby is her own. When Leah
       gathers supplies and kidnaps the baby, she is later hospitalized
       and sees a psychiatrist. Matt decides to move to a new area and

(Ruby, Lois)

strike out on his own with the baby. When he tells Leah of his
plans, she feels sadness but hopes the baby's life will be happier
than her own.

IL: Ages 11-18   RL: 6.5

7.21   Sherburne, Zoa. *Too Bad About the Haines Girl*. New York: William
       Morrow and Company, 1967. 189 pp. William Morrow, 1967 pap.

Seventeen-year old Melinda feels confused, worried, and ashamed
when she discovers she is pregnant. Melinda informs her boyfriend, Jeff, about her pregnancy, then refuses to see him or talk
to him. Melinda agonizes over what to do, considering running
away to an unwed mother's home or getting an abortion, which she
has been educated to think of as being morally wrong. Although
Jeff wants to marry Melinda, she asks him for money for an abortion. Jeff drives Melinda to the clinic, but once there, she finds
she cannot go through with it. On the night that Melinda is
crowned queen of a dance, she finally tells her parents about her
pregnancy. They make plans to meet with Jeff and his parents to
decide what to do next.

IL: Ages 11-18   RL: 7.0

7.22   Truss, Jan. *Bird at the Window*. New York: Harper and Row,
       1974. 215 pp.

Eighteen-year old Angela panics when she suspects that she is pregnant and even tries to make herself miscarry. She loves someone
other than Gordy, the older boy who is the father of her baby.
Also Angela has plans to travel through Europe during the summer.
Unable to tell her aloof mother or stern father about her pregnancy,
Angela confides only in a beloved teacher who advises her to get
an abortion. During her stay in Europe, Angela spends time with
her grandparents and makes an unsuccessful attempt to get an a-
bortion there. However, after Angela travels to a different country, she becomes ill and gives birth to a stillborn baby at a hospital. Still recovering from this, Angela is called back home where
her father is very ill with cancer. After her father's death, Angela discovers that she was not her father's child and that he married her mother to make Angela legitimate. Trying to do what her
father would have wanted, Angela agrees to go ahead and marry
Gordy. Only the sudden revelation that her deceased father was
not perfect makes Angela decide to forego marriage and turn to
writing as a career.

IL: Ages 14-18   RL: 7.5

7.23   Windsor, Patricia. *Diving for Roses*. New York: Harper and Row,
       1976. 248 pp.

Jean, a recent high-school graduate, has taken care of her ailing
mother for years while her father is away working in the city. With
no friends, Jean is very lonely and feels like a prisoner in her own

(Windsor, Patricia)

home. When Jean meets a friendly young man named Sasha camping
in the woods, she is attracted to him and the two become lovers.
Jean makes an unsuccessful attempt to obtain birth control. When
she begins noticing changes in her body, Jean believes that she
has venereal disease, but discovers that she is actually pregnant.
Sasha suggests an abortion but seeing that Jean wants to keep the
baby, he later asks Jean to marry him. Jean, however, claims she
could never leave her mother and in anger, Sasha tells Jean her
mother is really an alcoholic. When Jean comes to the realization
that Sasha is right, she confronts her mother. Jean's mother joins
Alcoholics Anonymous and becomes more confident and outgoing,
leaving Jean with no purpose in life. With a physician's help, Jean
tries to plan a life for herself after her baby is born.

IL: Ages 14-18   RL: 7.5

7.24 Zindel, Paul. *My Darling, My Hamburger*. New York: Harper and
Row, 1969. 168 pp. Bantam, 1972 pap.

Liz and Maggie become good friends and start to double-date during
their senior year of high school. Maggie, who is slightly overweight
and very self-conscious, gains confidence from the loud and popular Liz. Liz is unable to get along with her stepfather at home and
also has a recurring argument with her boyfriend, Sean, who wants
to engage in heavy petting. Liz and Sean break up over this issue
but after her stepfather accuses her of being a "tramp," Liz begins
to go along with Sean's wishes and eventually becomes pregnant.
At first Sean agrees to marry Liz, but then he decides to simply
give her money to finance an abortion. Maggie accompanies Liz
during the abortion and has to tell Liz's mother about it when com-
plications arise. On graduation day, Maggie is thankful that she
has improved her appearance and started to date, but she mourns
the fact that Liz is unable to participate in the ceremony.

IL: Ages 11-18   RL: 7.5

8.
Serious Illness and Death

Beyond sexual, financial, and emotional stresses that families are exposed to lies the possibility that sudden disaster may strike, crippling the family system and threatening its very survival. Probably one of the most catastrophic stresses that a family can face is serious illness and/or death of a family member. If the father becomes seriously ill or dies, a major portion of the family's livelihood is at stake. If the mother is ill or dies, not only is it likely that a significant portion of the family's income is threatened, her important supportive role in the family system is impacted as well. Lastly, the seriously ill child or a child's death can shake the very foundation of the family system to the point to where the parents may divorce or separate.

This chapter focuses on serious illness and death, generally of family members. The emphasis is on helping young people to cope with their own serious illness or that of a family member. Death is focused on through the eyes of young children and adolescents with the goal of helping them to better cope with the death phenomenon.

Serious Illness

Serious illness has a tremendous impact on children and adolescents. If a parent becomes seriously ill, it is not unusual for a small child to react to the illness in ways seemingly strange to the adult. For example, small children may blame themselves for the illness of a parent. Children in such a situation may well conclude that they caused the illness through their screaming or quarreling with a parent.

Adolescents have more of an awareness of the extent of a parent's illness. A major problem affecting the adolescent and other family members is a lack of communication about and denial of a parent's serious illness. Therapists generally believe that the illness of any family member should be discussed openly and freely. Many families faced with a family member's illness may deny its existence. Or they may attempt to cope with the illness by not directly talking about it to the sick family member. This kind of communication pattern is not helpful to the young person, the seriously ill family member, or to the well-being of the family system.

If a child becomes seriously ill, every member of the family is pro-
foundly affected - beginning, of course, with the child itself. There is
evidence suggesting that children who are gravely ill know more about
their illness than adults imagine. Research has found that children over
the age of four, even though they are not directly aware of the diagnosis,
often know the seriousness of their illness.[1]

Seriously ill children must develop coping mechanisms that well children do not have to contend with. It is not unusual for the ill child to
have to undergo surgery. This surgery may leave the child different
from the child's peers. The child may lose weight, lose hair to chemotherapy, or even lose a part of the body to amputation. Obviously, when
the child reenters the community, which includes the family, peer groups,
and school, the child will have misgivings. If the child does not receive
help for dealing with reentry into community life, the child may well become withdrawn and isolated from others and may regress to dependent
infantile behavior within the family system.[2]

The seriously ill child may have to learn to cope with family disharmony as well. When parents must spend a great deal of time helping the
child deal with its illness, the parents' marriage may become shaky. In
some cases, the marriage becomes stronger; however, for many marriages,
the child's illness has an opposite effect. When things get bad enough,
the child's parents should begin looking for outside therapy, both individual and family.

Death

Death was once both an expected and accepted part of living prior to
advanced industrialization. At the beginning of the twentieth century,
mortality rates were high, death during childbirth was frequent, and total life expectancy was brief when compared to life expectancy today.
Death occurred at home and family members prepared the departed for
burial. Given the high mortality rate prior to advanced industrialization,
children were exposed to death often. Death was an intricate part of
living.

Today, most children do not know how to respond to death since so
few of them are likely to lose a close family member. They know that
people die, but more often than not, these people are not closely related
to the child. When a parent or sibling dies, children must define for
themselves the appropriate manner in which to respond. What do we
presently know about how children respond to death?

Some research has been done on correlating children's understanding
of death with their chronological age. It should be kept in mind that
when using a child's chronological age for understanding a child's world,
only a limited picture is presented of how a child sees death. As with
all aspects of physical and psychological growth, children are not a very
homogeneous group and considerable variability among them is present.

Before the age of three, children have a limited understanding of
death. This is obviously due to the child's lack of experiential background
and inadequate symbolic capability. Little empirical research has been
done on the under three age group concerning death. We do know, however, that separation from significant others such as a parent, even for

a short period of time, is quite traumatic for the child under three years
of age.[3] When children this age lose a parent to death, there is considerable reaction to the loss, but little understanding of it on the part of
the child.

The existing research for the age group of three to five years is mea-
ger. Children in this age group also have a limited understanding of
death and view death in terms of wilted flowers, dead goldfish, etc. Many
children from three to five years old see death as "going away" or "going
to sleep."[4] Since the child in this age group has such an unrealistic understanding of death, the death of a person close to the child creates
unique problems. The child may assume that the dead person could return if they wanted to; when this return does not occur, the child not
only feels sadness but also possibly resentment for being abandoned.[5]

Empirical studies of the age group of five to ten years are more numerous than for younger children. Two important findings have emerged
from these studies that appear to be accurate for children five to ten
years of age. The first finding is that this age group begins to understand death as a biological process, giving the child a more realistic understanding of death.[6] Also reported is the finding that children between
five and ten become aware of the fact that everyone must die and that
death is universal.[7] In essence, this age group of children begins to
develop a more mature understanding of death.

Many empirical findings are reported concerning a child's understanding of death between the ages of ten and sixteen. Children in this age
group begin to develop a sophisticated understanding of death. They begin to see that death has many causes. An imagery of death becomes
highly developed. Children in this age group begin to ask questions a-
bout what happens after death. They also become concerned about the
significance of life and its basic meanings.

Our knowledge about how children understand and deal with death
is somewhat limited. Younger children from what we know have a lack of
understanding of death; older children have a more sophisticated understanding. Regardless of a child's age, however, children are not adequately taught to deal with death in modern society and many times require counseling or therapy when a close family member dies.

Criteria for Book Selection

This chapter includes books where the main character is a young person who must deal with serious illness and/or death of someone they are
close to. Most of the books concern serious illness or death of a member
of the young person's family such a parent, grandparent, or sibling. A
few of the books illustrate the effect on a young person when a friend or
pet dies. Other books selected for this chapter have main characters who
are the victims of a serious illness themselves.

Those characters in this chapter who have a serious illness themselves
are portrayed very realistically. They are generally adolescents who have
a complete understanding of the nature of their illness. Most of the books
concern young people faced with leukemia or other progressive illnesses;
others deal with less serious conditions. These books describe the feelings of rage, helplessness, resignation, and acceptance that the characters feel concerning their condition.

Other books illustrate a young person's reaction to serious illness in someone else. Books were selected where a parent, friend, or sibling is the victim of a grave illness. The young person's reaction to someone they love being seriously ill ranges from loneliness and sorrow to a feeling of relief if the person's condition improved. Books where the young person is made aware of the implications of a serious illness, particularly if it involves a parent, are the most helpful from a therapeutic point of view.

Books selected for this chapter where a young person has to deal with the death of someone they love, usually a family member, seem to exhibit a developmental perspective appropriate to the age of the book's main character. Those books for young children do not convey too much abstract information concerning death.[8] Most of these books deal with the death of a grandparent, with a few concerning the death of a parent or sibling. The books recognize and usually show tolerance for common reactions of young children to death - anger, withdrawal, refusal to eat, and even searching for the deceased person. Several of the characters attend funerals, each showing different rituals, practices, and beliefs.

Books in this chapter concerning death for older children make no attempt to mask the reality of death.[9] Certain books deal with the untimely death of a sibling, either from fatal illness, accident, or suicide. The death of a parent and the resulting trauma for the remaining parent and children in the family is the topic of other books. Many of the characters having a parent who dies find their lives greatly changed afterwards.

In using bibliotherapy for young people concerning the subjects of serious illness and/or death, great caution must be used. It is quite important to match the contents of a book with the child's situation. Young people who are seriously ill or who have a family member who is seriously ill should not be given false hope concerning the illness by reading about a situation which is not really similar to their own. Likewise, books where a serious illness is fatal are only appropriate for a young person whose parent, sibling, etc. is already deceased. Another aspect that must be considered for certain books in this chapter is the compatibility of rituals, practices, and beliefs concerning death with the background of the reader.

Helpful ways of coping with serious illness and/or death are evident in many of the books in this chapter. Some of the characters simply needed to talk out feelings and thoughts with a parent or peer. Other characters turned to counseling, either individual or group, in their efforts to deal with serious illness or death. Generally, the books in this chapter very realistically stress the long time period needed to adjust to death or serious illness, either in oneself or others.

NOTES

1. Robert Wernick, *The Family* (New York: Time-Life Books, 1974), p. 126.
2. Lynn Kagen-Goodheart, "Reentry: Living With Childhood Cancer," *American Journal of Orthopsychiatry* (Volume XLVII, No. 2, 1977): 651-658.

3. Henry B. Biller, *Paternal Deprivation* (Lexington, Massachusetts: Lexington Books, 1974).

4. Sylvia Anthony, *The Discovery of Death in Childhood and After* (New York: Basic Books, 1971), p. 52.

5. Everett S. Ostrovsky, *Children Without Men* (New York: Collier Books, 1962), p. 117.

6. Anthony, pp. 50-54.

7. Ibid.

8. Marsha Kabakow Rudman, *Children's Literature: An Issues Approach* (Lexington, Massachusetts: D.C. Heath and Company, 1976), p. 77.

9. Ibid.

BOOKS

8.1   Bartoli, Jennifer. *Nonna*. New York: Harvey House, 1975.   45 pp.

A young boy describes the sadness and quiet in his family after
his grandmother, Nonna, dies.   When his relatives gather at his
grandmother's house the day after the burial to divide up her belongings, the boy feels that Nonna should be there too.   His younger sister even searches through the house for Nonna.   As time passes, the family remembers all the good things about Nonna and at
Christmas, the boy's sister uses one of her grandmother's favorite
recipes.

IL: Ages 5-8   RL: 3.0

8.2   Beckman, Gunnel. *Admission to the Feast*. New York: Holt, Rinehart, and Winston, 1971. 114 pp.

Nineteen-year old Annika, a Swedish girl, is shocked when she is
informed by a doctor that her usual anemic condition has been diagnosed as leukemia.   Annika's mother is away on a trip so Annika
heads for a cottage in the woods to contemplate her disease.   In
writing a long letter to a friend who is in America, Annika explores
her disbelief and feelings of despair at having leukemia, even considering suicide.   She also writes of her parents' divorce and of
meeting her father after many years right before he died.   Unsure
of what her boyfriend's reaction to her illness will be, Annika wonders in her letter if they will ever again make love.   When her boyfriend calls and tells Annika that he knows about her leukemia, Annika ends the letter to her friend and waits for her boyfriend to
arrive, not sure what her future will hold.

IL: Ages 14-18   RL: 7.5

8.3   Blue. *Nikki 108*. see Ch. 2.

8.4   Blume. *Forever*. see Ch. 9.

8.5   Blume, Judy.   *Tiger Eyes*.   Scarsdale, NY: Bradbury Press, 1981.
206 pp.   Dell, 1982 pap.

When her father is killed during a hold-up of his store, it is hard
for fifteen-year old Davey, who held her father as he died, to recover.   Davey remains isolated in her home for days after the funeral, refusing to bathe or change clothes.   When school begins,
Davey's mother urges her to try to get back to her old routine,
but Davey starts to hyperventilate at school each day and sometimes
passes out.   Davey's mother decides that Davey and her younger
brother need to get away from the city and the three of them go
to spend some time with an aunt and uncle in New Mexico.   Davey
still has many bad moments when she is flooded with grief for her
father, but she begins to adjust with the help of new friends she
makes in New Mexico.   Of particular help is an older boy named
Wolf whose father is dying of cancer.   However, Davey's mother,
who complains of headaches and seldom leaves her room, is encouraged by Davey's aunt and uncle to see a counselor.   Davey's mother

(Blume, Judy)

starts to get out and even takes a job, but she lets Davey's aunt and uncle make all her decisions for her. Davey becomes resentful of her aunt and uncle's overprotectiveness. She is also upset about her mother starting to date, so Davey begins to receive counseling too. After going over the details of her father's death with a therapist, Davey feels a great sense of relief; she is also thrilled when her mother announces they are going back to New Jersey to make it on their own.

IL: Ages 11-18   RL: 5.0

8.6   Bosse. *The 79 Squares*. see Ch. 4.

8.7   Branfield. *Why Me?*   see Ch. 6.

8.8   Bunting, Eve. *The Happy Funeral*. New York: Harper and Row, 1982. 39 pp.

A young Chinese-American girl, Laura, cannot understand what her mother means when she says that Laura's grandfather is going to have a happy funeral. Laura watches her relatives that night at the funeral home as they place objects in her grandfather's casket and burn play money. She feels only sadness and cries herself to sleep that night. During the funeral procession the next day, Laura is surprised when she finds herself waving to people she knows and enjoying the band music. However, she is sad once again when her family arrives at the cemetery. Laura decides that although others are not happy at this time, perhaps her grandfather is happy because it was time for him to die.

IL: Ages 8-11   RL: 4.0

8.9   Buscaglia, Leo. *The Fall of Freddie the Leaf*. New York: Holt, Rinehart, and Winston, 1982. 27 pp.

Freddie the leaf first appears in Spring and becomes friends with other leaves on his branch. Daniel, Freddie's best friend, explains to Freddie that they are part of a large tree and that each leaf on the tree has a purpose such as giving shade to people. Freddie and his friends enjoy the hot days of Summer, but are shocked when Fall arrives with the first frost. All the leaves are happy about the beautiful colors they now turn. However, they are frightened when the wind blows some leaves off the tree. Daniel explains to Freddie and the others that Winter is approaching and all leaves must die, but they should not be afraid because it is just another one of the seasons that follow one after another.

IL: Ages 5-11   RL: 4.0

8.10 Byars, Betsy. *Good-bye, Chicken Little*. New York: Harper and Row, 1979. 101 pp. Scholastic, 1981 pap.

Feeling anxious and unprotected after his father's death in a mine several years before, Jimmie has given himself the nickname "Chicken

(Byars, Betsy)

Little" when he feels unable to join his friends in their adventures.
Jimmie is upset once again when his favorite uncle accidentally
drowns and Jimmie's mother, without thinking, blames Jimmie for
it. To help Jimmie overcome his undeserved guilt, Jimmie's mother
decides to have a family party where relatives can share happy memories of Jimmie's uncle. Jimmie's older sister also tells Jimmie about
the guilt she felt when their father died and how she overcame it.
Jimmie feels as if he is finally able to rid himself of most of his
negative feelings.

IL: Ages 8-11   RL: 5.5

8.11 Byars. *The Pinballs*. see Ch. 4.

8.12 Carner, Chas. *Tawny*. New York: Macmillan Publishing Company,
1978. 148 pp.

After the accidental death of his twin brother, twelve-year old Trey
has to deal with hurt, guilt, and loneliness. Trey's father brings
home an injured yearling doe and encourages Trey to nurse it back
to health. Trey's interest in the deer helps him to stop dwelling
on his past life with his brother. The warmth and concern shown
Trey by his parents also aid in Trey's recovery from the loss of
his twin. Trey reluctantly sets the deer free and feels ready to
face the first birthday since his brother died.

IL: Ages 11-14   RL: 7.5

8.13 Cate, Dick. *Never is a Long, Long Time*. Nashville: Thomas Nelson, 1976. 92 pp.

When his beloved dog dies, eleven-year old Billy mourns his loss,
unable to sleep at night and flooded with memories of good times
with the dog. When Billy asks his mother if they will get a new
dog, she tells him probably not because it's too hard losing something you love. The family is excited when Billy's older sister and
her husband announce that they're expecting a baby. Soon afterwards, Billy's grandmother, whom he is very close to, falls ill and
eventually needs to be hospitalized. Billy's family is saddened at
the thought of Christmas without grandmother; however, she is released from the hospital in time to enjoy the holidays. When spring
approaches, Billy feels that everything has fallen into place - his
sister's baby is born, his grandmother is regaining her strength,
and Billy's father announces that it's time to get a new dog.

IL: Ages 8-11   RL: 4.5

8.14 Cleaver, Vera and Bill. *Grover*. New York: J.B. Lippincott, 1970.
125 pp. New American Library, 1975 pap.

Eleven-year old Grover makes plans to spend an enjoyable summer
with his friends, not noticing or being told of his mother's serious
illness. When Grover's mother is taken to the hospital for an operation, Grover stays with his aunt and uncle who mention his mother

(Cleaver, Vera and Bill)

as little as possible. Grover senses that something is wrong and he fears that his mother is going to die; however, on her return home from the hospital, his mother appears to feel better and she insists on talking to Grover for hours at a time. When Grover's mother, unable to accept her condition becoming worse, commits suicide by shooting herself, Grover's father grieves constantly and becomes very withdrawn. Grover does not display any emotions over his mother's death, but he acts out some of his pain through his behavior with his friends. After a talk with a minister and a visit to his mother's grave, Grover feels better better about his mother's death and unsuccessfully tries to share his feelings with his grieving father. It is only through the support of Grover's housekeeper and his friends that Grover is able to rebuild his own life.

IL: Ages 11-14   RL: 5.5

8.15   De Paola, Thomas Anthony. *Nana Upstairs and Nana Downstairs*. New York: G.P. Putnam's Sons, 1973. 31 pp.

Tommy, who is four years old, loves to visit the house where his grandmother and great-grandmother live. Tommy and his great-grandmother share candy and stories and he takes meals upstairs to her. When Tommy's mother tells him his great-grandmother has died, he refuses to believe it until he sees her empty bed. When Tommy starts crying, his mother helps Tommy with his grief by telling him he can bring his great-grandmother back by remembering things about her.

IL: Ages 5-8   RL: 3.0

8.16   De Paola, Tomie. *Now One Foot, Now the Other*. New York: G.P. Putnam's Sons, 1981 pap. 43 pp.

Five-year old Bobby's best friend is his grandfather. They spend lots of time playing together and Bobby likes for his grandfather to tell him stories, especially about how his grandfather taught Bobby to walk. Bobby's grandfather suffers a stroke and must be hospitalized for several months. When his grandfather does finally come home, Bobby is frightened of him because of his inability to walk or talk. Bobby's parents tell him his grandfather will never get any better, but the little boy patiently tells his grandfather stories and eventually even helps his grandfather learn to walk once more.

IL: Ages 5-8   RL: 2.5

8.17   Dixon, Paige. *May I Cross Your Golden River?* New York: Atheneum, 1975. 262 pp. LC, talking book.

Eighteen-year old Jordan is part of a close-knit fatherless family with three brothers and a sister who are friends as well as siblings. Jordan attends a university with plans to be a lawyer and has an active social life. When Jordan develops a weakness in his knees

(Dixon, Paige)

after playing tennis one day, he visits his physician who suggests that Jordan have tests administered at the Mayo Clinic. There Jordan is diagnosed as having amyotrophic lateral sclerosis, a progressive fatal disease where muscles weaken and atrophy. Certain that the doctors are wrong, Jordan is angry for a period of time and even considers suicide, but eventually he accepts the disease. Jordan's mother resists over-protecting her son and his siblings express concern and respect Jordan's moods without showing pity. As Jordan's disease progresses, he must finally tell his girlfriend about it. He also makes plans to donate his body to science upon his death. A few weeks after participating in his brother's wedding and his nephew's christening - two events Jordan was determined to be alive for - Jordan collapses and is unable to talk to his family.

IL: Ages 11-18   RL: 7.0

8.18   Donovan, John. *I'll Get There. It Better Be Worth the Trip.* New York: Harper and Row, 1969. 189 pp. Dell, 1971 pap.

Thirteen-year old Davy has lived with his grandmother ever since his parents' divorce. When Davy's grandmother dies, his alcoholic mother reluctantly agrees to let Davy live with her. Davy misses his grandmother and must adjust to attending a private school in the city. Davy's mother is resentful and appears to be overwhelmed with having Davy and his dog in her apartment; Davy's father and stepmother genuinely like Davy and want him to visit often, but never offer to let Davy live with them. When Davy and a friend engage in some affectionate play, Davy fears that he is homosexual. Only after a talk with his father does Davy realize that what he and his friend did was quite normal for their age. Davy has a second death to contend with when his dog is run over by a car, but this time he is resigned to losing those you love.

IL: Ages 11-18   RL: 6.5

8.19   Gerson, Corrine. *Passing Through.* New York: The Dial Press, 1978. 193 pp. Dell, 1980 pap.

Still struggling with the pain of her older brother's suicide, fifteen-year old Liz finds herself constantly battling with her parents' values and even blaming them for his death. When Liz begins tutoring a teenage boy with cerebral palsy named Sam, she pours out her emotions to him and Sam in turn tells Liz about his difficulties in being handicapped. Although Liz's parents disapprove of Sam and feel that his family is beneath them socially, Liz continues her friendship with him. Eventually Liz shows Sam the last letter she received from her older brother right before his suicide, where her brother proclaims his homosexuality and the resulting pressures on him. When Liz's parents find her and Sam asleep on a bed and suspect that they've made love, Liz flees to the home of a young couple whom she babysits for and begs them to let her live there. Liz's parents find her brother's letter and even though they have a hard time accepting her brother's homosexuality, her parents

(Gerson, Corrine)

attempt to resolve some of their conflicts with Liz. Liz and Sam
drift apart, no longer feeling the need to share their thoughts and
emotions.

IL: Ages 11-18   RL: 9.0

8.20 Girion, Barbara. *A Tangle of Roots*. New York: Charles Scribner's
Sons, 1976. 154 pp. Dell, 1981 pap.

Beth, a high-school junior busy with school activities, is stunned
when her mother dies of a cerebral hemorrhage. Beth finds it
difficult, once the mourning period is over, to chatter with her
friends about school and she feels uncomfortable around her boyfriend. In addition, Beth's grandmother is constantly visiting her
house and becomes somewhat of a nuisance for Beth and her father.
Beth becomes angry when a neighbor asks her father to join a
single parent's group and she tries to spend more time with her
father so he won't feel lonely. This jeopardizes Beth's relationship
with her boyfriend and she is torn between family obligations and
her own social life. Beth is hurt when her father starts going out
with other people, but eventually she realizes that she and her
father must get on with their lives. Although Beth's house seems
empty without her mother, Beth discovers that her mother is still
very present in her memories as well as her father's.

IL: Ages 11-18   RL: 6.0

8.21 Greene. *Al(exandra) the Great*. see Ch. 11.

8.22 Greene, Constance C. *Beat the Turtle Drum*. New York: The Viking Press, 1976. 119 pp. Dell, 1979 pap. LC, talking book.

Twelve-year old Kate helps her younger sister, Joss, who is almost
eleven, earn money so that Joss can rent a horse. Joss has enough
money saved by her birthday and the two sisters, who are best
friends, eagerly await the arrival of the horse. Many happy summer
days follow with Joss giving rides to neighborhood children and
both girls talking until late in the night. While on a picnic, Joss
falls from high in a tree and is instantly killed. Kate and her parents attend Joss's funeral, numb with the shock of losing her.
Kate's parents turn to tranquilizers and alcohol to get through the
next few days. Kate finds herself wondering "Why not me?" and
feeling anger that her sister was taken away. When summer's end
is near, Kate realizes that school will start soon and life must go
on.

IL: Ages 11-14   RL: 4.0

8.23 Greenfield, Eloise. *Sister*. New York: Thomas Y. Crowell, 1974.
83 pp. LC, talking book.

A thirteen-year old black girl, Doretha, called Sister by everyone,
looks through her memory book and longs for the way her family
was before her father died of a heart attack. Now her mother works

(Greenfield, Eloise)

long hours at a laundry and never seems to smile. Doretha's older
sister, Alberta, had a best friend move away at the same time that
their father died and she can't bear the thought of anyone else
leaving her. Alberta constantly argues with their mother about
dropping out of school and leaves home for days at a time. At
school, the teachers unfairly compare Doretha to her older sister,
who is involved in fights and has failing grades. As Doretha thinks
back over all that has happened since her father's death, she finds
she can now accept some of the bad times and she resolves to use
her new-found strength to reach out to her mother and older sister
to bring her family back together once again.

IL: Ages 11-14   RL: 4.0

8.24   Hamilton, Virginia. *Sweet Whispers, Brother Rush*. New York:
Philomel Books, 1982.   215 pp.

Fourteen-year old Tree, who is black, is resentful because she is
left in charge of her older retarded brother. Tree prepares her
brother's meals and helps him dress. Her mother works away from
home and is only with her children a few hours on the weekend.
Tree believes that she sees a ghost that is her dead uncle and
learns from him facts about her family's past - that her mother beat
her retarded brother when he was small and that her father isn't
dead, he just left home. When Tree's brother develops a hereditary
illness and dies soon afterwards, Tree blames her mother for his
death and decides to run away from home. However, Tree discovers
that her mother may remarry and provide a better life for Tree.
Also, without the constant strain of watching her brother, Tree
may be able to lead a more "normal" life.

IL: Ages 11-18   RL: 7.0

8.25   Harlan, Elizabeth. *Footfalls*. New York: Atheneum, 1982.   128 pp.

Stevie, who is almost fourteen years old, is a serious runner and
a member of the school track team. Stevie's mother feels that her
running is unimportant and her father, who is recovering from a
serious operation, is too tired to show much interest in Stevie.
As her father's condition worsens, Stevie's family is under much
tension with Stevie and her younger brother often in conflict. Stevie's father must enter the hospital and Stevie's mother finally reveals to her children that their father has cancer. When her father
dies, Stevie feels emotionally numb at first and later angry at her
father. She stops running and has problems at school. When Stevie starts seeing the school counselor, she feels ready to run again
and is able to comfort her younger brother. Stevie also begins to
acknowledge her awakening sexual feelings for a boy on the track
team. Although Stevie still has periods of sadness, she tries to
accept her father's death and to remember some of the good times
they shared.

IL: Ages 11-14   RL: 7.0

8.26 Hautzig, Deborah. *Hey, Dollface*. see Ch. 9.

8.27 Holland, Isabelle. *Of Love and Death and Other Journeys*. New York:
      J.B. Lippincott, 1975. 159 pp. LC, talking book.

      Meg, who is fifteen years old, has spent most of her life traveling
      through Europe with her divorced mother and stepfather. Meg has
      never met her father, her parents having divorced before she was
      born, and she is hurt when her mother reveals the fact that Meg's
      father does not even know of Meg's existence. Meg's mother be-
      comes seriously ill and must undergo a cancer operation, from which
      she seems to rapidly recover. Then Meg discovers that her real
      father, who has finally been told about Meg by her mother, is com-
      ing to visit her for a few days. Meg is prepared to hate her father
      but she finds he is actually a nice person. Meg has a dream about
      her mother's death and soon afterwards, her mother does begin to
      decline and eventually dies. Unable to believe that the emaciated
      body they cremate could possibly be her mother, Meg feels only re-
      lief that it is all over. Only after she goes to live with her father
      and stepmother does Meg feel the reality of what has happened and
      allow herself to grieve.

      IL: Ages 14-18   RL: 8.5

8.28 Howe, James. *A Night Without Stars*. New York: Atheneum, 1983.
      178 pp.

      Eleven-year old Maria is frightened when she discovers she is sched-
      uled to have open-heart surgery. Although her family is very sup-
      portive, they are unable to answer Maria's many questions about
      her operation. Once at the hospital, Maria finds she cannot under-
      stand what the doctors and nurses tell her. The night before her
      operation, Maria seeks out a badly burned and deformed boy named
      Donald who has undergone many operations himself. Donald ex-
      plains the administration of anesthesia and other procedures in the
      operating room, reassuring Maria so that she is able to sleep. Af-
      ter her operation, Maria spends some time in the Intensive Care
      Unit and there a nurse finally explains to Maria all she wants to
      know about her heart condition. During the rest of her hospital
      stay, Maria helps Donald to face his disfigurement and to feel con-
      fidence in himself as a person.

      IL: Ages 11-14   RL: 6.0

8.29 Hughes, Monica. *Hunter in the Dark*. New York: Atheneum, 1982.
      131 pp.

      Sixteen-year old Mike, who has leukemia, runs away from home to
      go deer hunting by himself. During his time alone in the woods,
      Mike reflects on the past year since his leukemia was diagnosed.
      Mike's parents kept his disease a secret from him for months, say-
      ing his many blood tests were simply a check for anemia and mono.
      However, when he began chemotherapy and lost much of his hair,
      Mike suspected that his illness was serious and he asked the doctor
      to confirm his suspicions. During a period of remission, Mike per-
      suaded his overprotective parents to let him learn to drive and a

(Hughes, Monica)

friend also helped him prepare for his hunting trip. Although Mike finds himself unable to shoot a deer, he returns home feeling that he is a capable and worthy human being able to face anything.

IL: Ages 11-18   RL: 7.0

8.30 Hunt. *The Lottery Rose: A Novel.* see Ch. 4.

8.31 Kaplan, Bess. *The Empty Chair.* New York: Harper and Row, 1975. 243 pp. LC, talking book.

Nine-year old Becky, who is Jewish and lives during the time of the Great Depression, is ecstatic when her mother announces she is expecting a baby. Mama keeps postponing seeing a doctor and when her labor begins early, Mama and the baby both die. Grief-stricken, Becky feels very lonely and begins thinking her mother comes to her during the night. Relatives begin to search for a new wife for Becky's father which Becky and her younger brother resent very much. Becky's father does remarry eventually and Becky likes her new stepmother, but she feels guilty about it. Becky believes Mama walks through the house, resentful of Becky's stepmother and trying to punish family members. Becky's stepmother realizes that something is bothering Becky and finally Becky admits her fears to her father. He takes Becky to the cemetery to convince her that Mama is really gone. Becky's nightmares cease and she begins to have only good memories of Mama. Becky becomes closer to her stepmother and decides to call her "Mummy." Becky is a little apprehensive but very happy when her stepmother announces that a baby is on the way.

IL: Ages 8-11   RL: 4.0

8.32 Kellogg. *Like the Lion's Tooth.* see Ch. 4.

8.33 Klein. *Confessions of an Only Child.* see Ch. 10.

8.34 Krementz, Jill. *How it Feels When a Parent Dies.* New York: Alfred A. Knopf, 1982. 110 pp. LC, talking book.

Young people ranging in age from seven to sixteen years share their feelings at experiencing a parent's death. Some of the parents' deaths are recent while others happened several years ago. The parents' deaths occurred because of accidents, fatal diseases, and suicide. The children's stories portray many emotions felt at the time of a parent's death, including grief, anger, anxiety, and embarrassment.

IL: Ages 8-14   RL: 5.0

8.35 Lowry. *Anastasia Krupnik.* see Ch. 10.

8.36 Lowry, Lois. *A Summer to Die.* Boston: Houghton Mifflin, 1977. 154 pp. Bantam, 1979 pap. LC, braille.

(Lowry, Lois)

Thirteen-year old Meg and her sister Molly, who is fifteen, are dis-
mayed when their father announces that the family is going to move
to the country during his year's sabbatical. Meg and Molly have
very different interests, so it is difficult for the sisters to share
a bedroom in their new home. Molly becomes ill with frequent nose-
bleeds which keep her home from school and thus is often irritable.
When Molly needs to be hospitalized, Meg, who has always been envious of Molly's beauty, feels to blame due to an argument between
the two girls. On Molly's return home, Meg tries to cheer up her
listless sister and both girls become interested in a neighboring
couple who are expecting a baby. However, Molly has to return
to the hospital where she is diagnosed as having leukemia and the
family joins in their feelings of grief. Meg, who avoids visiting her
sister in the hospital, finally goes to tell her about the neighbors'
new baby; however, Molly is drugged and connected to machines,
so she barely responds. Molly dies and Meg and her parents prepare to leave their country home and try to go back to life in the
city.

IL: Ages 11-14   RL: 7.0

8.37 McLendon, Gloria H. *My Brother Joey Died*. New York: Julian Messner, 1982. 64 pp.

When her older brother dies of Reye's Syndrome, a young girl has
problems in accepting his death and attending his funeral. As she
mourns her brother's death, she feels the emotions of guilt, anger,
fear, and sadness. The girl's parents are lost in their own grief
so she receives comfort only from her grandparents. When she
starts experiencing behavioral problems at school, the girl is approached by a counselor and asked to join a grief support group
for young people. Her parents begin attending a support group
also and after a year, the girl's family appears better able to cope
with their loss.

IL: Ages 8-11   RL: 3.5

8.38 Madler, Trudy. *Why Did Grandma Die?* Milwaukee: Raintree Children's Books, 1980. 31 pp.

Young Heidi has a very close relationship with her grandmother,
who lives with Heidi's family. When Heidi's grandmother is hospitalized and later dies, Heidi is confused and upset that she will
not be with her grandmother again. After attending her grandmother's funeral, Heidi takes a walk with her father. He explains
to Heidi the necessity of grieving and the importance of remembering things about her grandmother.

IL: Ages 5-8   RL: 3.0

8.39 Mann, Peggy. *There Are Two Kinds of Terrible*. Garden City, NY:
Doubleday and Company, 1977. 132 pp. Avon, 1979 pap.

A young boy, Robbie, thinks it's terrible when he breaks his arm
and needs to wear a cast on it for most of the summer. However,

(Mann, Peggy)

he really feels bad when his beloved mother tells him she must go
to the hospital for a minor operation. Robbie finds himself at home
alone much of the time. Robbie's father, who has always been aloof,
becomes even less talkative and seems very sad. Finally Robbie's
father tells him that his mother is dying of cancer. When Robbie
visits her at the hospital, he cannot believe how pale and weak his
beautiful mother has become. Upon his mother's death, Robbie and
his father avoid each other. Robbie feels angry at his mother for
leaving him and at his father for not reaching out to him. Once
Robbie realizes how grief-stricken his father is, Robbie writes a
comforting note to his father. Robbie's father answers back and
father and son realize they must make a life together.

IL: Ages 8-11   RL: 4.5

8.40 Mazer, Norma Fox. *A Figure of Speech*. New York: Delacorte
Press, 1973. 197 pp. Dell, 1975 pap. LC, talking book.

Jenny, who is thirteen, has always been very close to Grandpa,
who lives in a basement apartment with Jenny's family. When Jenny's older brother gets married, he and his wife take over Grandpa's apartment and Grandpa is forced to share a small room with
one of his other grandsons. Grandpa seems to become disoriented
after this and his health starts to fail, causing Jenny's parents to
make a decision to put Grandpa in a "home." Jenny is outraged,
feeling that her family is being insensitive to her grandfather's
wishes. Jenny tells Grandpa about her parents' plans and the two
of them run away together to the farm Grandpa grew up on. Grandpa and Jenny exist for a week with only bare necessities. When
Grandpa wanders outside on a cold night and dies of exposure,
Jenny grieves and wonders if he took his own life. Upon finding
Jenny, her family appears to feel a sense of relief that the burden
of caring for Grandpa is gone.

IL: Ages 11-18   RL: 7.0

8.41 Mazer, Norma Fox. "Guess Whose Friendly Hands" in *Dear Bill,
Remember Me*. New York: Delacorte Press, 1976. 195 pp. Dell,
1978 pap. LC, talking book.

Eighteen-year old Louise, who has had two mastectomies and one
leg amputated, feels that she will die soon. However, her sister
and mother never mention Louise's approaching death. Louise resents the loss of her once beautiful body and the swollen face she
now has because of her chemotherapy. She feels ashamed that her
younger sister must bathe her and help her use a bedpan. Louise
also worries about all the extra expenses her mother must deal
with. Louise finally begs her mother to tell her the truth, and
once they talk about Louise's death, Louise feels at peace with herself.

IL: Ages 11-18   RL: 7.5

8.42 Mearian, Judy Frank. *Two Ways About It*. New York: The Dial Press, 1979. 166 pp.

Annie, who is eleven years old, has never had a good relationship with her older cousin Lou. Therefore, Annie is hesitant when she discovers that Lou is coming to spend the summer with Annie and her parents. During the course of the summer, Annie's mother discovers a lump in her breast and must be hospitalized for a mastectomy. When the lump is found to be malignant, Annie's father appears to be in a daze as he goes from work to hospital and then home. Annie finds that she is grateful for Lou's company. Lou becomes a great help to the family, doing housework and cooking, and the two cousins grow closer. Annie is too young to visit her mother's hospital room, so she must rely on phone calls and letters to communicate with her mother. Once Annie's mother's condition stabilizes and she returns home, Annie hesitantly questions about the operation and her mother explains the function of a prosthetic device. Annie is reluctant to see Lou leave at the end of the summer.

IL: Ages 11-14   RL: 6.5

8.43 Miles. *The Trouble with Thirteen*. see Ch. 9.

8.44 Orr. *Gunner's Run*. see Ch. 4.

8.45 Peck, Richard. *Close Enough to Touch*. New York: Delacorte Press, 1981. 133 pp. Dell, 1982 pap.

Seventeen-year old Matt has been dating Dory for almost a year when she dies of an aneurysm. It is painful for Matt to serve as a pallbearer at Dory's funeral and to visit her parents' home later that day. Matt's father doesn't know how to comfort his son, but his stepmother tries to talk things out with Matt. In attempting to get over the loss of Dory, Matt tries running long distances, staying away from school, and drinking alcohol to excess. Matt meets a very unusual girl, Margaret, whom he can confide in about his feelings of sorrow and bewilderment. With Margaret's help, Matt begins to get over the death of his former girlfriend.

IL: Ages 11-18   RL: 6.5

8.46 Peck, Richard. *Father Figure: A Novel*. New York: The Viking Press, 1978. 192 pp. New American Library, 1979 pap. LC, talking book.

Seventeen-year old Jim has never quite forgiven his father for divorcing his mother eight years ago. The divorce left Jim to assume the role of father to his younger brother Byron. When Jim's mother, who has a terminal illness, commits suicide, Jim and Byron see their father at the funeral. The boys continue to live with their grandmother and Jim is determined to accept responsibility for Byron's upbringing. He also tries to help Byron get over their mother's death. When Byron is hurt by a street gang, Jim feels guilty that he didn't take better care of his brother. Jim's grandmother, who feels she is unable to care for the boys, requests that their

(Peck, Richard)

father take them for the summer. During the summer, Jim and his
father avoid each other until they have a dispute over who should
care for Byron. Then Jim and his father develop a truce which
limits conversation between them as much as possible, creating an
unsettling summer for both of them and especially for Byron. Finally, under great tension, Jim reaches out to his father and asks
for an explanation of why his father left them so many years ago.
Jim and his father become closer, but another crisis occurs when
Byron decides he wants to live with his father permanently. It is
hard for Jim to let go of the responsibility he has always felt for
Byron, but he decides to turn over Byron's care to his father and
return to live with his grandmother. For the first time, Jim is able
to grieve his mother's death and start a life of his own.

IL: Ages 11-18   RL: 7.0

8.47   Pevsner. *And You Give Me a Pain, Elaine.* see Ch. 10.

8.48   Rabin, Gil. *Changes.* New York: Harper and Row, 1973. 149 pp.

Fourteen-year old Christopher moves to New York City with his
mother and grandfather shortly after his father's death. They are
forced to live in a tiny apartment which belongs to his mother's
sister-in-law. Christopher soon meets Peppy, who becomes his
first girlfriend. With memories of his father's death still in his
mind, Christopher witnesses his grandfather having a stroke which
leaves him blind. Christopher's grandfather does not accept his
blindness and soon has a heart attack, which forces Christopher's
mother to place him in a nursing home. Christopher and his girlfriend, whose mother died in a nursing home, are both horrified by
the decision. After a few visits to the home, Christopher refuses
to go anymore, upset at the changes in his grandfather. When his
grandfather dies, Christopher mourns his loss but is able to share
his emotions with his very understanding girlfriend.

IL: Ages 11-18   RL: 7.5

8.49   Ruby, Lois. "Spring" in *Arriving at a Place You've Never Left.*
New York: The Dial Press, 1977. 149 pp. Dell, 1980 pap.

Daniel, who is seventeen and dying of a terminal illness, is bitter
about his hospitalization and very uncommunicative toward his parents. He feels that he's being cheated, since he'll never be able
to go to college or drive to Mexico as he'd planned. Then Daniel
meets fifteen-year old Molly, also hospitalized with a terminal illness,
but with a different attitude toward death. Through his association
with Molly, Daniel is able to work through some of his bitterness
and better accept his impending death.

IL: Ages 11-18   RL: 8.0

8.50   Shecter. *Someplace Else.* see Ch. 5.

8.51   Smith. *Kick a Stone Home.* see Ch. 9.

8.52   Stevens, Margaret. *When Grandpa Died*. Chicago: Children's Press,
       1979. 31 pp.

       A little girl tells of the special relationship between herself and her
       grandfather, who lives with her family. They tell stories, go for
       walks, and work in the garden. When the little girl's grandfather
       becomes ill and later dies, she is angry with him for leaving her.
       The little girl finally cries and her father explains that she can say
       good-bye to her grandfather at the funeral the next day. As time
       passes, the little girl realizes her grandfather will never come back
       and she plans to tell her younger sister all about him someday.

       IL: Ages 5-8   RL: 2.5

8.53   Strasser, Todd. *Friends Till the End*. New York: Delacorte Press,
       1981. 199 pp. Dell, 1982 pap.

       Howie, a high-school senior, has problems adjusting to a new school
       after his parents move from Florida to Long Island. His only friend
       is David, who is on the soccer team and busy with other friends.
       When Howie is hospitalized and diagnosed as having leukemia, David
       reluctantly goes to visit him. There David learns about the chemo-
       therapy treatments and blood transfusions Howie must have. When
       Howie is able to return home during a remission, his parents are
       very overprotective of him but David tries to get Howie out to meet
       other people his age. Some of David's friends act as though they
       are afraid that Howie's cancer is contagious, but eventually people
       offer to tutor Howie with missed schoolwork and even agree to give
       blood when he needs it. When Howie returns to the hospital and
       his condition worsens, David is quite upset. It is even harder for
       David to accept the abrupt move of Howie's family back to Florida,
       with David never hearing from them again.

       IL: Ages 14-18   RL: 8.0

8.54   Tolan, Stephanie S. *Grandpa - and Me*. New York: Charles Scrib-
       ner's Sons, 1978. 120 pp.

       Eleven-year old Kerry and her older brother Matt are very fond of
       their grandfather, who has lived with them for years. When Grand-
       pa starts dressing and acting strangely, Kerry decides to spend
       more time with him. Kerry's parents notice that Grandpa seems to
       be living in the past and a physician diagnoses Grandpa as having
       senile dementia. Realizing that some plans must be made for Grand-
       pa's care, Kerry's parents discuss the possibility of placing him in
       a nursing home. Kerry is unsure of what the family should do and
       Matt strenuously objects to a nursing home. Grandpa, however,
       makes the decision for everyone by packaging and labeling all his
       personal belongings, then drowning himself. Afterwards, Kerry is
       sad at the loss of her grandfather, yet she has matured to the
       point to where she can understand his motives for suicide.

       IL: Ages 11-14   RL: 7.0

8.55   Truss. *Bird at the Window*. see Ch. 7.

8.56   Vogel. *My Twin Sister Erika*. see Ch. 10.

8.57   Voigt. *Dicey's Song*. see Ch. 10.

8.58   Wallace-Brodeur, Ruth. *The Kenton Year*. New York: Atheneum,
       1980. 93 pp.

Nine-year old Mandy must grow accustomed to life without her father when he is killed in an accident. Mandy is unable to attend
school and she is fearful that her mother will leave her too. Therefore, Mandy is relieved when her mother suggests that they begin
an early summer vacation in Kenton, a small rural community. Kenton and its people seem strange at first to Mandy, but soon she
and her mother make friends. Reluctant to face going back to the
city at summer's end, Mandy is pleased when her mother has a job
offer and they both agree to make Kenton their permanent home.
Mandy is apprehensive about her mother's interest in a man, but
her mother assures her that no one can ever take her father's
place. Christmas for Mandy is full of sadness and memories of her
father, as is the anniversary of his death. Mandy decides to erect
a memorial to her father so that she and her mother will never forget him, yet be able to start on a new life.

IL: Ages 8-11   RL: 6.5

8.59   York, Carol Beach. *Remember me When I am Dead*. New York: Else-
       vier/Nelson, 1980. 94 pp.

Thirteen-year old Sara and nine-year old Jenny have a hard time
facing their first Christmas since their mother's death. Although
Sara openly grieved her mother's death after the fatal accident,
Jenny has never accepted it. A year later, Jenny still has dreams
about her mother all the time and insists that her mother is alive.
The girls' father has remarried and their stepmother tries to make
the holidays special, knowing that everyone has memories of previous Christmases. A mysterious Christmas present for Jenny and a
letter addressed to her dead mother make the girls' father suspect
that Jenny is having emotional problems concerning her mother's
death. Actually Sara, who has always been jealous of Jenny, has
plotted in an attempt to have her younger sister sent away. To
Sara's horror, the girls' father and stepmother decide to send both
girls to boarding school for a change of environment.

IL: Ages 11-14   RL: 6.5

9.
Sexual Awareness

Most children and adolescents obtain their sexual attitudes and basic sexual repertoire from their peers rather than adults. Children are the most frequent agents of sexual mores; adults seem to play a minor role in this learning process. Often the child's understanding of human sexuality through such a process results in much misinformation that is carried through adolescence and even into adulthood.[1]

Children do learn about human sexuality from sources other than peer groups. Competing with the peer group, with obviously less influence, are parents and other significant adults in the child's life. Very young children learn about sexuality through the way their parents interact. If the child is accustomed to seeing its parents in affectionate embraces, this child will probably feel differently about sexuality than does a child whose family is carefully undemonstrative. When a child receives messages from a parent concerning sexuality, those messages are very important as they can create healthy attitudes or may well result in shame and guilt.[2] It is important that parents and other adults help children feel comfortable about their sexuality and help them to deal with their curiosity about this important part of their development.

The impact of the peer group is the most powerful during a child's adolescent years. Often parents are not able to deal adequately with the issues of sexuality and many schools are not sanctioned to deal with it as well; children thus turn to the peer group for answers about sexuality issues.[3] It is often through peers that children can engage in the information gathering and role modeling that helps produce their sexual life-style. Such a process of socialization for a young person may impact "healthy" as well as "unhealthy" sexual attitudes and behaviors in adulthood.

Even though children and adolescents receive much misinformation in the area of human sexuality, professionals who work with young people can be quite helpful if they consider the child's readiness to acquire sexual information. Three developmental stages of a child's sexual awareness have been identified that may help professionals working with children in this area. The three stages are the dormant stage, the awakened period, and the active stage.[4] The dormant stage lasts until about nine years of age. At this time, a child is not intensely concerned with sex, but is quite inquisitive about it. The awakened period lasts from age nine to about fourteen. Sexual curiosity and exploration are high during this phase. Young people from fourteen up to nineteen years of age are in the active stage of sexual development.[5] It should be kept in mind that these developmental stages are not rigid; a child's maturity must be considered as well as chronological age.

At each of these time periods, children have the developmental capacity to understand sexuality at various levels. The helping individual must be aware of these developmental periods and must not overload the child with information that does not fit the child's needs. For example, an explanation about human reproduction should be different for the nine-year old versus the seventeen-year old. A too detailed explanation will make little sense to the nine-year old. However, it is important that an explanation of human reproduction be detailed enough to meet the seventeen-year old's needs. The helping individual must be selective in approaching topics related to sexuality and must be sure to meet the child's needs based on the child's development.

Criteria for Book Selection

Books were selected for this chapter with the purpose of helping a young person to develop sexual awareness. The content of the books ranges from that which is suitable for the very young child to books concerning sexual issues which are appropriate for the adolescent reader. Because values and attitudes towards sexuality are conveyed in many books concerning sexual issues, an effort was made to avoid those books which tended to moralize or which conveyed myths about sex.

Young children who are in the dormant stage of sexual development, up until about the age of nine, are quite inquisitive about sex.[6] Therefore, books chosen for children in this stage deal with the birth process and anatomical differences, two areas which young children are quite curious about. Books selected for early adolescent children who are in the awakened period of sexual development deal with different issues. The characters in these books are curious about the sexual act and are concerned with such issues as masturbation, menstruation, and sexual preference. Some of these same books are suitable for adolescents in the active stage of sexual development as well. For those young people in the active stage, books were chosen concerning teenagers engaging in sex, with many of these books mentioning birth control and also venereal disease. Human sexuality issues related to rape are the topic of a few books selected.

Young people needing help in developing sexual awareness can gain much insight through reading books about various sexual issues. It is quite important for the young person to be given books which are compatible with the child's age and maturation. In using bibliotherapy to help develop a young person's sexual awareness, the books used can be vehicles for understanding and exploration and can lead to valuable discussions with the helping adult.

NOTES

1. Alfred C. Kinsey, Wardell B. Pomeroy, and Clyde E. Martin, *Sexual Behavior in the Human Male* (Philadelphia: W.B. Saunders, 1948).

2. Jules Henry, *On Shame, Vulnerability, and Other Forms of Self-Destruction* (New York: Random House, 1973).

3. Theodore Lidz, *The Person* revised ed. (New York: Basic Books, 1976), pp. 342-343.

4. William A. Block, *What Your Child Really Wants to Know About Sex and Why* (Englewood Cliffs, New Jersey: Prentice-Hall, 1972).

5. Ibid.

6. Ibid.

BOOKS

9.1   Anonymous. *Go Ask Alice*. see Ch. 2.

9.2   Banish, Roslyn. *I Want to Tell You About My Baby*. Berkeley:
      Wingbow Press, 1982. 46 pp.

      A small boy explains his feelings about his mother's pregnancy.
      He is excited about having a new baby and making preparations
      for it, yet he wishes his mother weren't so tired all the time. The
      boy enjoys having his grandparents take care of him when his par-
      ents go to the hospital and he is able to visit his mother and the
      new baby there. Once the baby comes home, the little boy helps
      his mother with baths and feedings. However, he resents the ba-
      by's crying and his having to play so quietly when the baby naps.
      The little boy's parents make sure that he still feels loved and has
      plenty of attention from them.

      IL: Ages 5-8   RL: 2.0

9.3   Bargar, Gary W. *What Happened to Mr. Forster?* New York: Clar-
      ion Books, 1981. 169 pp.

      With his mother dead and his father unknown to him, Louis lives
      with his deeply religious aunt. Tired of being taunted and called
      names at school, Louis decides to make his sixth grade year differ-
      ent. Louis and his classmates immediately like their new teacher,
      Mr. Forster, who makes school interesting and takes a personal in-
      terest in each student. Mr. Forster coaches Louis in softball,
      helps him to discover a talent for writing, and builds Louis's con-
      fidence in himself. However, several parents in the community are
      suspicious of Mr. Forster's male roommate and work to expose him
      as an unfit teacher. When Mr. Forster is fired after admitting that
      he is a homosexual, Louis is at first angry and confused. Later
      Louis becomes determined to not lose all the valuable things he has
      learned from Mr. Forster.

      IL: Ages 11-14   RL: 6.0

9.4   Blume, Judy. *Are You There God? It's Me, Margaret*. Scarsdale,
      NY: Bradbury Press, 1970. 149 pp. Dell, 1972 pap. LC, braille
      and talking book.

      Eleven-year old Margaret is apprehensive about her parents' move
      from New York City to the suburbs. However, she quickly makes
      some new friends at her school. Margaret and her friends form a
      secret club, with wearing a bra, starting menstruation, and boys
      as their main interests. Margaret's parents belong to different
      faiths and consequently her family does not attend church at all;
      yet Margaret starts talking to God about different early adolescent
      concerns she has. Margaret and her friends continue to discuss
      their developing bodies, the male anatomy, and how to kiss boys.
      Margaret decides to stop talking to God and once she finally begins
      to menstruate, her life seems to fall back into place.

      IL: Ages 11-14   RL: 3.5

9.5   Blume, Judy. *Forever.* Scarsdale, NY: Bradbury Press, 1975.
       199 pp. LC, braille and talking book.

       High school seniors Katherine and Michael are physically attracted
       to one another from the time that they meet. When Michael gets a
       key to his sister's apartment and he and Katherine make love, they
       both declare that their love will last forever. Since she has never
       engaged in lovemaking before, Katherine is somewhat surprised
       when Michael tells her he once had venereal disease. With the sup-
       port of her parents and grandmother, Katherine obtains birth con-
       trol pills from a clinic and she and Michael begin a serious relation-
       ship. At the same time, one of Katherine's friends tries to "help"
       the boy she is dating, who is suicidal and believes he may be homo-
       sexual. Another of Katherine's friends, who is unmarried and preg-
       nant, regrets her decision to give her baby up for adoption once
       it is born. In an attempt to separate Katherine and Michael for a
       short time, Katherine's parents get her a job at a summer camp.
       While there, Katherine and Michael faithfully exchange letters. How-
       ever, when Katherine learns of her grandfather's death, she turns
       to a college-age camp counselor, Theo, for comfort. Eventually
       Katherine realizes her feelings for Theo are becoming stronger so
       she tells Michael about the situation. Katherine and Michael part
       as friends, each sad that their relationship has ended.

       IL: Ages 14-18   RL: 7.5

9.6   Blume. *Then again, maybe I won't.* see Ch. 4.

9.7   Colman. *Diary of a Frantic Kid Sister.* see Ch. 10.

9.8   Donovan. *I'll Get There. It Better Be Worth the Trip.* see Ch. 8.

9.9   Donovan, John. *Remove Protective Coating a Little at a Time.*
       New York: Harper and Row, 1973. 101 pp. Dell, 1975 pap. LC,
       talking book.

       Fourteen-year old Harry describes some significant events in his
       life - his parents' hasty marriage when his mother became pregnant
       with him, his need to begin shaving and his first experiences with
       masturbation at eleven, and a recent unsuccessful sexual encounter
       with a girl at camp. Upon his return from summer camp, Harry
       can't understand the change in his parents; his father, who is
       vice-president of a very successful agency, doesn't come home sev-
       eral nights a week and Harry's mother becomes increasingly de-
       pressed and withdrawn. Harry meets and befriends an old woman
       whom he finds it is quite easy for him to confide in. His mother
       begins to see a psychiatrist and eventually is hospitalized for treat-
       ment. Harry grows closer to his father at this time, but he is
       confused when his father leaves on a vacation at the same time that
       Harry's mother comes home for a visit from the hospital. Harry
       continues to talk to his elderly friend, taking her food and blankets,
       but one day Harry finds that she has disappeared. Harry feels
       even more abandoned when his mother returns to the hospital with
       vague plans about going to college.

       IL: Ages 11-14   RL: 8.5

9.10 Eyerly. *The Phaedra Complex*. see Ch. 11.

9.11 Gerson. *Passing Through*. see Ch. 8.

9.12 Greene, Constance C. *I Know You, Al*. New York: The Viking
      Press, 1975. 126 pp. Dell, 1977 pap. LC, braille and talking
      book.

      Thirteen-year old Alexandria, nicknamed Al, is concerned because
      she is the only girl in her class who has not started menstruation.
      Al and her best friend discuss the subject at length, as well as
      sexual intercourse and artificial insemination. Al is also worried
      about her mother's newest boyfriend after she sees the two of them
      embracing. When Al's father, whom she has not seen for six years,
      comes to visit Al and invites her to attend his wedding, Al is re-
      luctant to go. However, once the wedding is over, Al finds that
      she likes her new stepmother and stepsiblings. She is also thrilled
      when she finally has her first menstrual period.

      IL: Ages 11-14   RL: 6.5

9.13 Hall, Lynn. *Sticks and Stones*. Chicago: Follett Publishing Com-
      pany, 1972. 220 pp. Dell, 1972 pap. LC, talking book.

      Sixteen-year old Tom and his recently divorced mother move to a
      small town to start a new life. Tom longs to establish a friendship
      with someone there, but only Floyd, a disheveled boy who is flunk-
      ing out of school, tries to be friends with Tom. Then Tom meets
      Ward, who has recently been discharged from the Army because of
      homosexual tendencies. Tom is unaware of Ward's past and the two
      become good friends. Floyd, who feels rejected, starts rumors a-
      bout Ward and Tom's relationship which spread through the whole
      high school. Teachers have a different attitude toward Tom and he
      is not allowed to participate in a music contest because of parental
      protests. Tom is horrified when he learns about his "homosexual"
      label but he doesn't want to worry his mother who is soon to be re-
      married. Under great mental stress due to isolation from other
      students, Tom is informed that he is failing his classes at school.
      When Tom is involved in an automobile accident that kills Floyd, he
      realizes how much the school gossip has damaged his life.

      IL: Ages 14-18   RL: 9.5

9.14 Harlan. *Footfalls*. see Ch. 8.

9.15 Hautzig, Deborah. *Hey, Dollface*. New York: William Morrow and
      Company, 1978. 151 pp. Bantam, 1980 pap. LC, talking book.

      Valerie and Chloe, both fifteen years old, become friends when they
      start attending a private school for girls. Although they both date
      occasionally, the two girls spend most of their free time together
      and especially enjoy their discussions on a wide range of topics, in-
      cluding sex. Valerie begins to sense a special attraction between
      Chloe and herself and worriedly questions her mother and a teacher
      about homosexuality. When Chloe's father dies, she spends much
      time with her mother and seems to avoid Valerie. After several

(Hautzig, Deborah)

weeks, the girls see each other once again and in consoling Chloe
about her father's death, Valerie physically caresses her. Valerie
flees in shame and she and Chloe avoid each other all summer.
Finally the two girls meet and discuss their feelings for each other,
exploring the possibility of whether either of them is a lesbian.
They decide to remain good friends and not worry so much about
the physical attraction between them.

IL: Ages 11-18   RL: 6.5

9.16 Herman, Charlotte. *The Three of Us*. Chicago: J. Philip O'Hara,
      1973. 126 pp.

Three fifth-grade girls form a secret club where they discuss many
topics, including sex. They are all very naive about sex and their
parents seem unwilling to give them any information about it. The
girls find and read pamphlets about menstruation and how a baby
is conceived. They also join in a campaign for a much needed sex
education course at their school.

IL: Ages 8-11   RL: 4.5

9.17 Holland, Isabelle. *The Man Without a Face*. New York: J.B. Lip-
      pincott, 1972. 159 pp. Dell, 1980 pap. G.K. Hall and Company,
      Large Print. LC, braille and talking book.

Fourteen-year old Charles, whose mother has been married and divorced several times, knows very little about his own father.
Charles has never had a close relationship with any of his stepfath-
ers and he and his older stepsister are constantly battling with
each other. Wanting to escape his two stepsisters and his mother,
who is about to marry once again, Charles decides to spend his
summer preparing for an entrance exam to get into a boarding
school. The only person at the summer beach colony Charles can
find to tutor him is Mr. McLeod, whose face is badly scarred from
burns. Although Mr. McLeod is very strict and requires much effort from Charles, the two become close friends and spend lots of
time together. Suffering from occasional mental blackouts due to
his inability to cope with memories of his father, Charles reaches
out to Mr. McLeod for physical reassurance but is gently rebuffed.
However, when his older stepsister purposely lets it leak out that
Charles's father was an alcoholic who died long ago, Charles runs
to Mr. McLeod for comfort and spends the night with him. The
next day Mr. McLeod tries to reassure Charles that what has happened between them resulted from stress and has no further meaning, but Charles doesn't go to see his tutor again. Only after
school has started does Charles return to visit Mr. McLeod as a
friend. Mr. McLeod, who has since died of a heart attack, leaves
a will with all his property going to Charles.

IL: Ages 11-18   RL: 7.0

9.18 Klein, Norma. *Naomi in the Middle*. New York: The Dial Press,
      1974. 53 pp. Archway, 1978 pap.

(Klein, Norma)

Seven-year old Naomi is excited about her mother's pregnancy.
Naomi's nine-year old sister, Bobo, is not so thrilled and claims
she may run away. Naomi, who already feels left out sometimes
when Bobo and her friends play, wonders what it will be like to
be the middle child of the family. The two sisters have quite frank
discussions of where babies come from with their mother. When
the baby is born, Naomi and Bobo stay with their grandmother and
Naomi is assured of her important place in the family.

IL: Ages 5-8   RL: 3.0

9.19 Lee. *Sycamore Year*. see Ch. 7.

9.20 Miklowitz, Gloria. *Did You Hear What Happened to Andrea?* New
      York: Delacorte Press, 1979. 168 pp. Dell, 1981 pap. LC, talk-
      ing book.

Fifteen-year old Andrea is raped which hitchhiking home from the
beach. Andrea is embarrassed and confused by all the proceedings
at the police station and she is unprepared for her parents' reaction to the incident. Andrea's mother wants to pretend the rape
never happened and her father wants to find the man who molested
Andrea and get revenge. Nauseated from the morning-after pills
she is given, Andrea isolates herself in her room for several days,
not wanting to face her friends or family. Constantly fearing that
the rapist will seek her out again, Andrea must force herself to return to work. She also tells her boyfriend about what has happened, but Andrea feels very uptight on dates with him. Andrea
begins calling a Rape Hotline to relieve the pressures she is under
and she finally convinces her parents to let her start seeing a
therapist. Andrea's therapy and the fact that her rapist is convicted and imprisoned help Andrea begin to rebuild her life.

IL: Ages 14-18   RL: 7.5

9.21 Miles, Betty. *The Trouble with Thirteen*. New York: Alfred A.
      Knopf, 1979. 108 pp. Avon, 1980 pap.

Annie and Rachel, twelve-year old best friends, share everything
including their worries about menstruation and about their developing bodies. When Rachel's parents announce that they are getting
a divorce, Rachel confides in Annie her mother's plan to move from
the suburbs to the city. At the same time, the two girls share
sadness when Annie's dog dies. Annie and Rachel both begin men-
struating and start to feel more at ease with the changes in their
bodies. When Rachel moves, Annie feels she has left one phase of
her life to begin a new one.

IL: Ages 11-14   RL: 6.0

9.22 Mohr. *In Nueva York*. see Ch. 2.

9.23 Mulford, Philippa Greene. *If It's Not Funny, Why Am I Laughing?*
      New York: Delacorte Press, 1982. 166 pp.

(Mulford, Philippa Greene)

Fifteen-year old Mimi seldom sees her career-oriented mother and she's having a hard time adjusting to her new stepmother, who sometimes sides with Mimi but more often sides with Mimi's dad over Mimi's privileges. Mimi also has mixed feelings about her best friend, Tuna, making love with her steady boyfriend. Tuna constantly talks about her love life and gives Mimi advice on how to develop a serious relationship with a boy Mimi is dating. Mimi, however, is not so sure that she wants a serious relationship and she finds herself laughing at all the wrong moments on dates. When the boys at Mimi's school develop a Virgin Pool and make bets on several girls, Mimi is horrified at such a cruel joke. One girl, who was talked into having sex, finds out about the bets and tries to set herself on fire. With all students at the high school shocked over what has happened, Tuna resolves to break up with her boyfriend whom she's become bored with. Mimi is glad she was not convinced by her friends to become involved in an adult relationship she was not ready for.

IL: Ages 14-18   RL: 7.0

9.24   Neufeld, John.   *Freddy's Book*.   New York: Random House, 1973. 132 pp.   Avon, 1975 pap.

Freddy is puzzled over certain words he sees on the bathroom wall. He also does not understand the erections he is starting to have. Longing to talk to his father who is away much of the time on business, Freddy questions his friends about sex and receives much misinformation.   Freddy gets no help from a librarian and his mother's answers to Freddy's questions don't satisfy him.   Finally Freddy's father returns home and gives Freddy a much needed explanation of sexual intercourse, answering all of Freddy's questions for the time being.

IL: Ages 8-11   RL: 5.0

9.25   O'Hanlon.   *Fair Game*.   see Ch. 2.

9.26   Peck, Richard.   *Are You in the House Alone?*   New York: The Viking Press, 1976.   156 pp.   LC, talking book.

Sixteen-year old Gail starts taking the pill and becomes sexually involved with Steve, a boy her parents don't approve of.   Gail's parents would rather she spend more time with her best friend, Alison, and Alison's boyfriend, Phil, whose parents are both prominent members of the community.   When Gail starts receiving prank phone calls and obscene notes from someone, she confides in Alison who advises Gail to keep quiet about it.   Gail considers going to her parents when the notes and phone calls continue, but she decides against it.   Finally, Gail turns to her school counselor, but receives no help there.   When babysitting one night, Gail answers the door to find Alison's boyfriend, Phil, standing there.   Phil, who has spied on Gail and Steve's lovemaking in the past, starts calling Gail terrible names and rapes her.   Gail must cope with the grueling ordeal of a hospital examination and police questioning.

(Peck, Richard)

Gail's rape does not come out into the open due to the position of
Phil's family, but when Phil injures another girl, he mysteriously
disappears from town.

IL: Ages 14-18   RL: 8.0

9.27 Scoppettone, Sandra. *Happy Endings Are All Alike*. New York:
Harper and Row, 1978. 202 pp.

Two high-school senior girls, Jaret and Peggy, are lovers. Only
Jaret's mother and Peggy's older sister know about the girls' relationship. Jaret and Peggy often meet in the woods. Mid, a disturbed boy who has always disliked Jaret, begins spying on them
in the woods and he plans to teach Jaret a lesson. When Peggy
decides to go out on a date with a boy she knows, Jaret heads for
the woods to think things over. There Mid finds her; he beats
Jaret and rapes her, then leaves her unconscious. Jaret's parents
find her and take her to a hospital. Despite Mid's threats to expose Peggy and herself as lovers, Jaret names Mid as her rapist
and he is arrested. Mid claims that seeing the two girls together
in the woods drove him to commiting rape and the authorities consider giving him a lighter sentence because of this. When the
whole story goes to the press and small town prejudice arises a-
gainst the two girls, a frightened Peggy tells Jaret that they are
through. On the day before both girls leave for college, Peggy
seeks out Jaret insisting she still loves Jaret but is unsure whether
the two can have a future.

IL: Ages 14-18   RL: 6.5

9.28 Scoppettone, Sandra. *Trying Hard to Hear You*. New York: Harper
and Row, 1974. 264 pp. LC, braille.

Camilla, who is sixteen, has a major role in a summer stage production and is friends with most of the cast. She is particularly happy
to be working with Jeff, her next-door neighbor and best friend.
Camilla starts dating the assistant manager of the production, Phil.
No one can figure out why Jeff and Phil act so secretive at rehearsals until they are discovered kissing each other at a party. The
rest of the cast taunt Jeff and Phil with the label "queer" and some
of the males start to physically abuse them. Camilla is very emotionally distraught and cannot bring herself to accept Jeff and
Phil's homosexual relationship. When Jeff is almost tar and feath-
ered by the group and Phil is killed in an automobile accident suspected to be suicide, all of the stage cast, but particularly Camilla,
feel much guilt.

IL: Ages 14-18   RL: 8.5

9.29 Smith, Doris Buchanan. *Kick a Stone Home*. New York: Thomas
Y. Crowell, 1974. 152 pp. LC, braille.

Fifteen-year old Sara, who is more interested in sports than in
school or dating, frustrates her mother when she insists on playing

(Smith, Doris Buchanan)

football with a group of boys. Sara's parents have been divorced
for three years, yet Sara still cannot accept the divorce or her
father's remarriage. Sara only has one girlfriend, Kay, and they
confide in each other about the difficulties of having their parents
divorced and dealing with stepparents. Sara turns to her dog for
companionship as well and she greatly mourns his death when the
dog is hit by a car. A boy at Sara's school begins acting very
friendly to her and Sara is pleased at the attention. However,
when the boy grabs at Sara's body in public, Sara is humiliated
and is even more convinced that she won't date. A summer job at
a veterinarian's office makes Sara consider the possibility of becoming a veterinarian herself. Still determined to have Sara date, her
mother arranges a date for Sara but Sara feels uncomfortable with
the boy. Finally, Sara asks a boy in her class to a party and is
delighted when she thoroughly enjoys his company.

IL: Ages 11-14   RL: 4.5

9.30 Steptoe, John. *Marcia*. New York: The Viking Press, 1976.
      81 pp.

Marcia, a fourteen-year old black girl who lives in the projects with
her mother, is confused by her sexual feelings for her boyfriend.
Afraid of getting pregnant, Marcia keeps rebuffing her boyfriend
until they eventually break up. Marcia is comforted when she discovers that her best friend is having similar problems and both
girls agree that they want to make love but don't feel ready. When
Marica turns to her mother with her problems, her mother is very
understanding and offers to take Marcia to a physician for birth
control. Marcia then feels as if she's more in control of her life.
Marcia makes up with her boyfriend, but is still in no hurry to
begin a sexual relationship with him.

IL: Ages 11-18   RL: 3.5

9.31 Steptoe, John. *My Special Best Words*. New York: The Viking
      Press, 1974. 27 pp.

Young Bweela, who lives with her father and baby brother, describes their daily routine. She tells about their "special" words
including the family's personal bathroom language. Bweela and her
brother enjoy taking a bath together and are comfortable with their
bodies. To her father's delight, Bweela is even able to toilet-train
her brother.

IL: Ages 5-8   RL: 2.0

9.32 Stolz. *Leap Before You Look*. see Ch. 3.

9.33 Sullivan, Mary. *What's This About Pete?* Nashville: Thomas Nel-
      son, 1976. 125 pp.

Fifteen-year old Peter worries that he may be homosexual because
his body is not muscular and he enjoys sewing. His father and a

(Sullivan, Mary)

coach at school even imply that Peter may be gay. Peter feels
even more confused because he likes motorcycle riding which he
considers "macho." When a man propositions him, Peter decides to
visit the school guidance counselor. Through his session with the
counselor, Peter gains more knowledge about homosexuality and he
is encouraged to accept himself regardless of what his future sexual
preference turns out to be.

IL: Ages 11-18   RL: 7.0

9.34 Tolan, Stephanie S. *The Last of Eden*. New York: Frederick
      Warne, 1980. 154 pp.

Fifteen-year old Michelle is glad to return to boarding school after
a turbulent summer spent with her widowed mother. She becomes
immediate friends with her new roommate Marty, a troubled girl who
lives with her father and stepmother. When a rumor develops a-
bout a homosexual relationship between Marty and an art teacher,
Michelle defends her friend only to later discover that Marty is
having such a relationship with another student. Marty becomes
so involved with her lover that she moves out of Michelle's room.
After Marty's lover takes an overdose of drugs, Marty transfers to
another school. Lonely at the loss of her friend, Michelle tries to
sort out her feelings.

IL: Ages 11-18   RL: 7.5

9.35 Wells. *None of the Above*. see Ch. 11.

9.36 Windsor. *Diving for Roses*. see Ch. 7.

9.37 Winthrop. *A Little Demonstration of Affection*. see Ch. 10.

9.38 Zindel, Paul. *I Never Loved Your Mind*. New York: Harper and
      Row, 1970. 181 pp. Bantam, 1972 pap.

Seventeen-year old Dewey, who has dropped out of school, begins
working at a hospital. When Dewey meets twenty-year old Yvette
at the hospital, he is very attracted to her although he doesn't
understand some of her strange behaviors. Eventually Dewey
starts dating Yvette and is invited to the apartment she shares
with three male musicians. Dewey and Yvette make love and he is
on top of the world. However, the next day Yvette refuses to
speak to Dewey. When Dewey attends a party given by Yvette's
friends, he better understands her unconventional life-style but
he finds he is unable to forget her.

IL: Ages 14-18   RL: 8.5

9.39 Zindel. *My Darling, My Hamburger*. see Ch. 7.

10.
Sibling Relationships

A child's siblings are clearly some of the most important people impacting a child's development. Siblings who grow up together must be aware of each other's unique characteristics and must learn to share time with parents, as well as love, possessions, and physical space. Siblings must learn to adapt to each other; this process impacts how children deal with others outside the family system.

Much research has been conducted on birth order, an important factor in determining how a child relates to siblings and others. Essentially, birth order becomes an important factor because it influences how the child sees itself and the way that a child functions interpersonally and intrapsychically at various levels. A child's prolonged interaction with more dominant or submissive siblings will impact a long chain of competitive or noncompetitive attitudes that will shape the child's reactions in the future when separated from younger or older brothers or sisters. Within the confines of the family system, the child develops ways of viewing the self and behaviors that will bring success or nonsuccess in various situations in adult life. A child's ordinal position will become a lifelong component of the child's psychosexual identification and self-esteem, influencing the child's relationships with spouse, friends, coworkers, and eventually the child's own children.[1]

The research on ordinal position in the family has been conducted for virtually decades. Some of this research does not agree; however, there are some consistent findings that have emerged in the literature. The research has for the most part suggested that the first born child has identifiable characteristics that differ from later born children. The first born appears to be more serious, more highly motivated in academic endeavors, and generally is more successful.[2] Children born in the middle of the birth order have been found not to have the same high motivation as first borns and also have a tendency to be more prone to problem behaviors.[3] Last born children have been found to have lower self-esteems than first born children and are more likely to experience stress and conflict during development.[4] It is noted that there are exceptions to the above findings and not all children fit nicely into each category. Regardless of the degree of impact ordinal position has on a child's development, most children survive their imposed birth position and lead normal and happy lives in adulthood.

Some of the more problematic areas occurring between siblings is sharing parental time, learning to share physical space and possessions, the arrival of a new sibling in the family system, and sibling rivalry. Each of these problems can be handled with minimal stress and conflict if parents are aware of ways of dealing with them.

The sharing of parental time and learning to share with each other are especially difficult in large families where both parents work. In such a family system, the parents should make special efforts after work to provide quality time with each child. Parents can accomplish this by having a specific time period set aside for play and interaction each day with their children. Obviously, with large families, this interaction will by necessity be in a group form - a vehicle through which quality interaction can be provided if well planned. This interaction teaches children how to share not only parental time, but also how to share physical space and possessions. Naturally, demands on parental time and learning to share are problems in smaller family units as well.

When a new baby arrives in a family, this may well be one of the more traumatic events in the lives of older siblings. Again, if parents are skillful, the arrival of a new family member can be relatively smooth with minimal problems if the older siblings are aware of what a new baby means and are given the chance to learn about babies. Older siblings need to be able to express their anger, anxiety, fear, etc. concerning the new arrival. It should also be noted that each sibling will react differently to a new baby; this is determined greatly by the child's age and ordinal position in the family unit.

The last issue, sibling rivalry, is an ongoing problem in all family systems. Most siblings bicker and fight with each other throughout their development; this conflict gradually changes and takes new forms with the passage of time. Even though the rivalry never ends even into adulthood, parents play an important role in helping their children deal with this continuing problem. Parents should help their children communicate with each other about their rivalry and impress upon them that the conflict is normal, but should be expressed in socially acceptable ways.

Criteria for Book Selection

Books which focus on sibling relationships were selected for this chapter. These books offer a wide range of family settings, with various books representing two-parent and one-parent families, as well as families where a grandparent, etc. is the primary parent. Siblings in these books are portrayed very realistically, with disharmony among siblings stressed as well as friendship between siblings.

Certain books chosen for this chapter deal with the arrival of a new baby. Feelings of jealousy that an older sibling experiences when a new baby is born are focused on. Several of the characters understandably worry that the baby will take parental time and attention away from them. The most helpful books concerning the arrival of a new baby illustrate the older sibling feeling important by helping the parents care for the new baby.

Other books describe the relationship between siblings when one of the siblings is handicapped, either mentally or physically. The non-handicapped sibling(s) often feel resentment about the extra time parents had to spend with their handicapped brother or sister. Older siblings are often portrayed as having to help with mentally retarded brothers or sisters - this took away from time spent with peers. Those siblings with mentally retarded brothers or sisters also feel embarrassment when people stare or ask thoughtless questions. A common element in these books, however, is the strong bond of love and the sense of family that the non-handicapped child feels for a handicapped sibling.

Many of the books selected for this chapter merely deal with the problem of sibling rivalry between both younger children and adolescent siblings. The most helpful books on this topic do not impose feelings of guilt on anyone, but rather recognize a certain degree of sibling conflict as being normal and healthy. Younger siblings, who are sometimes portrayed by animal characters, are in conflict over issues ranging from the sharing of parental time to difficulties in playing together. The majority of the books on sibling rivalry which involve younger characters focus on conflict through the eyes of the youngest child in the family.[5]

Books which deal with sibling rivalry between pre-adolescent and adolescent children also depict conflicts over the sharing of parental time. In addition, personality differences, sharing of possessions, and conflicts over privileges are cause for arguments in various books. Although these books quite realistically portray siblings of all ages as disliking each other and engaging in arguments at times, the majority of the books on sibling rivalry also illustrate moments of closeness and cooperation between siblings.

In using bibliotherapy for young people experiencing problems with sibling relationships, there are no clear-cut solutions. Parental behavior is quite critical in easing sibling problems. At times, professional counseling in the form of individual or family treatment is required to soothe family relationships. Some siblings eventually outgrow some of their difficulties and this is hinted at in certain books in this chapter. Other books illustrate ways of lessening sibling rivalry without totally getting rid of it. Through reading about other siblings, children experiencing sibling relationship problems can see that their feelings are not abnormal and that there are acceptable ways of relating to each other.

NOTES

1. Alfred Adler, *The Science of Living* (Garden City, New York: Doubleday, 1969).

2. Luciano L'Abate and Leonard T. Curtis, *Teaching the Exceptional Child* (Philadelphia: W.B. Saunders Company, 1975), pp. 254-255.

3. Ibid.

4. Ibid.

5. Marsha Kabakow Rudman, *Children's Literature: An Issues Approach* (Lexington, Massachusetts: D.C. Heath and Company, 1976), p. 18.

BOOKS

10.1   Alexander. *To Live a Lie.* see Ch. 3.

10.2   Alexander, Martha. *Nobody Asked Me If I Wanted a Baby Sister.*
        New York: The Dial Press, 1971. 28 pp. Dial Press, 1977 pap.

A little boy can't understand why everyone is paying so much attention to his new baby sister. Putting his little sister in his
wagon, the boy tries to offer her for sale and even give her away.
When the boy takes her to a friend's house, his baby sister cries
and no one can make her stop except her big brother. Not quite
so jealous now, the boy takes her home and decides his baby sister isn't so bad after all.

IL: Ages 5-8   RL: 2.0

10.3   Baldwin, Ann. *A Little Time.* New York: Viking Press, 1978.
        119 pp.

Ten-year old Sarah loves her retarded four-year old brother Matt,
but she resents him at times. Sarah and her siblings are embarrassed to invite friends over and Matt is a drain on their mother's
energy. Sarah's father is very sympathetic to Sarah's feelings
and he and Sarah's mother even discuss the possibility of putting
Matt in a special boarding school. When Sarah's mother becomes
ill and is hospitalized, the whole family must pitch in to care for
the house and meet all of Matt's needs. Once Sarah's mother returns home, she is still weak and it is necessary to place Matt in
foster care. Although the family members enjoy the relief of not
having the constant responsibility for Matt, they all miss him and
eventually decide to bring him back home. Plans are made, however, to not ignore the needs of other family members.

IL: Ages 8-11   RL: 6.0

10.4   Banish. *I Want to Tell You About My Baby.* see Ch. 9.

10.5   Blume, Judy. *Superfudge.* New York: E.P. Dutton, 1980.
        166 pp. Dell, 1981 pap. LC, talking book.

Peter, a fifth grader, is horrified and claims he will run away when
his parents announce they are expecting a baby. Peter feels that
he has enough problems coping with his precocious, obnoxious
four-year old brother, Fudge. Once the new baby, nicknamed
Tootsie, arrives, Peter feels that he is neglected and Fudge's development begins to regress into bed-wetting, etc. Peter's parents
soon tell the children the family will be moving from New York
City to Princeton for a year and Peter threatens to run away a-
gain. Peter soon adjusts to his new school there although Fudge,
who is in kindergarten now, proves to be embarrassing for Peter.
Peter is sometimes disgusted with Tootsie's messiness, but he is
also excited along with Fudge and his parents in watching Tootsie
learn to crawl, walk, and talk.

IL: Ages 8-11   RL: 4.0

10.6   Branfield. *Why Me?* see Ch. 6.

10.7   Bunin, Catherine and Sherry. *Is That Your Sister?* New York:
        Pantheon Books, 1976.   35 pp.

        Six-year old Catherine and her four-year old sister are both a-
        dopted.   With the help of her mother, Catherine explains to her
        friends how children like her sister and herself live in foster homes
        until an adoption agency finds a "forever family" for them.   She
        tells about the social worker's visits and how her adoptive parents
        went to court to legally adopt her after Catherine had lived with
        them for six months.   Catherine says that she and her sister don't
        think about being adopted that much, but just concentrate on all
        being a family together.

        IL: Ages 5-8   RL: 3.0

10.8   Byars. *The Pinballs.* see Ch. 4.

10.9   Byars, Betsy. *The Summer of the Swans.* New York: Viking Press,
        1970.   142 pp.   Viking Press, 1972 pap.

        Sara, her older sister, and her ten-year old retarded brother
        Charlie, all live with their aunt.   The children's mother is dead
        and their father left them years ago and never visits.   During her
        fourteenth summer, Sara feels quite restless; she is jealous of her
        older sister's beauty and her dating and she resents feeling re-
        sponsible for Charlie.   When Charlie wanders away from home one
        night, Sara and her aunt panic, knowing that Charlie isn't capable
        of asking anyone for help.   Joe, a boy Sara's age whom she has
        previously disliked, helps Sara search the woods for Charlie.   Af-
        ter Joe and Sara find Charlie, Sara feels a great sense of relief
        and is more appreciative of Charlie.   She also gladly accepts a
        date with Joe.

        IL: Ages 11-14   RL: 6.0

10.10   Cleaver, Vera and Bill. *I Would Rather Be a Turnip.* New York:
        J.B. Lippincott, 1971.   159 pp.   New American Library, 1976 pap.

        Twelve-year old Annie, who has no mother, is accustomed to life
        with her father and their housekeeper Ruth.   When her older sis-
        ter's illegitimate son, who is eight, comes to live at Annie's house,
        Annie receives much harassment from her friends.   Annie adamant-
        ly makes up her mind to dislike Calvin, although her father insists
        that Annie treat Calvin like a brother.   Annie fantasizes about
        Calvin contracting a fatal disease and she even runs away from
        home for a brief period of time in an effort to escape her new fam-
        ily situation.   Shunned by her friends whose parents won't allow
        them to associate with her, Annie is forced to spend more time with
        Calvin.   Annie discovers through some research at the library that
        several famous people were also illegitimate; this and Annie's res-
        cue of Calvin from a dangerous situation develops a permanent
        bond between the two.

        IL: Ages 11-14   RL: 5.0

10.11 Cleaver, Vera and Bill. *Me Too*. New York: J.B. Lippincott,
1973. 158 pp. New American Library, 1975 pap. LC, braille
and talking book.

Twelve-year old Lydia has a retarded twin sister Lorna, whom
Lydia's father has always been ashamed of. Lydia is shocked when
her father leaves home and her mother announces that she cannot
afford to keep Lorna at her special school for the summer. Determined to be Lorna's teacher all summer and to raise Lorna's a-
chievement level to equal her own, Lydia ignores her friends and
all her outside interests. Lydia believes her father will come home
to stay if she can make Lorna, who functions at the level of a
five-year old, a duplicate of herself. Only when Lydia is in a
dangerous situation and Lorna cannot understand her need for
help does Lydia accept the fact that Lorna will always have limitations. With plans for Lorna to go back to her special school at
the end of the summer, Lydia realizes that her father will probably not return.

IL: Ages 11-14   RL: 8.0

10.12 Clifton, Lucille. *Everett Anderson's Nine Month Long*. New York:
Holt, Rinehart, and Winston, 1978. 25 pp.

Everett, who has a new stepdaddy, feels that something special is
going to happen. His mother tells Everett how much she loves
him and announces that a new baby is on the way. Everett feels
that he's not getting the attention from Mama that he used to get.
However, during a walk with his stepdaddy, Everett is reassured
that he will always be special because he's the firstborn. Everett's
stepdaddy also tells him that there's enough love in their family
to share with a new family member.

IL: Ages 5-8   RL: 3.0

10.13 Clymer, Eleanor. *My Brother Stevie*. New York: Holt, Rinehart,
and Winston, 1967. 76 pp. LC, braille.

Twelve-year old Annie and her eight-year old brother, whose father is dead, have lived with their grandmother since their mother
left them several years ago. Annie and Stevie both feel unwanted
and unloved and Annie feels that she must be responsible for her
younger brother. When Stevie starts playing with older boys and
getting into trouble, Annie does not tell her grandmother about it
but turns to Stevie's teacher, Miss Stover, instead. Soon both
children grow very close to Miss Stover and when she resigns her
position to care for her sick mother, Annie and Stevie run away
to visit her. Annie and Stevie spend a few days with Miss Stover,
her mother, and the foster children her mother cares for. Upon
their return to their grandmother's house, Stevie's behavior improves and Annie feels less resentful.

IL: Ages 8-11   RL: 5.5

10.14 Colman, Hila. *Diary of a Frantic Kid Sister*. New York: Crown
Publishers, 1973. 119 pp. Archway, 1974 pap.

(Colman, Hila)

Eleven-year old Sarah dislikes her sixteen-year old sister, Didi, and she decides to write down her feelings in a diary. Didi borrows Sarah's clothes and is given more privileges. Sarah is unfairly compared to her older sister by teachers at school. Sarah is also jealous of the very close relationship between Didi and the girls' mother. To add to Sarah's troubles, she is upset over a friend's shoplifting and she constantly worries about her menstruation beginning. The girls' mother becomes depressed and goes for psychiatric help due to pre-menopausal problems. During a family counseling session, Sarah begins to better understand her feelings about herself, her mother, and Didi. The relationship between the two sisters improves when Sarah and Didi realize that they need to respect each other's differences.

IL: Ages 11-14   RL: 4.5

10.15 Danziger, Paula. *Can You Sue Your Parents for Malpractice?* New York: Delacorte Press, 1979. 152 pp. Dell, 1981 pap.

With a younger sister who makes a pest of herself telling jokes and an older sister who is beautiful and full of poise, life seems hard for fourteen-year old Lauren. Her parents' battles and her father's domineering attitude toward everyone in the family also upset Lauren. Lauren's mother refuses to admit that her daughters are growing up, so Lauren must help her younger sister understand her developing body. Lauren's college-age sister is thrown out of the house when she announces her plans to live with her boyfriend. Faced with many conflicts concerning friends and school, Lauren feels that her parents haven't given her the confidence to face these situations. Lauren starts to date Zack, who has a good relationship with his divorced mother. With the help of Zack, an understanding teacher, and her older sister, Lauren is better able to deal with the problems of growing up.

IL: Ages 11-14   RL: 5.5

10.16 Danziger. *The Pistachio Prescription.* see Ch. 3.

10.17 Dixon. *May I Cross Your Golden River?* see Ch. 8.

10.18 Fox, Paula. *Blowfish Live in the Sea.* Scarsdale, NY: Bradbury Press, 1970. 116 pp. Dell, 1972 pap. LC, braille.

Twelve-year old Carrie lives in New York with her parents and eighteen-year old half-brother Ben. Ben's father left him and his mother when he was young. For the last year, Ben has been acting strangely - giving away all his possessions, not going to school, refusing to work. Carrie, who idolizes her older brother, does not understand the change in him and her parents are unable to cope with it as well. When Ben receives a message to meet his father in Boston, he and Carrie make the trip together. Carrie is shocked at the seedy hotel where they find Ben's father, who is drunk and slovenly dressed. Although Ben's father is obviously an alcoholic who lies about his successful business deals, Ben

(Fox, Paula)

likes him and sends Carrie home by herself. Once home, Carrie
misses Ben terribly but she realizes that Ben, in trying to help
his father, has found a purpose in life.

IL: Ages 11-18   RL: 6.5

10.19 Grant, Eva. *Will I Ever Be Older?* Milwaukee: Raintree Children's
Books, 1981. 31 pp.

David, a seven-year old, is resentful of his older brother Steven.
David has to wear Steven's outgrown clothes, has to go to bed
earlier, and is unfairly compared to his older brother by teachers
at school. The boys' mother tries to point out advantages to being
the youngest, but it doesn't seem to help David much and he wishes he were an only child. However, when Steven goes to a weekend camp, David finds that he misses his older brother and is glad
to welcome him home.

IL: Ages 5-8   RL: 3.0

10.20 Greene. *Beat the Turtle Drum.* see Ch. 8.

10.21 Heide, Florence Parry. *The Wendy Puzzle.* New York: Holiday
House, 1982. 119 pp.

Dodie, a junior high-schooler, and her family are all puzzled by
the behavior of Dodie's older sister Wendy. During her senior
year of high school, Wendy has become obsessed with ecology and
seems to constantly be yelling at people about it, especially her
family members. Dodie is afraid to eat junk food or take showers
for fear of being verbally attacked by Wendy. Dodie's mother and
father avoid conversations with Wendy and Dodie's four-year old
sister hides from Wendy whenever she's around. For a while, Dodie thinks Wendy may be in love, but she discovers that Wendy is
simply in love with the world. Although Wendy's classmates taunt
her and call her "weird," when a chemical spill occurs in their
town and everyone must be evacuated, Dodie's family and others
begin to realize that Wendy's ideas on ecology are indeed important.

IL: Ages 11-14   RL: 5.5

10.22 Hoban, Lillian. *No, No, Sammy Crow.* New York: Greenwillow Books,
1981. 29 pp.

Sammy Crow, who is old enough for school, is scolded by his mother and others for sucking his thumb and carrying around a blanket. Sammy's older sister, Sheila, tattles on him and the two of
them quarrel frequently. When Sammy is kidnapped by the Robin
brothers, however, Sheila forgets their differences and comes to
his rescue. Sammy decides to give up his blanket to warm his
mother's newest egg. Sammy's mother declares that he is a big
boy now and praises her two children for working together.

IL: Ages 5-8   RL: 3.0

10.23   Kingman. *Head Over Wheels*. see Ch. 6.

10.24   Klein, Norma. *Confessions of an Only Child*. New York: Pantheon
        Books, 1974. 93 pp. Dell, 1975 pap. LC, braille.

        Eight-year old Antonia, nicknamed Toe, has mixed feelings when
        her parents announce that they're expecting a baby. Toe has al-
        ways liked being an only child and her best friend informs her a-
        bout all the unpleasant things that accompany a baby. However,
        when Toe's mother has the baby prematurely and it dies, Toe is
        very sad and she realizes that she had really been looking forward
        to having a sibling. Toe tries to cheer up her mother who becomes
        depressed after her return home from the hospital. Her mother
        soon becomes pregnant again and Toe is genuinely happy when her
        baby brother is born.

        IL: Ages 8-11   RL: 3.0

10.25   Klein. *Naomi in the Middle*. see Ch. 9.

10.26   Lasker, Joe. *He's My Brother*. Chicago: Albert Whitman and Com-
        pany, 1974. 37 pp.

        An older brother describes the problems that Jamie, an eight-year
        old with learning disabilities, encounters at school and home. Ja-
        mie doesn't have many friends and is often teased. It is hard for
        him to learn to tie his shoes and hang up his clothes at home.
        School is very difficult for Jamie; he often pounds out a rhythm on
        his desk and becomes mixed up if the room gets noisy. Jamie's
        parents are very understanding when he's had a bad day and his
        older brother plays games with Jamie or tells him stories to make
        him feel better.

        IL: Ages 5-8   RL: 2.0

10.27   Lexau. *Emily and the Klunky Baby and the Next-Door Dog*. see Ch. 3

10.28   Little, Jean. *Take Wing*. Boston: Little, Brown, and Company,
        1968. 176 pp.

        Laurel, a young teenager, worries about her seven-year old broth-
        er, James, who is very dependent on her. Laurel assumes respon-
        sibility for taking care of James from changing his wet bed to
        dressing him, and has little time for friends. Both of Laurel's
        parents, but especially her mother, make excuses for James and
        pretend that he is no different from other children his age. When
        Laurel's mother breaks her hip and must be hospitalized for sever-
        al weeks, an aunt comes to care for Laura and her siblings. Laur-
        el resents her aunt taking over most of James's care, but she
        finds she is able to spend more time with her peers. The aunt,
        who has felt that James needed special help for some time, is able
        to encourage Laurel's parents to seek professional advice about
        James. James is diagnosed as being "mentally retarded" and plans
        are made for his enrollment in a special classroom.

        IL: Ages 11-14   RL: 5.5

10.29   Lowry, Lois. *Anastasia Krupnik*. Boston: Houghton Mifflin, 1979.
113 pp. Bantam, 1981 pap. LC, braille and talking book.

Ten-year old Anastasia is upset when she finds out she's about to
become a sister. She vows that she'll leave home until her parents
decide to let Anastasia choose the baby's name. Anastasia also
falls in love for the first time and ponders over what religion she
wants to be. Anastasia begins having long talks with her senile
grandmother. When her grandmother dies, Anastasia is saddened
and goes with her father to the nursing home to pick up grandmother's belongings. Soon afterward, the baby is born and Anastasia becomes involved with its care. She decides it may not be
so bad to have a brother after all.

IL: Ages 8-11   RL: 6.0

10.30   Lowry. *A Summer to Die*. see Ch. 8.

10.31   Neville. *Garden of Broken Glass*. see Ch. 2.

10.32   Peck. *Father Figure: A Novel*. see Ch. 8.

10.33   Peterson, Jeanne. *I Have a Sister - My Sister is Deaf*. New
York: Harper and Row, 1977. 32 pp. LC, talking book.

A girl describes the many things her five-year old sister, who is
deaf, can do as well as the sounds her sister will never be able
to hear. The older girl communicates with her little sister by using her hands, face, and eyes to express things. She also stomps
the ground or waves her hands to get her deaf sister's attention.
The five-year old deaf girl is taught by her mother to speak and
read lips and she attends a regular school. The older girl tells
her friends that her deaf sister's ears don't hurt, but her feelings
do when people don't understand.

IL: Ages 5-8   RL: 2.5

10.34   Pevsner, Stella. *And You Give Me a Pain, Elaine*. New York: The
Seabury Press, 1978. 182 pp. Archway, 1981 pap. LC, talking
book.

Thirteen-year old Andrea feels that her parents focus most of their
attention on her sixteen-year old sister Elaine. Andrea's mother
tries to change Elaine, arguing with her about being popular and
getting better grades, but Elaine only grows more willful and sarcastic. Andrea finds herself turning to her older brother Joe, who
is in college, for advice on school and boys. When Elaine runs
away with her boyfriend, everyone in the family is upset except
Andrea. She is more disturbed by Elaine's return several weeks
later. After Elaine and her parents spend some time in counseling,
family relations improve. Andrea and Elaine are both shocked,
however, when their brother Joe is killed in a motorcycle accident.
For a while, Andrea blames herself for Joe's death but gradually
comes to accept it. She and Elaine grow closer as they each struggle to work out the problems of maturing.

IL: Ages 11-14   RL: 6.0

10.35   Pfeffer, Susan Beth. *What Do You Do When Your Mouth Won't Open?*
        New York: Delacorte Press, 1981. 114 pp. Dell, 1982 pap.

Twelve-year old Reesa has always been a rival of her pretty older
sister Robby. When Reesa wins an essay contest, she and her
parents are delighted. However, Reesa discovers she must read
her essay aloud, something she has a phobia about, and in despair
Reesa visits a psychologist. Robby taunts Reesa about the situation, jealous of all the attention her sister is getting. Eventually
the girls call a truce and with the support of Robby and the psychologist she visited, Reesa is able to read her essay before a
crowd with ease.

IL: Ages 11-14   RL: 6.0

10.36   Platt. *Chloris and the Freaks.* see Ch. 11.

10.37   Platt. *Chloris and the Wierdos.* see Ch. 3.

10.38   Rabe, Berniece. *The Girl Who Had No Name.* New York: E.P. Dut-
        ton, 1977. 149 pp. LC, talking book.

Twelve-year old Girlie, who is growing up during the time of the
Depression, is taken by her father to live with one of her sisters
after her mother's death. Girlie is certain that her father, who
has always rejected her and refused to give her a name at birth,
will eventually come to take her home. However, Girlie ends up
in a turmoil of being sent to live with one sister after another.
Girlie's oldest sister is pregnant with a second child and has little
money; another sister has a son that creates trouble for Girlie;
still another sister falls ill and is unable to care for Girlie. Girlie
discovers that her father has always felt that Girlie's difficult birth
eventually led to his wife's death; therefore, out of guilt, her
father has always denied that Girlie was his child. Weary of living
with her sisters and feeling unwanted, Girlie sets out to convince
her father that she is indeed his daughter. Although her father
is still unconvinced, he agrees to informally adopt Girlie and give
her a name.

IL: Ages 11-14   RL: 6.0

10.39   Reynolds. *Will the Real Monday Please Stand Up.* see Ch. 2.

10.40   Roberts. *Don't Hurt Laurie!* see Ch. 4.

10.41   Shreve, Susan. *The Masquerade.* New York: Alfred A. Knopf,
        1980. 184 pp. Dell, 1981 pap.

When her father is arrested for embezzlement, eighteen-year old
Rebecca finds her siblings and her mother relying on her to keep
the family going. Rebecca's mother, who has suffered a previous
breakdown, cannot cope with selling their large home and taking a
job and she must return to a mental institution. Rebecca's sixteen-
year old sister stops attending school and runs away for a brief
period of time. Rebecca, who has been accepted at Yale, wonders
at her chances of attending school there. After Rebecca's father

(Shreve, Susan)

pleads guilty to his charge and is imprisoned, Rebecca refuses to visit him and feels as if her life has really fallen apart. Unable to deal with her siblings' demands, Rebecca begins staying out late and engaging in petting with boys she really doesn't like. When Rebecca's mother improves enough to return home, Rebecca makes the painful decision to delay attending Yale for a semester. She also visits her father in prison in an effort to draw the family together as much as possible.

IL: Ages 11-18   RL: 6.5

10.42 Shyer. *My Brother, the Thief*. see Ch. 4.

10.43 Shyer, Marlene Fanta. *Welcome Home, Jellybean*. New York: Scribner's Sons, 1978. 152 pp. Scholastic, 1980 pap. LC, talking book.

After spending several years in residential training centers, Geraldine, who is thirteen and mentally retarded, moves back home with her parents and twelve-year old brother Neil. Geraldine is noisy and disturbs the neighbors; she also makes a mess of Neil's and his parent's belongings. Neil cannot practice the piano without being disturbed by Geraldine. He also has his homework either disrupted or ruined by Geraldine until Neil is on the verge of being expelled from school. Neil's father, unable to tolerate their home situation any longer, moves out and encourages Neil to come with him. Neil, however, is beginning to understand his sister's actions and wants to stay and help his mother teach Geraldine some things. When Geraldine makes a disturbance at a school event, Neil runs out of the school in embarrassment and is determined to go live with his father. However, at the last minute, Neil feels he cannot be a quitter like his father and decides to stay where he is needed with his sister.

IL: Ages 11-14   RL: 5.5

10.44 Smith, Janice. *The Monster in the Third Dresser Drawer*. New York: Harper and Row, 1981. 86 pp.

Young Adam not only has to cope with a move to a new house, but also with a new baby sister. During the move, Adam clings to his old toys and remembers all the good times in his old house. Once Adam is settled in his new bedroom, he finds he must share his room with his baby sister. Adam feels as if his parents are always telling him that he's too loud or in the way. When Adam starts to misbehave, his parents finally realize how resentful he is of the new baby. However, after his baby sister is moved into a room of her own, Adam finds that he is lonely for her at night.

IL: Ages 5-8   RL: 3.0

10.45 Sobol, Harriet. *My Brother Steven Is Retarded*. New York: Macmillan Publishing Company, 1977. 26 pp.

(Sobol, Harriet)

Eleven-year old Beth describes life with her retarded brother Steven. She explains that "retarded" means Steven can't learn or understand things like everyone else and she tells how Steven's brain was damaged when he was born. Beth relates her different feelings toward her brother - love, anger, embarrassment. She says she feels left out sometimes because her parents spend so much time with Steven. Beth is hurt when other kids say she is retarded too. Beth describes the special school Steven attends and the skills he learns there. Beth says she just hopes her brother will always be happy.

IL: Ages 11-14   RL: 3.5

10.46   Stolz. *What Time of Night Is It?* see Ch. 3.

10.47   Tolan. *The Liberation of Tansy Warner.* see Ch. 3.

10.48   Van Leeuwen, Jean. *Amanda Pig and Her Big Brother Oliver.* New York: The Dial Press, 1982. 56 pp.

Amanda is frustrated and feels left out when her older brother Oliver is able to do physical activities and play games which are too difficult for her. Likewise, Oliver is annoyed when his little sister tries to copy everything he does and when she refuses to let him dictate how they will play. Mother and Father Pig, with humor and great understanding, are able to soothe relationships between the two siblings.

IL: Ages 5-8   RL: 2.5

10.49   Viorst, Judith. *Alexander and the Terrible, Horrible, No Good, Very Bad Day.* New York: Atheneum, 1972. 32 pp. Atheneum, 1976 pap. LC, talking book.

Young Alexander knows from the moment he wakes up that it will be a bad day. In addition to problems at school, where he loses his best friend, Alexander has several conflicts with his two older brothers as well. Alexander gets wrongfully blamed for a fight with one of his brothers and he is upset when his two brothers get colorful tennis shoes and Alexander has to settle for white ones. Alexander's evening is miserable too when, among other things, one brother takes back his pillow and the other brother gets to sleep with the cat. Alexander feels better, however, when his mother assures him that some days are just like that.

IL: Ages 5-8   RL: 3.0

10.50   Vogel, Ilse-Margret. *My Twin Sister Erika.* New York: Harper and Row, 1976. 54 pp.

Seven-year old identical twins Inge and Erika are so skillful at deceiving other people that they sometimes wonder about their own identity. The two girls have mixed feelings about each other - jealousy, rivalry, love, and even hatred. When Erika suddenly

(Vogel, Ilse-Margret)

dies after a short illness, Inge mourns and feels as if a part of herself is gone. Inge also feels guilty because of the sometimes intense rivalry between her sister and herself in the past. Inge's mother, however, helps her to realize that love was the dominant feeling she had for her sister.

IL: Ages 5-8   RL: 3.0

10.51 Voigt, Cynthia. *Dicey's Song*. New York: Atheneum, 1982. 196 pp.

When their mother abandons them and is later admitted to a mental hospital, thirteen-year old Dicey and her younger sister and brothers make a long journey to the home of their grandmother. Dicey is relieved to have Gram shoulder some of her responsibilities, but she still worries about her siblings. Her brother James is quite intelligent but has problems making friends; Sammy is a fighter and gets into mischief frequently; Maybeth has musical talent but appears to have a learning disability that affects her schoolwork. With her independent nature and quick mind, Dicey also has problems with classmates and teachers at school. Dicey finds she is maturing physically and beginning to notice boys as well. Gram is forced to apply for public assistance to provide for the four children and when she receives an unencouraging report from the mental hospital, she investigates adoption of Dicey and her siblings. Dicey wonders about the sadness in Gram, who will not speak of the past. When Dicey and Gram visit the hospital where her mother is dying, Dicey begins to understand how hard life was for her mother with no husband and constant poverty. She also grows closer to Gram as the two make arrangements when Dicey's mother dies.

IL: Ages 11-14   RL: 6.0

10.52 Wells, Rosemary. *A Lion for Lewis*. New York: The Dial Press, 1982. 28 pp.

When young Lewis plays make-believe with his older brother and sister, he is always given the least desirable role - the baby, the patient, etc. Lewis puts on a lion suit and chases his brother and sister around, pretending that he has been swallowed. Then he is given equal standing with his older siblings. This makes Lewis feel much better about himself.

IL: Ages 5-8   RL: 2.5

10.53 Winthrop, Elizabeth. *A Little Demonstration of Affection*. New York: Harper and Row, 1975. 152 pp. Dell, 1977 pap. LC, talking book.

Sixteen-year old John and thirteen-year old Jenny have always excluded their asthmatic brother, Charley, who is fourteen, from their activities. However, when John goes away for the summer, Jenny and Charley suddenly find themselves spending a lot of time

(Winthrop, Elizabeth)

together. When Charley's dog dies, he and Jenny hold each other close in their sorrow and are surprised at the emotions their contact arouses. Because their parents have never shown signs of affection around the children, Charley and Jenny are later troubled by their physical contact that night. As the summer passes, Jenny becomes possessive of her brother to the point of ignoring her friends. Eventually Charley begins to avoid Jenny and she becomes isolated in her loneliness and guilt over loving her brother. Finally, Jenny's father, who has seldom talked to his children about any personal issues, approaches Jenny and reassures her that her emotions concerning her brother are "normal."

IL: Ages 11-18   RL: 7.5

10.54 Wright, Betty. *My Sister is Different*. Milwaukee: Raintree Children's Books, 1981. 31 pp.

Carlo is resentful of and embarrassed by his older retarded sister Terry. Carlo hates always having to take Terry with him wherever he goes, especially when other children laugh at her or adults stare. However, when Carlo intentionally lets Terry wander away in a department store, he becomes frantic with worry until he finds her. Carlo begins to think of all the good qualities Terry possesses. Although Carlo still doesn't always feel like having his sister tag along, he realizes how much love there is between them.

IL: Ages 8-11   RL: 3.0

11.
Stepparents

The majority of men and women who divorce eventually remarry. This is also true for a significant number of those who lose a spouse because of death. A large proportion of these remarriages are likely to involve children. For many of these children, the transition into a reconstituted family - a family system created from elements of other broken families - creates little trouble in adjusting and achieving a positive relationship with their new stepparent. However, some children have considerable difficulties in adjusting to their new families and stepparents.

The research literature is sparse in studies related to adjustment levels of children with stepparents. Although limited in numbers, several studies have given insight into the special problems experienced by the children of stepparents.

Age of the child appears to be an important factor in a child's adjustment. Younger children seem to have a closer and more affectionate relationship with stepparents than do older children; the adolescent has the greatest problem in adjustment. Children also appear to adapt more easily to stepparents when the previous marriage has been broken by divorce rather than by death.[1]

An obvious problem encountered between children and stepparents is the complex role structure that has been created through a reconstituted family. The child who has a stepparent is also likely to have stepsiblings, stepaunts, stepuncles, and stepgrandparents. Some children, no doubt, have problems adjusting to these new immediate and extended family members. Role confusion may result for all, especially the child.[2] For example, this complex role structure becomes extremely difficult for children during holidays or birthdays. The child may well have to celebrate special days at three or more different households involving people who are steprelatives that the child may see no more than once a year. Happy events, such as a child's birthday, may well turn into complex and frustrating situations for the child because of role confusion.

A major problem related to role functioning and confusion between children and stepparents is that the stepparent has difficulty in assuming completely the parenting role. One clinical study found that regardless of how hard the stepparent tries to be a parent for the stepchild, success is never complete.[3] It is not unusual for the stepchild to say to the stepparent during an argument, "My real father would never get angry at me the way you do all the time." Even if the stepparent makes a great effort to be an ideal parent, the child will often continue to idolize the absent biological parent.

Stepparents must usually share the parental role with a previous parent. At times, the stepparent may be expected to completely replace the biological parent from whom the child is separated. The stepparent can easily become resentful when this expectation is not realized, thus adding tension to the relationship with the stepchild. Bernard has found considerable resentment of men and women toward their stepchildren; one third of divorced men and forty-four per cent of divorced women were found not to be affectionate toward children acquired through remarriage.[4]

There are other factors that can create problems between children and stepparents related to family roles. One problem is the expectation by stepparents that their stepchild should automatically love them because they are now a family. The stepchild is likely to resent the new parent and may well say, "I will never love you, never!" Even if the child makes an effort to love the new parent, the stepparent at times may be hypersensitive about the relationship and misinterpret these loving behaviors and emotions negatively. Finally, as with most parents, the stepparent may interpret behavioral or emotional problems of the child as due to their own personal shortcomings as a parent. As with any parent, such an attitude or feeling is difficult to deal with.

Another strain that often complicates roles in a reconstituted family is when both parents bring stepchildren into a remarriage. Competition and rivalry arise among the stepsiblings. The stepparents may also have a tendency to favor their own children over their stepchildren. This particular kind of familial situation can be very conflict prone, especially if the children are older.

Criteria for Book Selection

Books selected for this chapter deal with children who have stepparents. Children whose parents remarried in these books did so after a divorce or after a spouse's death. Several of the books illustrate the addition of stepsiblings, as well as a stepparent, to a child's life.

A few characters in these books appear to be quite happy when their parents announce that they are remarrying. However, the majority of the young people who are characters in the books in this chapter initially feel resentment toward their new stepparent. Some of the characters feel that they are losing a mother or father to a new stepparent; certain characters seem to still be adjusting to a parental divorce when a stepparent arrives on the scene. The majority of the characters resent the new stepparent's first attempts in trying to discipline them or give them advice.

The addition of new stepsiblings to a character's life is also usually portrayed as being traumatic in most of the books in this chapter. Often stepsiblings in these books would first meet at their parents' wedding. Feelings of jealousy and rivalry often flared up between stepsiblings, particularly those who resided in the same home after a remarriage. However, most of the young people in these books who are stepsiblings eventually work out their difficulties with each other; a few who are close in age even become good friends.

The birth of a new baby to a parent and stepparent is the topic of a few books in this chapter. The apprehensions children felt toward the arrival of a new stepsibling appear to be similar to those of any child worried about the arrival of a new baby in the family.

For bibliotherapy purposes, most characters in the books in this chapter appear to eventually work out any problems related to the remarriage of their parents. Many characters came to the helpful realization that they could love a stepparent and still maintain a close relationship with the parent not living at home. Certain books also portrayed good communication among all members of the newly formed family; talking things out was an essential tool in these books for airing gripes and learning to accept each other's differences.

NOTES

1. James Walter and Nick Stinnett, "Parent-Child Relationships: A Decade of Research," *Journal of Marriage and the Family* (Volume 33, 1971): 70-116.
2. L. Duberman, *The Reconstituted Family: A Study of Remarried Couples and Their Children* (Chicago: Nelson-Hall Company, 1975).
3. Irene Fast and Albert C. Cain, "The Stepparent Role: Potential for Disturbances in Family Functioning," *American Journal of Orthopsychiatry* (Volume 36, 1966): 485-490.
4. Jessie Bernard, *Remarriage: A Study of Marriage* (New York: Dryden Press, 1956).

BOOKS

11.1   Adler, C.S. *Footsteps on the Stairs*. New York: Delacorte
         Press, 1982. 151 pp.

         Thirteen-year old Dodie, whose mother seems to always be criti-
         cizing her, has become very fond of her new stepfather Larry.
         Therefore, she does not look forward to her stepfather's two chil-
         dren visiting them during the summer. Dodie is overweight and
         likes to clown around while Anne, her stepsister, is quiet and
         beautiful. Both girls are in competition for Larry's attention with
         Anne's younger brother seeming to be the only one happy with
         the situation. Anne is still bitter about her parents' divorce and
         she berates Dodie's mother. In solving a mystery, the two step-
         sisters grow closer and Dodie and her mother talk about how to
         improve their relationship. The summer ends with plans for Lar-
         ry's children to spend more time with him, Dodie, and her mother.

         IL: Ages 11-14   RL: 6.5

11.2   Adler, C.S. *In Our House Scott Is My Brother*. New York: Mac-
         millan, 1980. 139 pp. Bantam, 1982 pap.

         Jodi and her father have lived alone for three years since the
         death of Jodi's mother. When her father suddenly decides to re-
         marry, Jodi not only finds herself with a new stepmother, but al-
         so a thirteen-year old stepbrother Scott. Jodi's stepmother tries
         to remodel everything in the house and wants to remodel Jodi as
         well, taking her shopping for a whole new wardrobe. Scott is an
         embarrassment to Jodi at school, where they totally avoid each
         other. However, at home Scott and Jodi talk and he confides to
         her that he's a shoplifter. Jodi discovers that her stepmother
         has a problem as well with drinking. Just when the new marriage
         starts to look shaky, Jodi and Scott realize what good friends
         they've become.

         IL: Ages 11-14   RL: 7.0

11.3   Ashley, Bernard. *Break in the Sun*. New York: S.G. Phillips,
         1980. 185 pp.

         Patsy, a girl around twelve years old, has been desperately un-
         happy ever since her mother has remarried. Patsy's stepfather
         regularly abuses Patsy, both verbally and physically, and Patsy's
         mother, busy with a new baby, doesn't stand up for Patsy. Pat-
         sy has even started wetting the bed at night, which greatly em-
         barrasses her. When Patsy meets an older girl involved with a
         touring summer theatre group, Patsy decides to run away with
         the theatre group. Distraught over Patsy's disappearance, Pat-
         sy's mother informs the police but they are unable to help. Pat-
         sy's stepfather and Patsy's only friend, an overweight boy with
         problems of his own named Kenny, take a train in search of Patsy.
         Kenny has a tremendous dislike of Patsy's stepfather but after
         spending much time talking with the man, Kenny begins to better
         understand him. Patsy's stepfather was beaten himself as a boy

(Ashley, Bernard)

and frequently ran away from home. Patsy runs away from the theatre group and is found by her stepfather and Kenny. Feeling trapped, she prepares to jump from a high structure. At the last minute, sensing a different attitude from her stepfather, Patsy descends to start over again with her stepfather.

IL: Ages 11-14   RL: 6.0

11.4   Bates, Betty. *Bugs in Your Ears*. New York: Holiday House, 1977. 128 pp. Archway, 1977 pap. LC, braille.

Thirteen-year old Carrie is disappointed when her mother decides to get remarried. Carrie's new stepfather has three children of his own and it's crowded when they all move into a house together. Carrie has to share a room with her stepsister and she attends a different school where she's in the same class as one of her stepbrothers. Carrie's stepsiblings seem to dislike her and feel that Carrie's mother is trying to take over their house. When Carrie's new stepfather insists on adopting her, she grows even more resentful. Eventually, all the children realize what a strain their parents are under and they save their money so that the whole family can celebrate their parents' one-month anniversary.

IL: Ages 11-14   RL: 5.5

11.5   Berger, Terry. *Stepchild*. New York: Julian Messner, 1980. 63 pp.

David, a young boy whose parents have been divorced for two years, is upset when his mother announces her plans to remarry. David still misses his father and wishes his parents could get back together. At his mother's wedding, David meets his new step-brother and stepsister and senses that they are unhappy as well. David resents the changes in his life after his mother remarries: he moves to an apartment; he dislikes the word "stepson;" he doesn't like being disciplined by his stepfather. However, David finds that his stepfather is trying to be fair and the two begin working together and talking more. David comes to the realization that it is possible to love his stepfather without taking away from the close relationship he maintains with his father.

IL: Ages 8-11   RL: 2.5

11.6   Childress. *A Hero Ain't Nothin' but a Sandwich*. see Ch. 2.

11.7   Clifton. *Everett Anderson's Nine Month Long*. see Ch. 10.

11.8   Clifton, Lucille. *Everett Anderson's 1-2-3*. New York: Holt, Rinehart, and Winston, 1977. 30 pp.

Everett, a young black child, thinks that one is a lonely number but two is just right with he and his mother doing things together. He is a little worried about his mother starting to like Mr. Perry so much, because Everett thinks the apartment might get too

(Clifton, Lucille)

crowded if Mr. Perry was always there. During a walk with Everett, Mr. Perry tells Everett that he doesn't expect to take his
daddy's place but wants to just be given a chance to be himself.
Everett decides then that the number three may work out just
fine.

IL: Ages 5-8   RL: 3.0

11.9   Donovan. *I'll Get There. It Better Be Worth the Trip.* see Ch. 8.

11.10 Elfman. *A House for Jonnie O.* see Ch. 7.

11.11 Eyerly, Jeannette. *The Phaedra Complex.* New York: J.B. Lippin-
       cott, 1971. 168 pp. Archway, 1971 pap.

Laura, a high-school junior, feels that everything is changed when
her mother gets remarried, even her mother's last name. She has
difficulty attending her mother's wedding and is resentful that
she will be left behind during her mother and stepfather's honeymoon. Once they return, however, Laura's life with her mother
and stepfather falls into a pattern. When Laura becomes interested
in a boy she meets, she can't understand why her new stepfather
appears so jealous of the boy and is so upset when Laura comes
in late from a date. Laura's mother and stepfather begin to argue
frequently and her mother seems to withdraw from the world. After her mother takes an overdose of pills and refuses to let Laura
visit her at the hospital, Laura realizes that the relationship between herself and her stepfather has visibly been getting out of
bounds. It takes much time for the three of them to reestablish
themselves as a family and it is decided that Laura should go away
to school.

IL: Ages 14-18   RL: 8.0

11.12 Francis, Dorothy. *The Flint Hills Foal.* Nashville: Abingdon,
       1976. 124 pp. Scholastic, 1978 pap.

Ten-year old Kathy dislikes her new stepbrother Jay and she feels
as if her new stepmother is constantly scolding her. Feeling a
distance between herself and her father as well, Kathy begins
spending much time at a horse ranch helping the owner. When a
foal from the ranch runs away, Kathy rescues it and nurses it
back to health. Jay sometimes helps Kathy with the horse, but
still annoys her with his teasing and bragging. Kathy discovers
that Jay is afraid of horses; this knowledge makes her better understand Jay's actions. Eventually Kathy realizes that she has
also misinterpreted some of her stepmother's actions and that Jay
and his mother want to include Kathy in their new family.

IL: Ages 8-11   RL: 4.5

11.13 Green, Phyllis. *Ice River.* Reading, MA: Addison-Wesley, 1975.
       48 pp.

(Green, Phyllis)

Dell, a young boy whose parents are divorced, lives with his mother and stepfather. Dell's father often fails to show up for his promised Sunday visits and when Dell discovers that his mother is pregnant, he feels all alone except for his pet dog. When Dell's dog jumps into the river and cannot be found and Dell learns from his stepfather on the same day that his mother has had a miscarriage, the double loss is too much for him. Dell cries in his stepfather's arms, voicing his sadness at the changes in his life and the realization that his father will probably never visit him again. Dell's stepfather seems to understand Dell's feelings and the two are happy when Dell's dog returns home that night.

IL: Ages 8-11   RL: 2.5

11.14 Greene, Constance C. *Al(exandra) the Great*. New York: The Viking Press, 1982. 133 pp.

Thirteen-year old Alexandra and her friend pack in preparation for Al's trip to visit her father and stepmother. Al has some feelings of anger toward her father because of his remarriage. She is also reluctant to leave her divorced mother and worries about her mother always being tired because of long hours at work. When Al convinces her mother to see a doctor and she is put in the hospital with pneumonia, Al has to stay with her friend. The two girls have an argument and discover that they are envious of each other - Al because her friend has a stable family life and her friend because Al gets to go on trips to visit her father. With her mother just getting out of the hospital, Al decides it's her responsibility to care for her mother. She reluctantly calls her father to cancel her vacation plans and is pleased when he and her stepmother tell Al how proud they are of her.

IL: Ages 11-14   RL: 6.5

11.15 Greene, Constance C. *Getting Nowhere*. New York: The Viking Press, 1977. 121 pp. LC, talking book.

Mark, who is fourteen, resents his father getting remarried, while his twelve-year old brother likes their new stepmother. Mark feels left out when his dad and stepmother have their own plans each weekend. Mark is especially jealous of the new car his dad buys for his stepmother and he makes a long scratch mark on its side. He becomes even more hostile when his father hits him during an argument between them. Mark is also invited to a party that doesn't exist by some pranksters from his school. When Mark takes his younger brother and a friend for a joyride in his stepmother's car and has an accident injuring the two other boys, his dad and stepmother consider sending him to a psychiatrist.

IL: Ages 11-14   RL: 6.5

11.16 Greene, Constance C. *I and Sproggy*. New York: The Viking Press, 1978. 155 pp. Dell, 1981 pap.

(Greene, Constance C.)

Ten-year old Adam, who lives with his divorced mother, is glad
when his father and his new stepmother move into his neighborhood. However, Adam hates the idea of sharing his father with
his stepsister Sproggy, who is also ten. Adam is rude to Sproggy
from the start and he is furious when his friends ask Sproggy to
join their club. Adam's mother is quite supportive when he dis-
cusses his problem with her but she leaves the solution up to Adam. When Adam sees Sproggy being teased by some neighborhood
girls, he comes to her rescue. Sproggy is grateful and does a
favor for Adam as well, making Adam realize that having a stepsister isn't so bad.

IL: Ages 8-11   RL: 5.0

11.17   Greene. *I Know You, Al*. see Ch. 9.

11.18   Hanlon, Emily. *The Swing*. Scarsdale, NY: Bradbury Press, 1979.
        209 pp. Dell, 1981 pap.

Both eleven-year old Beth and thirteen-year old Danny consider
a swing to be their private refuge from problems at home. Beth,
who is deaf, wishes to be more independent and resents her mother's overprotective attitude. Beth's speech sounds strange to
most people and some children make fun of her. Danny is still
grieving over the death of his father several years ago. His mother has remarried and Danny resents his strict stepfather. Although
Danny's stepfather appears to love Danny, Danny feels he has lost
his mother and nothing Danny does seems to please his stepfather.
When Danny tells a lie to save face with his stepfather, Beth's
freedom is affected and she thrashes out verbally at Danny. The
whole neighborhood becomes caught up in Danny's lie until he finally must confess the truth to his stepfather. Eventually Beth
and Danny begin to meet at the swing; they start to understand
each other's problems as they share their feelings with each other.

IL: Ages 11-14   RL: 5.5

11.19   Holland. *Of Love and Death and Other Journeys*. see Ch. 8.

11.20   Hunter, Evan. *Me and Mr. Stenner*. New York: J.B. Lippincott,
        1976. 157 pp.

Eleven-year old Abby does not want her parents to divorce and
she is confused when she and her mother move into a house with
Mr. Stenner. When Abby realizes that Mr. Stenner is also getting
a divorce so that he can marry her mother, she is embarrassed
about their living together and is determined not to like Mr. Stenner. Abby also resents Mr. Stenner playing father to her, but
eventually Abby decides she can't help but like him a little. When
both divorces are finalized and Abby's mother marries Mr. Stenner,
Abby accompanies them on their honeymoon to Italy and she grows
very close to her stepfather. Finally Abby comes to the realization
that she can love both her father and her stepfather without having to make a choice between them.

(Hunter, Evan)

IL: Ages 11-14   RL: 7.0

11.21   Kaplan. *The Empty Chair*. see Ch. 8.

11.22   Klein, Norma. *Mom, the Wolf Man, and Me*. New York: Pantheon
        Books, 1972. 128 pp. Avon, 1974 pap. G.K. Hall and Company,
        Large Type. LC, talking book.

Eleven-year old Brett likes living alone with her mother, who has
never married. Although some of Brett's friends are eager for
their divorced mothers to remarry, Brett has never particularly
wanted a father. However, when Brett meets a nice bearded man
named Theo, she introduces him to her mother and the two begin
dating. Theo begins staying overnight at Brett's apartment and
Brett, aware that her mother and Theo make love, asks her mother if she plans to have a baby. Brett's grandmother is convinced
that Brett's mother and Theo will get married, so Brett tries to
convince Theo that he wouldn't like married life. Brett's mother,
upon her announcement that she will marry Theo, tries to reassure
Brett that she and Theo will try to make as few changes in Brett's
life as possible.

IL: Ages 11-14   RL: 6.5

11.23   Mazer, Harry. *Guy Lenny*. New York: Delacorte Press, 1971.
        117 pp. Dell, 1972 pap.

Twelve-year old Guy has lived alone with his father for seven
years since his mother left them both to marry someone else.
Therefore, Guy resents the intrusion of his father's new girlfriend,
who seems to take over their house and tries to be a surrogate
mother to Guy. Guy's mother unexpectedly returns, wanting to
see him and giving him gifts. When she asks Guy to live with
her and his stepfather, Guy refuses to even consider it. Still
holding a grudge against his mother for deserting him, Guy ex-
pects his father to back up his refusal. Guy discovers, however,
that his father has asked Guy's mother to take Guy so that he
can remarry. Feeling unwanted and wishing he were dead, Guy
runs away. Upon his return, Guy feels alienated from all the a-
dults deciding what is best for him and he decides to rely only
on himself in the future.

IL: Ages 11-14   RL: 5.0

11.24   Mulford. *If It's Not Funny, Why Am I Laughing?* see Ch. 9.

11.25   O'Hanlon. *Fair Game*. see Ch. 2.

11.26   Okimoto, Jean Davies. *My Mother is not Married to my Father*.
        New York: G.P. Putnam's Sons, 1979. 109 pp. Archway, 1981
        pap.

Fifth grader Cynthia and her little sister Sara feel sad when they
discover that their parents are getting divorced. Sara makes a
vow to clean her room in an effort to get her father to return and

(Okimoto, Jean Davies)

Cynthia worries about her mother's moodiness. However, the girls enjoy their visits to their father's apartment and going special places with him on weekends. When both their parents begin dating other people, the girls are at first resentful. Cynthia soon discovers, however, that she really likes the man her mother is dating. When their mother announces she is remarrying, Cynthia and Sara look forward to meeting their new stepbrothers.

IL: Ages 8-11   RL: 4.0

11.27   Pevsner, Stella. *A Smart Kid Like You*. New York: The Seabury Press, 1975. 216 pp. Scholastic, 1976 pap.

Twelve-year old Nina has difficulties in accepting her parents' divorce and she resents her father getting remarried. Nina is stunned on her first day at junior high school when she discovers that her new math teacher is her stepmother. Nina's friends convince her that they should all start a campaign to harass her stepmother during class so she will quit her job. Nina is also troubled because her working mother has little time to talk to her and has started to date other people. After a day spent with her father, Nina begins to understand her father's needs and feels more accepting of his new family. Nina decides to call a truce with her stepmother at school. Nina and her mother also begin to communicate better and Nina feels that things may work out after all.

IL: Ages 11-14   RL: 6.0

11.28   Pfeffer, Susan Beth. *Marly the Kid*. Garden City, NY: Doubleday and Company, 1975. 137 pp. LC, braille and talking book.

Unable to live with her sarcastic divorced mother, fifteen-year old Marly runs away from home to live with her father and stepmother Sally. Marly soon finds that Sally is willing to listen and offer advice to her much like a friend. When Marly experiences difficulties with a teacher at school and is suspended, her father, Sally, and several fellow students come to her aid. Marly's mother also appears to support Marly. Although Marly decides to remain living with her father and stepmother, Sally persuades Marly to try to improve relations with her mother.

IL: Ages 11-18   RL: 6.5

11.29   Platt, Kin. *Chloris and the Freaks*. Scarsdale, NY: Bradbury Press, 1975. 217 pp. Bantam, 1976 pap. LC, braille.

Fourteen-year old Chloris worries her younger sister Jenny when she predicts that their mother and stepfather will soon divorce. Chloris still idolizes the girls' dead father and heartily dislikes their stepfather. Jenny, on the other hand, has always been fond of their stepfather and has even come to think of him as her father. Jenny questions a friend whose parents are divorcing and closely watches her mother and stepfather. When their stepfather goes out of town and the girls' mother brings home a male friend,

(Platt, Kin)

Jenny is quite upset and cannot understand why Chloris welcomes
the man. Jenny's mother soon demands a divorce and to Jenny's
dismay, her stepfather reluctantly agrees to it. Once the girls
and their mother move to an apartment, Jenny is shocked when
Chloris, now seeing a psychiatrist, reveals her plans to get rid of
their mother's newest boyfriend.

IL: Ages 11-18   RL: 7.0

11.30   Roberts. *Don't Hurt Laurie!*   see Ch. 4.

11.31   Shyer. *My Brother, the Thief*.   see Ch. 4.

11.32   Smith. *Kick a Stone Home*.   see Ch. 9.

11.33   Vigna, Judith.   *Daddy's New Baby*.   Chicago: Albert Whitman and
        Company, 1982.   29 pp.

A young girl whose parents are divorced resents her remarried
father's new baby. When she visits her father, the girl has to
share a room with the baby and share her father's attention as
well. Preparing for an outing, the girl helps her father dress and
feed the baby. She also saves the baby from a near disaster.
Discovering that only she can make the baby stop crying, the
girl becomes more fond of her half-sister.

IL: Ages 5-8   RL: 2.0

11.34   Vigna, Judith.   *She's Not My Real Mother*.   Chicago: Albert Whit-
        man and Company, 1980.   30 pp.

Miles, whose parents are divorced, spends a weekend with his
father and stepmother. Miles is determined to not like his new
stepmother no matter how hard she tries to be friends with him.
When his father has work to do on Sunday, Miles reluctantly ag-
grees to attend an Ice Show with his stepmother. Once there,
Miles purposely gets lost just to worry his stepmother, but he begins to get scared after a while. When his stepmother finally lo-
cates him, Miles decides to be her friend when she does not tell
his father about the incident.

IL: Ages 5-8   RL: 2.0

11.35   Wells, Rosemary.   *None of the Above*.   New York: The Dial Press,
        1974.   182 pp.   Avon, 1975 pap.

Marcia, whose widowed father has remarried, feels inadequate a-
round her well-educated stepmother and stepsister Chrissy. Marcia feels pushed by her stepmother and struggles through college
prep courses in high school, which causes her to develop an ul-
cer. Although Marcia's father is kind to her, he lets her stepmother take over all facets of Marcia's life. Marcia's older married
sister returns home pregnant from an extra-marital affair and Marcia is hurt when her father and stepmother insist on her sister

(Wells, Rosemary)

getting an abortion and leaving immediately. Despite efforts from
Chrissy to discuss topics such as boys and sex, Marcia feels they
can never develop a close relationship. Marcia begins dating a
boy her stepmother disapproves of and the two try unsuccessfully to have sexual intercourse. Marcia becomes frustrated with
trying to help her boyfriend overcome his sexual problems. She
has pressures at home as well about passing college entrance ex-
ams. When Marcia and her boyfriend realize they love each other,
she decides to eventually marry him rather than go to college.

IL: Ages 14-18   RL: 7.5

11.36   Wolitzer, Hilma. *Out of Love*. New York: Farrar, Straus, and
        Giroux, 1976. 147 pp. LC, talking book.

Thirteen-year old Teddy, who lives with her mother and younger
sister, can't understand how her parents fell out of love and got
a divorce two years ago. Although her new stepmother is nice
to Teddy, visits to see her father and stepmother are still painful
for Teddy. Deciding her stepmother's attractiveness must have
lured her father, Teddy embarks on a plan to encourage her mother to wear make-up and begin exercising, as well as to stop smoking. Teddy and her best friend Maya become interested in improving their appearances as well when they begin talking to boys at
school. However, Maya's extremely overprotective parents deny
Maya any type of a social life and she runs away briefly in rebellion. When Teddy discovers that her new stepmother is pregnant,
she is shattered. Eventually, however, Teddy gives up her unrealistic dream of her parents reuniting and she begins to admire
her mother's independence and courage.

IL: Ages 11-14   RL: 7.0

11.37   Wolkoff, Judie. *Happily Ever After · · · Almost*. Scarsdale, NY:
        Bradbury Press, 1982. 215 pp.

Eleven-year old Kitty and her younger sister Sarah have adjusted
to their parents' divorce and are fond of the man their mother
plans to marry. However, the two sisters are not so sure how
they feel about their future stepbrother R.J., a troubled boy with
a very demanding mother. Once Kitty's mother has remarried,
the girls find themselves with a friendly set of stepgrandparents
who welcome them as part of the family. The sisters are delighted
when they discover that their remarried father and his new wife
are expecting a baby. When R.J.'s mother secretly plans to move
to London, his father goes to court for custody and R.J. moves
into Kitty and Sarah's house. The sisters find that R.J. has his
good qualities. All three children look forward to the birth of
another baby when Kitty's mother announces her pregnancy.

IL: Ages 11-14   RL: 6.5

11.38   York. *Remember me When I am Dead*. see Ch. 8.

11.39   Zindel. *My Darling, My Hamburger*. see Ch. 7.

Author Index

Includes authors and joint authors.
Numbers refer to individual entry number.

Addy, Sharon, 4.1
Adler, C.S., 3.1, 11.1, 11.2
Alexander, Anne, 3.2
Alexander, Martha, 10.2
Allen, Marjorie N., 6.1
Amdur, Nikki, 5.2
Ames, Mildred, 3.3
Anderson, Mary, 4.3
Anonymous, 2.1
Arrick, Fran, 4.5
Ashley, Bernard, 4.7, 11.3

Baldwin, Ann, 10.3
Banish, Roslyn, 9.2
Bargar, Gary W., 9.3
Barness, Richard, 2.2
Bartoli, Jennifer, 8.1
Bates, Betty, 11.4
Bauer, Marion Dane, 4.9
Beckman, Gunnel, 7.1, 8.2
Berger, Terry, 3.4, 11.5
Berry, James, 2.3
Blue, Rose, 2.4, 3.6
Blume, Judy, 3.7, 4.10, 4.11, 6.3,
    8.5, 9.4, 9.5, 10.5
Bosse, Malcolm J., 4.12
Brandenberg, Franz, 5.7
Branfield, John, 6.4
Bridgers, Sue Ellen, 4.13
Bunin, Catherine, 10.7
Bunin, Sherry, 10.7
Bunting, Eve, 8.8

Buscaglia, Leo, 8.9
Butterworth, William E., 2.5
Byars, Betsy, 4.14, 8.10, 10.9

Carner, Chas, 8.12
Cate, Dick, 8.13
Chaikin, Miriam, 5.8
Childress, Alice, 2.6
Christman, Elizabeth, 7.3
Cleaver, Bill, 8.14, 10.10, 10.11
Cleaver, Vera, 8.14, 10.10, 10.11
Clifton, Lucille, 5.9, 10.12, 11.8
Clymer, Eleanor, 4.15, 10.13
Colman, Hila, 3.10, 10.14
Cone, Molly, 3.11
Corcoran, Barbara, 3.12, 6.5
Cormier, Robert, 4.17

Dacquino, V.T., 6.6
Danziger, Paula, 3.13, 3.14, 4.18,
    10.15
DePaola, Thomas Anthony, 8.15
DePaola, Tomie, 8.16
Dixon, Paige, 2.7, 8.17
Dizenzo, Patricia, 7.4
Donovan, John, 8.18, 9.9

Elfman, Blossom, 7.5
Eyerly, Jeanette, 7.6, 7.7, 11.11

Fanshawe, Elizabeth, 6.8
Fox, Paula, 10.18

Francis, Dorothy, 11.12

Gerson, Corrine, 3.15, 8.19
Girion, Barbara, 8.20
Goff, Beth, 3.16
Gold, Sharlya, 4.20
Goldman, Katie, 3.17
Grant, Eva, 10.19
Green, Phyllis, 4.21, 11.13
Greene, Constance C., 8.22, 9.12,
   11.14, 11.15, 11.16
Greene, Shep, 2.10
Greenfield, Eloise, 3.19, 8.23

Hall, Lynn, 9.13
Hallman, Ruth, 6.11
Hamilton, Dorothy, 2.11
Hamilton, Virginia, 8.24
Hanlon, Emily, 4.23, 11.18
Harlan, Elizabeth, 8.25
Harris, Marilyn, 4.24
Hautzig, Deborah, 4.25, 9.15
Haywood, Carolyn, 5.10
Heide, Florence Parry, 3.20, 4.26,
   10.21
Helmering, Doris Wild, 3.21
Herman, Charlotte, 9.16
Hermes, Patricia, 6.13
Hinton, Nigel, 7.9
Hinton, Susan E., 2.13
Hlibok, Bruce, 6.14
Hoban, Lillian, 10.22
Hoff, Sydney, 5.11
Holland, Isabelle, 2.14, 2.15, 8.27,
   9.17
Howe, James, 8.28
Hughes, Monica, 8.29
Hughes, Shirley, 5.12
Hunt, Irene, 4.27
Hunter, Evan, 11.20
Hurwitz, Johanna, 5.13

Irwin, Hadley, 3.25

Jones, Penelope, 5.14

Kaplan, Bess, 8.31
Kelley, Sally, 6.16
Kellogg, Marjorie, 4.28
Kenny, Kevin, 2.17
Kent, Deborah, 6.17
Kerr, M.E., 4.29
Kingman, Lee, 2.19, 6.18
Klein, Norma, 3.26, 9.18, 10.24,
   11.22
Krementz, Jill, 8.34

Krull, Helen, 2.17

Lasker, Joe, 6.19, 10.26
Lee, Mildred, 7.11
Levine, Edna S., 6.20
Lexau, Joan M., 3.27, 3.28
Little, Jean, 10.28
Lowry, Lois, 5.15, 8.36, 10.29
Luger, Harriett, 4.30, 7.12
Lyle, Katie Letcher, 7.13
Lynch, Marietta, 3.38

Mack, Nancy, 6.21
MacLachlan, Patricia, 4.31
McLendon, Gloria H., 8.37
Madison, Winifred, 7.14
Madler, Trudy, 8.38
Manley, Deborah, 5.16
Mann, Peggy, 3.29, 8.39
Mathis, Sharon Bell, 6.23
Mazer, Harry, 2.22, 11.23
Mazer, Norma Fox, 2.23, 3.31,
   8.40, 8.41
Mearian, Judy Frank, 8.42
Miklowitz, Gloria, 9.20
Miles, Betty, 9.21
Milford, Jerry, 5.17
Milford, Sue, 5.17
Milton, Hilary, 6.24
Minshull, Evelyn, 7.15
Mohr, Nicholasa, 2.24
Moore, Emily, 3.33
Morgan, Alison, 4.37
Mulford, Philippa Greene, 9.23
Myers, Walter Dean, 2.25

Neufeld, John, 4.39, 9.24
Neville, Emily Cheney, 2.26
Newfield, Marcia, 3.34
Norris, Gunilla Brodde, 2.27

O'Dell, Scott, 2.28
O'Hanlon, Jacklyn, 2.29
Okimoto, Jean Davies, 11.26
Orr, Rebecca, 4.42

Park, Barbara, 3.36
Paterson, Katherine Womeldorf,
   4.44
Peck, Richard, 8.45, 8.46, 9.26
Perry, Patricia, 3.38
Peter, Diana, 6.25
Petersen, Palle, 6.26
Petersen, P.J., 4.45
Peterson, Jeanne, 10.33
Pevsner, Stella, 10.34, 11.27

Pfeffer, Susan Beth, 3.40, 10.35, 11.28
Philips, Barbara, 4.47
Platt, Kin, 3.42, 4.49, 11.29
Powers, Bill, 7.17
Prince, Alison, 7.18

Rabe, Berniece, 6.28, 10.38
Rabin, Gil, 8.48
Reynolds, Pamela, 2.33
Rinkoff, Barbara Jean Rich, 4.50
Roberts, Willo Davis, 4.51
Rosenberg, Maxine B., 6.29
Ruby, Lois, 4.52, 4.53, 4.54, 7.19, 7.20, 8.49

Sallis, Susan, 4.56
Samuels, Gertrude, 2.34
Schulman, Janet, 5.19
Schwartz, Sheila, 3.43
Scoppettone, Sandra, 2.35, 6.31, 9.27, 9.28
Seabrooke, Brenda, 2.36
Sharmat, Marjorie Weinman, 5.20, 5.21
Shecter, Ben, 5.22
Sherburne, Zoa, 7.21
Shreve, Susan, 10.41
Shura, Mary Francis, 5.23
Shyer, Marlene Fanta, 4.60, 10.43
Smith, Doris Buchanan, 4.61, 4.62, 9.29
Smith, Janice, 10.44
Smith, Nancy Covert, 4.63
Sobol, Harriet, 10.45
Southall, Ivan, 6.32
Stein, Sara, 6.33
Steptoe, John, 9.30, 9.31
Stevens, Margaret, 8.52
Stolz, Mary, 3.46, 3.47
Strasser, Todd, 2.38, 8.53
Sullivan, Mary, 9.33

Thomas, William E., 6.34
Thompson, Vivian L., 5.26
Tolan, Stephanie S., 3.48, 8.54, 9.34
Trivers, James, 2.39
Truss, Jan, 7.22

Van Leeuwen, Jean, 10.48
Vigna, Judith, 11.33, 11.34
Viorst, Judith, 10.49
Vogel, Ilse-Margret, 10.50
Voigt, Cynthia, 10.51

Wahl, Jan, 6.35
Wallace-Brodeur, 8.58
Watson, Wendy, 5.28
Wells, Rosemary, 10.52, 11.35
White, Paul, 6.36
White, Wallace, 2.40
Windsor, Patricia, 7.23
Winthrop, Elizabeth, 6.38, 10.53
Wojciechowska, Maia Rodman, 2.42
Wolf, Bernard, 6.39, 6.40, 6.41
Wolitzer, Hilma, 4.65, 11.36
Wolkoff, Judie, 11.37
Wood, Phyllis Anderson, 5.29
Wright, Betty, 10.54

York, Carol Beach, 8.59
Young, Helen, 6.42

Zelonsky, Joy, 6.43
Zindel, Paul, 7.24, 9.38

Title Index

Numbers refer to individual entry number.

About Handicaps: An Open Family Book for Parents and Children Together, 6.33

Admission to the Feast, 8.2

Alexander and the Terrible, Horrible, No Good, Very Bad Day, 10.49

Al(exandra) the Great, 11.14

All Kinds of Prickles, 4.37

Amanda Pig and Her Big Brother Oliver, 10.48

The Amazing Memory of Harvey Bean, 3.11

Amelia Quackenbush, 4.20

Anastasia Again, 5.15

Anastasia Krupnik, 10.29

And You Give Me a Pain, Elaine, 10.34

Angel Dust Blues, 2.38

Anna's Silent World, 6.39

Are You in the House Alone?, 9.26

Are You There God? It's Me, Margaret, 9.4

Arriving at a Place You've Never Left, 4.52, 4.53, 4.54, 7.19, 8.49

The Balancing Girl, 6.28

Beat the Turtle Drum, 8.22

Belonging: A Novel, 6.17

The Big Hello, 5.19

Bird at the Window, 7.22

Blind Flight, 6.24

Blowfish Live in the Sea, 10.18

Blubber, 4.10

Bonnie Jo, Go Home, 7.6

A Book for Jodan, 3.34

The Boy Who Drank Too Much, 2.10

Break in the Sun, 11.3

Breakaway, 6.11

Bring to a Boil and Separate, 3.25

Bugs in Your Ears, 11.4

But I Thought You Really Loved Me, 7.15

Can You Sue Your Parents for Malpractice?, 10.15

The Cat Ate My Gymsuit, 4.18

Changes, 8.48

Chester, 5.23

Chloris and the Freaks, 11.29

Chloris and the Wierdos, 3.42

The Chocolate War, 4.17

Claire and Emma, 6.25

Close Enough to Touch, 8.45

Confessions of an Only Child, 10.24

Connie's New Eyes, 6.40

Daddy's New Baby, 11.33

A Dance to Still Music, 6.5

Dear Bill, Remember Me, 2.23, 8.41

Deenie, 6.3

Diary of a Frantic Kid Sister, 10.14

Dicey's Song, 10.51
Did You Hear What Happened to Andrea, 9.20
Dinky Hocker Shoots Smack, 4.29
Diving for Roses, 7.23
The Divorce Express, 3.13
Don't Call Me Fatso, 4.47
Don't Feel Sorry for Paul, 6.41
Don't Hurt Laurie!, 4.51
Don't Make Me Smile, 3.36

Eddie's Valuable Property, 5.10
The Elephant Tree, 4.30
Emily and the Klunky Baby and the Next-Door Dog, 3.27
The Empty Chair, 8.31
Everett Anderson's Nine Month Long, 10.12
Everett Anderson's 1-2-3, 11.8

Fair Day, And Another Step Begun, 7.13
Fair Game, 2.29
The Fall of Freddie the Leaf, 8.9
The Falling-Apart Winter, 4.63
Father Figure: A Novel, 8.46
A Figure of Speech, 8.40
The Flint Hills Foal, 11.12
Footfalls, 8.25
Footsteps on the Stairs, 11.1
Forever, 9.5
Freddy's Book, 9.24
Friends Till the End, 8.53

Garden of Broken Glass, 2.26
Getting Free, 7.9
Getting Nowhere, 11.15
Gila Monsters Meet You at the Airport, 5.20
The Girl Who Had No Name, 10.38
Go Ask Alice, 2.1
Good, Says Jerome, 5.9
Good-bye, Chicken Little, 8.10
Grandpa-and Me, 8.54
The Great Gilly Hopkins, 4.44
Grover, 8.14
Growing Anyway Up, 4.26
Growing Up in a Hurry, 7.14
Gunner's Run, 4.42
Guy Lenny, 11.23

Happily Ever After ... Almost, 11.37
Happy Endings Are All Alike, 9.27
The Happy Funeral, 8.8
Head Over Wheels, 6.18

Headman, 4.49
Heads You Win, Tails I Lose, 2.14
A Hero Ain't Nothin' but a Sandwich, 2.6
Heroin Was My Best Friend, 2.3
He's My Baby Now, 7.7
He's My Brother, 10.26
Hey, Dollface, 9.15
Hey, That's My Soul You're Stomping On, 3.12
HOME is Where They Take You In, 2.36
A House for Jonnie O, 7.5
How Does it Feel When Your Parents get Divorced?, 3.4
How I Put My Mother Through College, 3.15
How it Feels When a Parent Dies, 8.34
Hunter in the Dark, 8.29

I and Sproggy, 11.16
I Can Stop Any Time I Want, 2.39
I Can't Always Hear You, 6.43
I Have a Sister - My Sister is Deaf, 10.33
I Have Two Families, 3.21
I Know You, Al, 9.12
I Never Loved Your Mind, 9.38
I Should Worry, I Should Care, 5.8
I, Trissy, 3.31
I Want to Tell You About My Baby, 9.2
I Would Rather Be a Turnip, 10.10
Ice River, 11.13
If It's Not Funny, Why Am I Laughing?, 9.23
I'll Get There. It Better Be Worth the Trip, 8.18
I'm Not Moving, 5.14
In Nueva York, 2.24
In Our House Scott Is My Brother, 11.2
In the Wings, 3.17
Irving and Me, 5.11
Is That Your Sister?, 10.7
It Ain't All for Nothin', 2.25
It's Not the End of the World, 3.7
It's Not What You Expect, 3.26
It's Too Late for Sorry, 4.23

Jamie's Tiger, 6.35
Janet at School, 6.36

Kathleen, Please Come Home, 2.28

The Kenton Year, 8.58
Kick a Stone Home, 9.29
Kiss the Candy Days Good-bye, 6.6
The Last of Eden, 9.34
Last Was Lloyd, 4.61
The Late Great Me, 2.35
Lauren: A Novel, 7.12
Leap Before You Look, 3.46
Let the Balloon Go, 6.32
The Liberation of Tansy Warner, 3.48
Like Mother, Like Me, 3.43
Like the Lion's Tooth, 4.28
A Lion for Lewis, 10.52
Lisa and her Soundless World, 6.20
Lisa, Bright and Dark, 4.39
Listen for the Fig Tree, 6.23
Listen to Me!, 2.2
A Little Demonstration of Affection, 10.53
A Little Time, 10.3
Long Time Between Kisses, 6.31
The Lottery Rose: A Novel, 4.27
Luke Was There, 4.15

Maggie and the Good-bye Gift, 5.17
Mama One, Mama Two, 4.31
The Man Without a Face, 9.17
Marathon Miranda, 6.38
Marcia, 9.30
Marly the Kid, 11.28
The Masquerade, 10.41
May I Cross Your Golden River?, 8.17
Me and Mr. Stenner, 11.20
Me Day, 3.28
Me Too, 10.11
Member of the Gang, 4.50
Mia Alone, 7.1
Mitchell is Moving, 5.21
Mom, the Wolf Man, and Me, 11.22
Mommy and Daddy are Divorced, 3.38
The Monster in the Third Dresser Drawer, 10.44
A Month of Sundays, 3.6
Moving, 5.28
Moving Molly, 5.12
My Brother Joey Died, 8.37
My Brother Steven Is Retarded, 10.45
My Brother Stevie, 10.13
My Brother, the Thief, 4.60
My Dad Lives in a Downtown Hotel, 3.29
My Darling, My Hamburger, 7.24

My Friend Leslie: The Story of a Handicapped Child, 6.29
My Mother is Not Married to my Father, 11.26
My Sister is Different, 10.54
My Special Best Words, 9.31
My Twin Sister Erika, 10.50

Nana Upstairs and Nana Downstairs, 8.15
Naomi in the Middle, 9.18
Never is a Long, Long Time, 8.13
The New Boy is Blind, 6.34
A New House, 5.16
New Neighbors for Nora, 5.13
A Nice Italian Girl, 7.3
Nice New Neighbors, 5.7
Nick Joins In, 6.19
A Night Without Stars, 8.28
Nikki 108, 2.4
No, No, Sammy Crow, 10.22
Nobody Asked Me If I Wanted a Baby Sister, 10.2
None of the Above, 11.35
Nonna, 8.1
Notes for Another Life, 4.13
Now Is Not Too Late, 2.15
Now One Foot, Now the Other, 8.16

Of Love and Death and Other Journeys, 8.27
One Dark Night, 2.40
One of Us, 5.2
One, Two, Three - AH-CHOO!, 6.1
An Open Mind, 4.56
Out of Love, 11.36

Pass Me a Pine Cone, 5.29
Passing Through, 8.19
The Peter Pan Bag, 2.19
The Phaedra Complex, 11.11
Phoebe, 7.4
The Pinballs, 4.14
The Pistachio Prescription, 3.14

Rachel, 6.8
Remember me When I am Dead, 8.59
Remove Protective Coating a Little at a Time, 9.9
Run, Shelley, Run!, 2.34
The Runaway's Diary, 4.24

Sad Day, Glad Day, 5.26
Sally Can't See, 6.26
Second Star to the Right, 4.25
The 79 Squares, 4.12

She's Not My Real Mother, 11.34
Silent Dancer, 6.14
The Silver Coach, 3.1
Sister, 8.23
A Smart Kid Like You, 11.27
Someplace Else, 5.22
Something to Count On, 3.33
Sometimes My Mom Drinks Too Much,
   2.17
Starting with Melodie, 3.40
Steffie Can't Come Out to Play,
   4.5
Step on a Crack, 4.3
Stepchild, 11.5
Sticks and Stones, 9.13
Straight Mark, 2.11
The Summer of the Swans, 10.9
A Summer to Die, 8.36
Superfudge, 10.5
Sweet Whispers, Brother Rush, 8.24
The Swing, 11.18
Sycamore Year, 7.11

Take My Walking Slow, 2.27
Take Wing, 10.28
Talk About a Family, 3.19
A Tangle of Roots, 8.20
Tangled Butterfly, 4.9
Tawny, 8.12
Terry on the Fence, 4.7
A Test of Love, 7.17
That Was Then, This Is Now, 2.13
Then again, maybe I won't, 4.11
There Are Two Kinds of Terrible,
   8.39
The Three of Us, 9.16
Tiger Eyes, 8.5
To Live a Lie, 3.2
Toby Lived Here, 4.65
Too Bad About the Haines Girl, 7.21
Tough Chauncey, 4.62
Tracy, 6.21
Trouble with Explosives, 6.16
The Trouble with Thirteen, 9.21
Trying Hard to Hear You, 9.28
Tuned Out, 2.42
The Turkey's Nest, 7.18
Two Ways About It, 8.42

Under the Influence, 2.5

Walk My Way, 2.7
Walkie-Talkie, 4.21
The War on Villa Street, 2.22
We Didn't Mean To, 4.1
Welcome Home, Jellybean, 10.43

The Wendy Puzzle, 10.21
What Are Friends For?, 3.3
*What Difference Does it Make,
   Danny?*, 6.42
What Do You Do in Quicksand?, 7.20
*What Do You Do When Your Mouth
   Won't Open?*, 10.35
What Happened to Mr. Forster?,
   9.3
What if They Knew?, 6.13
What Time of Night Is It?, 3.47
*What's the Matter with the Dob-
   sons?*, 3.10
What's This About Pete?, 9.33
When Grandpa Died, 8.52
When the Sad One Comes to Stay,
   3.20
*Where is Daddy? The Story of a
   Divorce*, 3.16
Why Did Grandma Die?, 8.38
Why Me?, 6.4
Will I Ever Be Older?, 10.19
*Will the Real Monday Please Stand
   Up*, 2.33
Would You Settle for Improbable?,
   4.45

Subject Index

Numbers refer to individual entry number.

Abandonment (see Parental, abandonment)
Abortion, 3.26, 7.6, 7.14, 7.24,
11.35
Absent parent (see Death, Divorce,
Separation, marital)
Abuse and neglect (see Child abuse
and neglect)
Accidents, 2.5, 2.19, 3.14, 6.18,
6.24, 6.32, 8.10, 8.12, 8.22,
8.34, 8.58, 9.13, 11.15
Adolescent idiopathic scoliosis (see
Handicaps, scoliosis)
Adoption, 6.38, 7.7, 7.12, 7.19,
9.5, 10.7
Aged, 3.20, 4.12, 4.37, 4.42,
5.15, 9.9
Alcoholics Anonymous, 2.15, 2.35,
7.23
Alcoholism
of child, 2.5, 2.10, 2.25, 2.35,
2.39, 4.11, 4.12
of parent, 2.7, 2.14, 2.15, 2.17,
2.22, 2.23, 2.25, 2.26, 2.27,
2.29, 2.34, 2.36, 4.27, 4.30,
4.42, 4.45, 4.49, 4.62, 6.23,
7.23, 9.17, 10.18, 11.2
Allergies, 6.1
Angel dust, 2.38
Anorexia nervosa, 4.25
Asthma (see Handicaps)

Baby (see Sibling, new baby)

Battered child (see Child abuse
and neglect)
Behavioral problems, 2.1, 2.2,
2.10, 2.13, 3.31, 3.33, 3.36,
4.37, 6.42, 8.37, 10.13, 10.44,
11.3
Birth control, 7.23, 9.5, 9.26,
9.30
Blacks, 2.6, 2.25, 3.19, 3.28,
4.50, 5.9, 6.23, 8.23, 8.24,
9.30, 9.31, 10.12, 11.8
Blindness (see Handicaps)
Boy-girl relationships, 2.13, 2.14,
2.23, 2.28, 2.35, 3.42, 4.23,
4.29, 6.11, 6.18, 6.23, 6.31,
7.1, 7.3, 7.4, 7.5, 7.7, 7.9,
7.11, 7.12, 7.13, 7.14, 7.17,
7.18, 7.19, 7.20, 7.21, 7.22,
7.23, 7.24, 8.2, 8.5, 8.17,
8.19, 8.20, 8.25, 8.45, 8.48,
9.5, 9.20, 9.23, 9.28, 9.30,
10.9, 10.15, 10.34, 10.41,
11.11, 11.35
Braces on body/limbs (see Handicaps)
Broken homes (see Death, of parent, Divorce, Separation, marital)
Brother (see Sibling)

Cancer (see Illnesses)
Cerebral palsy, 6.21, 6.32, 6.33,
8.19

Child abuse and neglect, 2.10,
2.15, 2.22, 2.26, 2.27, 4.3, 4.7,
4.14, 4.27, 4.28, 4.42, 4.51,
4.53, 4.62, 8.24, 11.3
Counseling
of child, 2.1, 2.3, 2.6, 2.10,
2.33, 2.38, 3.15, 3.36, 4.3,
4.9, 4.11, 4.15, 4.18, 4.25,
4.29, 4.31, 4.39, 4.56, 4.63,
6.4, 6.16, 7.20, 8.5, 8.25,
8.37, 9.20, 9.33, 10.14, 10.34,
10.35, 11.10, 11.29
of parent, 2.33, 3.15, 3.43,
4.25, 4.63, 8.5, 8.37, 9.9,
10.14, 10.34
Crippled (see Handicaps)

Dating (see Boy-girl relationships
and Parental, dating)
Deafness (see Handicaps)
Death
of father, 7.22, 8.5, 8.10, 8.23,
8.25, 8.34, 8.48, 8.58, 9.15
of friend, 4.14, 4.27, 4.42,
8.45, 9.13, 9.17
of grandparent, 4.37, 5.22, 8.1,
8.8, 8.15, 8.18, 8.38, 8.40,
8.48, 8.52, 8.54, 9.5, 10.29
of mother, 8.14, 8.20, 8.27,
8.31, 8.34, 8.39, 8.46, 8.59,
10.38, 10.51
of pet, 4.37, 6.4, 8.13, 8.18,
9.21, 9.29, 10.53
of sibling, 2.4, 8.12, 8.19,
8.22, 8.24, 8.36, 8.37, 10.34,
10.50
Delinquency, juvenile, 2.2, 2.13,
4.45, 4.49
Depression, 2.4, 3.43, 4.13, 4.17,
4.31, 4.39, 4.63, 9.9, 10.14,
10.24
Detention center, 2.2, 2.39, 4.7,
4.45, 4.49, 4.53
Diabetes (see Illnesses)
Diet/dieting, 2.14, 4.18, 4.25,
4.29, 4.47, 4.61, 6.4, 6.6
Divorce, 3.1, 3.2, 3.3, 3.4, 3.6,
3.12, 3.13, 3.14, 3.15, 3.16,
3.17, 3.21, 3.25, 3.27, 3.28,
3.29, 3.31, 3.33, 3.34, 3.36,
3.38, 3.40, 3.42, 3.46, 4.13,
4.56, 7.5, 8.18, 8.27, 8.46,
9.13, 9.17, 9.21, 9.29, 11.1,
11.5, 11.13, 11.20, 11.23, 11.26,
11.27, 11.28, 11.29, 11.36

Down's syndrome (see Mental retardation)
Drinking (see Alcoholism)
Drugs, 2.1, 2.2, 2.3, 2.4, 2.6,
2.11, 2.13, 2.14, 2.19, 2.24,
2.28, 2.38, 2.42, 4.5, 4.18,
4.25, 4.29, 4.39, 9.34

Emotional problems, 2.14, 2.26,
3.12, 3.42, 4.11, 4.21, 4.65,
7.20, 8.59, 9.27, 11.15, 11.23,
11.29
Epilepsy, 6.13, 6.42
Exceptional children (see Handicaps, Learning disabilities,
Mental retardation)

Fighting, 2.13, 2.27, 4.17, 4.23,
4.49, 4.62
Foster home, 2.34, 4.14, 4.15,
4.31, 4.44, 4.62, 4.65, 7.7,
10.3, 10.7
Funerals, 8.5, 8.8, 8.20, 8.37,
8.38, 8.45, 8.46, 8.52

Gangs, 2.22, 4.7, 4.12, 4.17,
4.49, 4.50
Grandparent
death of (see Death, of grandparent)
illness of (see Illness, of grandparent)
living in child's home, 8.16,
8.38, 8.40, 8.48, 8.52, 8.54
Great-grandparent, 8.15
Grief, 8.1, 8.5, 8.8, 8.10, 8.12,
8.13, 8.14, 8.15, 8.18, 8.19,
8.20, 8.22, 8.25, 8.27, 8.31,
8.34, 8.36, 8.37, 8.38, 8.39,
8.40, 8.46, 8.52, 8.54, 8.58,
9.5, 9.15, 10.50, 11.18
Guide dog (see Seeing eye dog)

Half brother/half sister (see Sibling)
Handicaps
asthma, 3.14, 6.38, 10.53
blindness, 5.2, 6.17, 6.23,
6.24, 6.26, 6.34, 6.40, 8.48
braces on body/limbs, 6.3
cerebral palsy (see Cerebral
palsy)
deafness, 6.5, 6.11, 6.14,
6.20, 6.25, 6.35, 6.39, 6.43,
10.33, 11.18

multiple, 6.29
multiple sclerosis, 6.31
prosthesis, 6.41, 8.42
quadriplegia, 6.18
scoliosis, 6.3
speech problems, 4.21, 6.16,
    7.14
spina bifida (see Spina bifida)
visual impairment, 6.29
Hearing aid, 6.20, 6.25, 6.29,
    6.35, 6.39, 6.43
Heart trouble, 8.28
Heroin, 2.3, 2.4, 2.6, 2.28
Hitchhiking, 4.24, 9.20
Homosexuality
female, 2.34, 9.15, 9.27, 9.34
male, 2.24, 8.18, 8.19, 9.3, 9.5,
    9.13, 9.17, 9.28, 9.33
Hyperactivity, 4.21

Illness
of friend, 8.53
of grandparent, 8.13, 8.16, 8.52
of parent, 4.56, 5.22, 7.22, 8.5,
    8.14, 8.25, 8.27, 8.42, 8.46,
    10.3, 10.28, 11.14
of sibling, 8.17, 8.24, 10.50
Illnesses
amyotrophic lateral sclerosis,
    8.17
cancer, 7.22, 8.5, 8.25, 8.27
cardiac conditions (see Heart
    trouble)
diabetes, 6.4, 6.6
leukemia, 8.2, 8.29, 8.36, 8.53
Reye's syndrome, 8.37
terminal, 8.17, 8.41, 8.49

Juvenile delinquency (see Delin-
    quency, juvenile)

Language problems (see Handicaps,
    speech problems)
Learning disabilities, 10.26, 10.51
Lesbianism (see Homosexuality,
    female)
Leukemia (see Illnesses)
LSD, 2.13, 2.42

Marijuana, 2.11, 2.19, 2.33, 2.34,
    2.39, 2.42, 4.23
Mastectomy, 8.41, 8.42
Masturbation, 4.11, 6.3, 9.5
Menstruation, 3.46, 9.4, 9.12,
    9.16, 9.21, 10.14

Mental hospital, 2.5, 2.19, 2.35,
    4.13, 4.52, 4.65, 9.9, 10.41,
    10.51
Mental illness
of adolescent, 4.3, 4.9, 4.26,
    4.29, 4.39, 4.52, 4.54
of parent, 2.35, 4.13, 4.31,
    4.63, 4.65, 9.9, 10.41, 10.51
Mental retardation, 4.23, 4.27,
    8.24, 10.3, 10.9, 10.11, 10.28,
    10.43, 10.45, 10.54
Middle child (see Sibling)
Miscarriage, 2.28, 7.9, 7.17,
    7.22, 10.24, 11.13
Mourning (see Grief)
Moving, 3.2, 3.6, 3.34, 4.11,
    4.26, 4.63, 5.2, 5.7, 5.8, 5.9,
    5.10, 5.11, 5.12, 5.13, 5.14,
    5.15, 5.16, 5.17, 5.19, 5.20,
    5.21, 5.22, 5.23, 5.26, 5.28,
    5.29, 6.5, 7.11, 8.18, 8.48,
    9.4, 9.21, 10.5, 10.44, 11.4,
    11.5, 11.29
Multiple sclerosis (see Handicaps)
Murder, 4.53

Neglect (see Child abuse and ne-
    glect)
New baby (see Sibling)
New home (see Moving)
Nursing home, 8.48, 10.29

Obesity (see Overweight)
Old age (see Aged)
Operation, 8.14, 8.25, 8.27,
    8.28, 8.39
Overprotection (see Parental,
    overprotection)
Overweight, 2.14, 4.10, 4.18,
    4.29, 4.47, 4.61, 11.1, 11.3

Parent/parents
adoptive (see Adoption)
death of (see Death, of parent)
divorce of (see Divorce)
fighting between, 2.14, 3.7,
    3.10, 3.17, 3.19, 3.40, 3.46,
    4.24, 7.4, 10.15
illness of (see Illness, of par-
    ent)
mental illness of (see Mental
    illness, of parent)
remarriage of (see Stepparent)
separation of (see Separation,
    marital)

stepparent (see Stepparent)
suicide of (see Suicide, of parent)
Parental
  abandonment, 3.47, 3.48, 4.15,
    4.37, 4.44, 4.60, 8.24, 11.23
  absence (see Death, Divorce,
    Separation, marital)
  abuse (see Child abuse and neglect, Sexual abuse)
  alcoholism (see Alcoholism)
  dating, 3.4, 3.13, 3.14, 3.14,
    3.21, 3.26, 3.42, 3.43, 4.26,
    8.20, 9.12, 11.22, 11.26
  overprotection, 4.61, 6.32, 6.34,
    7.22, 8.29, 8.53, 11.36
Parole, 2.2
Pets, 2.7, 2.26, 4.37, 4.51, 4.62,
  5.2, 5.10, 5.11, 5.12, 5.19,
  5.22, 5.23, 6.1, 6.4, 8.12, 8.13,
  8.18, 9.21, 9.29, 11.13
Physical handicaps (see Handicaps)
Pregnancy, 2.28, 4.20, 7.1, 7.3,
  7.4, 7.5, 7.6, 7.9, 7.11, 7.12,
  7.13, 7.14, 7.15, 7.17, 7.18,
  7.19, 7.21, 7.22, 7.23, 7.24,
  9.5
Premarital sex, 2.1, 7.1, 7.3, 7.4,
  7.5, 7.6, 7.7, 7.9, 7.11, 7.12,
  7.13, 7.14, 7.15, 7.17, 7.18,
  7.19, 7.20, 7.21, 7.22, 7.23,
  7.24, 9.5, 9.9, 9.23, 9.26, 9.30,
  9.38, 11.35
Prison, 2.13, 2.25, 10.41
Probation, 2.39, 4.12, 4.50
Prosthesis (see Handicaps)
Prostitution, 4.5
Pupil-teacher relationships (see
  Teachers)

Quadriplegia (see Handicaps)

Rape, 9.20, 9.26, 9.27
Remarriage (see Stepparent)
Retardation (see Mental retardation)
Reye's syndrome (see Illnesses)
Rivalry (see Siblings)
Running Away, 2.1, 2.7, 2.19,
  2.34, 3.7, 3.11, 3.15, 3.40, 4.5,
  4.7, 4.24, 4.28, 4.62, 5.11, 6.5,
  6.11, 6.31, 7.5, 7.9, 8.23, 8.40,
  10.13, 10.41, 11.3, 11.23, 11.36

School
  behavior, 3.17, 3.33, 3.36,
    4.21, 5.22, 5.29, 8.5, 11.27,
    11.28
  classmate relationships, 4.10,
    4.61, 5.2, 5.10, 6.8, 6.13,
    6.17, 6.19, 6.21, 6.28, 6.29,
    6.34, 6.36, 6.38, 6.43, 7.5,
    9.3, 9.13, 9.16, 9.33, 9.34,
    10.51
  truancy, 4.30, 4.61, 10.18
Seeing eye dog, 6.40
Seizures, 6.13, 6.42
Self-concept, 4.18, 4.20, 4.42,
  4.50, 4.60, 6.43, 9.3
Senility, 8.54, 10.29
Separation, marital, 2.14, 3.7,
  3.10, 3.11, 3.19, 3.20, 3.26,
  3.43, 3.47, 3.48, 7.1, 10.11,
  10.43
Sexual abuse, 2.29, 4.28, 11.11
Shoplifting, 2.2, 2.27, 3.3, 4.3,
  4.11, 4.20, 4.28, 4.50, 4.60,
  10.14, 11.2
Sibling
  death of (see Death, of sibling)
  half brother/half sister, 4.60,
    10.18, 11.33
  illness of (see Illness, of sibling)
  love for, 2.42, 4.14, 4.60, 5.9,
    6.25, 8.10, 8.17, 8.22, 8.25,
    8.36, 9.31, 10.5, 10.7, 10.9,
    10.10, 10.11, 10.18, 10.19,
    10.22, 10.26, 10.28, 10.33,
    10.34, 10.44, 10.45, 10.51,
    10.53, 10.54, 11.1, 11.2
  mentally retarded, 4.23, 8.24,
    10.3, 10.9, 10.11, 10.28,
    10.43, 10.45, 10.54
  middle, 3.14, 9.18, 10.9, 10.15,
    10.21
  new baby, 9.2, 9.18, 10.2,
    10.5, 10.12, 10.22, 10.24,
    10.29, 10.44, 11.3, 11.13,
    11.33, 11.36, 11.37
  responsibility for, 3.2, 3.27,
    3.47, 8.46, 9.31, 10.3, 10.9,
    10.11, 10.13, 10.28, 10.38,
    10.41, 10.43, 10.51, 10.54,
    11.33
  rivalry, 2.26, 2.33, 3.14, 3.48,
    4.20, 6.4, 7.14, 8.59, 9.2,

9.17, 10.2, 10.5, 10.10, 10.12,
10.14, 10.15, 10.19, 10.21,
10.22, 10.34, 10.35, 10.48,
10.49, 10.50
stepbrother/stepsister, 4.51,
9.12, 9.17, 11.1, 11.2, 11.4,
11.5, 11.12, 11.16, 11.35,
11.37
suicide of (see Suicide, of sibling)
twins, 6.18, 8.12, 10.50
Sister (see Sibling)
Speech problems (see Handicaps)
Spina bifida, 6.36
Stealing, 2.6, 2.25, 4.7, 4.30,
4.44, 4.45, 4.60, 7.9, 10.41
Stepbrother/stepsister (see Sibling)
Stepparent
father, 2.6, 2.29, 2.34, 3.42,
4.14, 4.47, 4.51, 4.60, 6.5,
7.5, 7.20, 7.24, 8.24, 8.27,
10.12, 11.1, 11.3, 11.4, 11.5,
11.8, 11.11, 11.13, 11.18,
11.20, 11.22, 11.23, 11.26,
11.29, 11.37
mother, 3.15, 8.18, 8.31, 8.45,
8.59, 9.12, 9.23, 9.29, 11.2,
11.12, 11.14, 11.15, 11.16,
11.23, 11.27, 11.28, 11.33,
11.34, 11.35, 11.36, 11.37
Stuttering (see Handicaps, speech
problems)
Suicide
of friend, 2.34, 9.28
of grandparent, 8.40, 8.54
of parent, 8.14, 8.34, 8.46,
11.11
of sibling, 4.28, 8.19
Surgery (see Operation)

Teachers, 2.4, 2.17, 2.35, 3.33,
4.9, 4.18, 5.29, 6.3, 6.14, 6.16,
6.20, 6.25, 6.26, 6.28, 6.40,
6.42, 6.43, 9.3, 10.13, 10.15,
11.28
Theft (see Shoplifting, Stealing)
Truancy (see School)
Twins (see Sibling)

Unwed mother's home, 7.11, 7.15
Unwed parents
father, 7.7, 7.20
mother, 7.3, 7.5, 7.18

Vandalism, 4.1, 4.12, 11.15
Venereal disease, 9.5
Visual impairment (see Handicaps)

Weight control (see Diet/dieting)
Wheelchair, use of, 4.21, 4.56,
6.8, 6.19, 6.21, 6.28, 6.36